Pakistan: failure in national integration

The Southern Asian Institute of Columbia University seeks a deeper knowledge of that vast and tumultuous area stretching from Pakistan in the West to Indonesia and the Philippines in the East. To understand the problems facing its leaders and diverse peoples requires sustained study and research. Our publications are intended to contribute to that better understanding.

Rounaq Jahan examines the problem of national integration in Pakistan. She analyzes why former President Ayub's constitutional innovations, economic policies, and approaches to bureaucratic recruitment and political participation were inadequate and even contributed to the disintegration of Pakistan.

Pakistan: failure in national integration

ROUNAQ JAHAN

Columbia University Press

1972 New York and London

Rounaq Jahan is Associate Professor of Political Science at Dacca University, Bangladesh.

Copyright © 1972 Columbia University Press
Printed in the United States of America

Library of Congress Cataloging in Publication Data

Jahan, Rounaq.
   Pakistan: failure in national integration.
    1. Pakistan—Politics and government. 2. Pakistan—Social conditions. 3. Pakistan—Economic conditions. I. Title.
   DS384.J34   320.9'549   72-3771   ISBN 0-231-03625-6

TO MY MOTHER
AND
TO THE MEMORY OF
MY FATHER

Preface

ONE OF the traumatic events of 1971 was the disintegration of Pakistan and the emergence of the new nation state, Bangladesh. The study traces the gradual process of east-west disintegration in Pakistan that resulted in 1971 in the breakup of the country. It is a policy-oriented study, and I focus mainly on the Ayub period (1958–69) in Pakistan's history. The purpose of this study is not to frame any general theory regarding political development or national integration; rather, I try to show how difficult application of theories is in an empirical situation. Ayub was hailed in the sixties by many political scientists as a great "modernizer" and an "innovator"; and, indeed, he undertook a number of development-oriented policies. Here I analyze the actual workings of some of these policies and evaluate their impact on the problem of national integration in Pakistan.

The study originated five years ago as a Ph.D. dissertation at Harvard University. When my academic adviser, the late Professor Merle Fainsod, suggested the topic, I was at first reluctant to undertake the necessary research. Given the Ayub regime's strict control of the press and writing in general, it would be difficult to collect materials and to write on this controversial political issue. I also knew that my objectivity would be questioned by those who disagreed with my conclusions. But because the issue was so challenging, and because no comprehensive study of it had yet been attempted, I decided to undertake this research. I collected data and conducted interviews in Pakistan during the spring and summer of 1968 and wrote the dissertation a year later in the spring and summer of 1969. I then edited the dissertation for publication, which essentially meant cutting its size by half, during 1969-70, when I spent the year at the Southern Asian Institute of Columbia University. In November 1970 I went to Dacca, and since communications between Dacca and New York were problematic throughout 1971, publication of the book was delayed. While the manuscript was at the press, the disintegration of Pakistan became complete, and Bangladesh, formerly East Pakistan, emerged as a sovereign nation state. Except for the addition of an epilog, I decided not to alter any part of the manuscript which had been submitted to Columbia University Press in November 1970, since I thought the study would be more interesting for not having been written on the basis of hindsight. The epilog is an attempt not so much to update events as to analyze the birth of Bangladesh in the light of the whole study.

Many people have made this book possible. I am particularly grateful to late Professor Merle Fainsod, who was an invaluable teacher, friend, and guide during my stay at Harvard. He read through the study at all stages and offered ready and useful criticisms. I remember especially the difficult spring and summer of 1969, when, though hard pressed by tremendous problems on campus, he willingly made time to read my dissertation. Most gratefully I acknowledge my all-too-obvious debts, intellectual and otherwise, to Professor Samuel P. Huntington. I owe to him my interest in comparative politics. Over the years he remained a constant source of encouragement and help. I am also indebted to Professor Rupert Emerson, who first aroused my interest in the problems of nationalism, and to Professor Francis G. Hutchins, who read my dissertation and offered valuable comments.

I am grateful to the Southern Asian Institute of Columbia University, particularly to Professors Stanley Heginbotham, Wayne A. Wilcox, and

Howard Wriggins. Professors Wilcox and Wriggins read the manuscript in its entirety and suffered through its various stages with patience and good humor. They have made possible a considerable degree of improvement in the syntax, style, and structure of the study.

Abdus Sattar made useful comments on the earlier drafts and Mohiuddin Alamgir helped in the collection of some statistical data. Gustav and Hanna Papanek helped in many ways, as did Professor James Q. Wilson. I am grateful to my professors at Dacca University and the many people I interviewed in Pakistan, whose association had helped me in gaining insight into Pakistani politics.

I am indebted to Professor Alex Inkles for giving me the permission to use his survey materials on Pakistan. I am also grateful to Michelle Kamhi and Karen Mitchell, who edited the manuscript for readability and style, Jesse Goodale, who labored hard on checking the footnote references, and Mrs. Carole Greszler, who typed the manuscript. Thanks are also due to my numerous friends in Cambridge, New York, and Dacca who helped with criticisms and suggestions at various times. Finally, I am grateful to my parents for their unstinting encouragement and emotional sustenance, and particularly to the memory of my deceased father, without whose interest, support, and urging my career could not have taken this shape. But while I owe a great deal to many people, it is, of course, my book and hence my responsibility.

Cambridge, Massachusetts   *Rounaq Jahan*
May 1972

Contents

one / Introduction: the problem of national integration   1
two / Background: east-west imbalance, 1947–58   9
three / The decade of Ayub (1958–68): an overview   51
four / The regime's attempt at nation-building through economic development   67
five / Bureaucracy and nation-building   91
six / The basic democracies and political parties   109
seven / The 1962 constitution and East Pakistani political movements   143
eight / Dilemmas of political development in Pakistan   179
epilog / The disintegration of Pakistan and the birth of Bangladesh   185

Statistical appendix, 205   Bibliography, 217   Index, 239

Pakistan: failure in national integration

one / Introduction: the problem of national integration

MANY of the new states of Asia and Africa, as Rupert Emerson has pointed out, "are not yet nations in being but only nations in hope."[1] Nationalism in these countries came as a negative phenomenon. It was a movement more against Western colonialism than for a positive, coherent, national identity. Unlike the European countries, where nationalism accompanied or followed industrial and democratic revolutions, and where common language and culture were key elements in the growth of nation states,[2] the new states of Asia and Africa found the mixed seeds of their nationalisms planted in essentially diverse traditional social soils. The challenges of the "integration crisis" lay in the future.[3]

[1] Rupert Emerson, *From Empire to Nation*, p. 94.
[2] John H. Kautsky, ed., *Political Change in Underdeveloped Countries*, p. 33. For a detailed analysis of the development of nationalism in Europe, see Hans Kohn, *Nationalism: Its Meaning and History;* Carlton J. Hayes, *Essays on Nationalism;* Hans Kohn, *Prophets and Peoples.*
[3] Lucian W. Pye, *Aspects of Political Development*, p. 65. According to Pye, political development in the new states involves six crises: i.e., crises of identity, legitimacy, penetration, participation, integration, and distribution. These six crises may appear in different sequences, but all of them must be successfully met before a society can become a modern nation state.

Language and cultural factors are often not supportive of the growth of a single nationalism in these new states, a great many of which have "illogical" boundaries cutting across tribes and nationality groups or which contain within themselves "subnational" groups whose leaders aspire to lead an independent nation state. The social group cleavages in multicultural states are both horizontal (i.e., ethnic, religious, linguistic, tribal) and vertical (i.e., class, caste, sectarian). The most immediate loyalties of the vast majority of people in these states go to units other than the nation state. The primary task faced by the leaders of the new African and Asian states, therefore, is to transform "primordial sentiments"[4] into "civil sentiments," to create a national identity out of, or superior to, parochial identities, to build a nation state out of multiple subnational groups—a nation state not merely "in form and by international courtesy"[5] but also in political and governmental reality.

The term "nation-building" has both a mechanistic and a voluntaristic aspect. It suggests, in the words of Karl W. Deutsch,

> ... an architectural or mechanical model. As a house can be built from timber, bricks, and mortar in different patterns, quickly or slowly, through different sequences of assembly, in partial independence from its setting, and according to the choice, will and power of its builders, so a nation can be built according to different plans, from various materials, rapidly or gradually, by different sequences or steps, and in partial independence from its environment.[6]

Though nation-building is a problem shared by both developing and developed countries, there are important differences between the two. In developed countries, where there is a preexistent, well-formed, national ideology, a national elite, and national institutions, the problem is essentially found in the need to integrate one or more alienated groups into the already existing system. In the developing countries, on the other hand, there is often no such preexisting "sovereign" system, and

---

[4] Clifford Geertz, "The Integrative Revolution," in Geertz, ed., *Old Societies and New States*. Geertz defines a primordial sentiment as "one that stems from the givens of—or, more precisely, as culture is inevitably involved in such matters, the assumed givens of social existence: immediate contiguity and kin connections mainly, but beyond them the givenness that stems from being born into a particular religious community, speaking a particular language or even a dialect of a language, and following particular social practices" (p. 109).

[5] Pye, *Political Development*, p. 37.

[6] Karl W. Deutsch and William J. Foltz, eds., *Nation-Building*, p. 3.

the problem is thus twofold: first, to create a national ideology, a national elite, and national institutions, in short, to build a nation where there was none before; and second, to integrate the various groups into the newly created national system.

Nation-building, or national integration (the terms are used interchangeably in the current literature on political development), is a multidimensional problem. As Myron Weiner suggests, it may involve five tasks:[7] the creation of a sense of territorial nationality; the establishing of a national central authority; the bridging of the elite-mass gap; the creation of a "minimum" value consensus; and the devising of integrative institutions and behavior. In this study, national integration is broadly defined as the creation of a national political system which supersedes or incorporates all the regional subsystems. The special emphasis here is on ethno-cultural group conflicts in Pakistan's plural society and on the consequent problem of integration.

In the newly emerging states of Africa and Asia, the problems of nation-building are compounded by the fact that the ruling elite must perform the seemingly independent and sometimes contradictory tasks of state-building and nation-building simultaneously. In Europe, by contrast, the ruling elites generally faced the task of nation-building only after having built the state.[8] While state-building requires the creation and concentration of authority and an emphasis on the role of government in the social process (what David Easton has called the output functions), nation building, especially in states with several subnational groups, often calls for dispersal of power and an emphasis on responsiveness in the political process (Easton's input functions).[9] The prime necessity of the state's survival as an independent international entity often pushes the governing elite to concentrate on state-building at the cost of nation-building. By overemphasizing the need for the concentration of authority, the maintenance of law and order, economic development, and the establishment of an efficient administrative apparatus, the ruling elite in the new states often underestimates the need to nourish and strengthen the political process. Most new governments find it difficult

[7] Myron Weiner, "Political Integration and Political Development," *The Annals of the American Academy of Political and Social Sciences*, CCCLVIII (1965), 52–64.

[8] Joseph R. Strayer, "The Historical Experience of Nation-building in Europe"; and Karl J. Friedrich, "Nation-building?"; chaps. 1 and 2, respectively, in Deutsch and Foltz.

[9] David Easton, *A Systems Analysis of Political Life*.

to share power and enter into a political dialogue with the subnational groups in order to develop a national ideology, and above all to tolerate an acceptable level of instability in the system. In the absence of adequate policies for nation-building, however, the cohesion of the state becomes tenuous. The new states must therefore strike a rather delicate and difficult balance between nation-building and state-building efforts. The two processes are potentially complementary; but unless they are carefully balanced, they work at cross purposes and undermine each other.

Though integration is a vital problem of the new states, only a few studies have systematically measured and analyzed the nation-building efforts of these states.[10] Most available studies are concerned with explicating indices for the analysis of modernization, social change, and political development.[11] National integration is generally treated as a part of the broader problems of political development and modernization. But though they are interrelated problems, the process of creating an integrated nation and the process of achieving a developed, modern polity often require different sets of policies. Hence, there is a need to examine nation-building as a separate and distinct problem.

In the case of Pakistan, as we shall see, a disequilibrium arose in the development of the country's different sectors, i.e., in economic development, modernization, state-building, and nation-building. The failure to develop adequate nation-building policies, in spite of success in other sectors, endangered the viability of the state. In Pakistan, as in many new states, especially those with numerous subnational groups, there has been an imbalance in the distribution of power

---

[10] Karl W. Deutsch, *Nationalism and Social Communication*, is a path-breaking study which suggests indices for the measurement of national integration. For the analysis of the problems of integration in specific countries, see Selig S. Harrison, *India;* James S. Coleman and Carl G. Rosberg, eds., *Political Parties and National Integration in Tropical Africa;* Lucian W. Pye, *Politics, Personality and Nation Building;* Kalman H. Silvert, ed., *Expectant Peoples;* Geertz, *Old Societies,* Howard Wriggins, *Ceylon.*

[11] Daniel Lerner, *The Passing of Traditional Society;* Cyril E. Black, *The Dynamics of Modernization;* David E. Apter, *The Politics of Modernization;* Lucian W. Pye, ed., *Communications and Political Development;* Gabriel A. Almond and Sidney Verba, *The Civic Culture;* Joseph La Palombara, ed., *Bureaucracy and Political Development;* Gabriel A. Almond and Lucian W. Pye, eds., *Political Culture and Political Development;* La Palombara and Weiner, eds., *Political Parties and Political Development;* Karl W. Deutsch, "Social Mobilization and Political Development," *American Political Science Review,* LV (1961), 493–514; Samuel P. Huntington, *Political Order in Changing Societies.*

5 / *Introduction: the problem of national integration*

among those groups. One or two "subnations," because of their early exposure to modernization, have tended to monopolize administrative, economic, and political power and, thus, to become dominant as the "national" elite. This elite, partly because it is modern in outlook and partly because of the necessities of survival, has put a premium on goals of economic development, social change, modernization, and state-building, objectives requiring both the creation and the concentration of power.[12] But the concentration of power in the hands of this elite has meant concentration of power in the hands of a single subnation group, to the exclusion of others.

Politics in Pakistan, as in the new states in general, is still best characterized as the politics of status, and there are few political links between the elite and other groups. While policy innovation for modernization and economic development undertaken by the elite leads to the social mobilization of others subnational groups, the elite is reluctant to share its newly concentrated political power with newly mobilized groups. There is thus a lag between "mobilization" modernization in the economic sector and "representative" modernization in the political sector.

Pakistan is in many ways typical of the new states. It falls into the category of what Clifford Geertz calls "old societies and new states."[13] It shares with other new states many features — a long history of colonial domination, a plural society, and a so-called traditional socioeconomic political structure. Pakistan is truly a new state and a new nation. It is a state which "almost no one had foreseen and few could credit in advance as even a possibility."[14] The claim of the "Pakistani nation" was first put forth, in partial form, as late as 1940, and the state was created legally when India became independent in 1947. For Pakistan, therefore, state-building and nation-building can be easily differentiated, since both the state and the nation had to be consciously and deliberately built almost from scratch after independence.

The most formidable problem of nation-building in Pakistan after the state's inception was the integration of the Bengali subnation. The urgency of this problem is underscored by the fact that the Bengalis

---

[12] See Frederick Frey, *The Turkish Political Elite*, pp. 406–19.
[13] Geertz, *Old Societies*.
[14] Emerson, *From Empire to Nation*, p. 92.

were not merely the largest ethno-cultural subgroup in Pakistan but actually constituted a majority (54 percent) of the country's total population. At the time of independence the Bengalis had little representation in the civil-military bureaucracy, the professions, or the entrepreneurial class. As a result, the Punjabis and the migrants from northern and western India—who "modernized" early—though ethnically and linguistically a minority, became the national elite of Pakistan from the outset. The new state, threatened by external danger and internal crisis, addressed itself primarily to state-building and economic development. Thus the "output sector," where Bengali representation was nil, was developed with little regard for the "input sector," where Bengali representation could have been substantial. Without doubt, the emphasis on state-building efforts made Pakistan a more viable political unit, but it led to the growing alienation of the Bengalis. Neglect of nation-building policies eroded the thin veneer of Pakistani national identity, and by the end of the 1960s East and West Pakistan were on the brink of separation. In 1971 a civil war was the culmination of these trends of contradictory priorities of political development.

From the viewpoint of East and West Pakistan's integration, the second decade of Pakistan's existence, the Ayub period, was a critical time. The Ayub regime, like military regimes elsewhere, assumed power to "save the country from disintegration," and promised a fresh start at nation-building. As a proof of his intentions, Ayub Khan visited East Pakistan within ten days of the military coup, and pledged that the domination of East Pakistan by West Pakistan would cease.[15] In subsequent years his regime undertook an unprecedented publicity campaign, emphasizing that it had done more for East Pakistan than had any previous government. And indeed the regime did adopt some policies responsive to Bengali demands. The intensity and extent of the Bengali drive for autonomy at the end of Ayub's decade therefore puzzled many casual observers of the Pakistani political scene. However, as an analysis of the actual workings and consequences of the Ayub regime's nation-building policies will show, there was, as before, an imbalance in the development of different sectors, an imbalance which inevitably intensified Bengali alienation.

[15] *Dawn* (Karachi), October 22, 1958.

Unlike most military regimes, the Ayub regime pursued a deliberate policy of political institution-building. Several questions will be examined here to gauge the capabilities of these institutions for national integration: (1) *Were these institutions structurally integrative?* Was East Pakistan's numerical representation in these institutions equal to that of West Pakistan? Were there any built-in devices whereby representatives from the two wings could work out a consensus on fundamental problems within these institutions? Were the linkages created by these institutions vertical or horizontal? (2) *Were these institutions functionally integrative?* That is, did they succeed in giving the Bengalis a sense of identity with the national political system? Did they provide for effective Bengali participation? Were they "responsive" to Bengali demands? Did they give the Bengalis a share in political power? (3) *Finally, did these institutions gain legitimacy in the country as a whole, and especially in East Pakistan?* What was the extent of compliance with and support for—two essential attributes of legitimacy—these institutions in East Pakistan?

With respect to the Ayub regime's economic and administrative policies, it is important to determine whether those policies succeeded in gaining Bengali support for a "national" economy and administration or, on the contrary, led to greater Bengali demands for a separate and autonomous economy and administration for East Pakistan. The analysis also assesses the effect of the lag between the regime's performance in the economic and the political sectors. This created a disequilibrium in the national system. While Ayub Khan's economic growth policies resulted in the creation of new forces, his political institutions, with their limited capacities for mobilization and participation were unable to reconcile these forces, and the regime was toppled in the resulting social turbulence.[16]

Since the regime was highly "elitist" in nature, a pertinent question is whether the power elite was representative. Was Bengali representation in the power structure any more equitable than in the pre-1958 period? Did the elite structure undergo any changes that significantly affected east-west integration?

[16] Here Huntington's differentiation between political modernization and political development is closely followed. While Ayub's economic policies led to increased social mobilization and greater complexity of the polity, the political structure he created was unable to manage the increased load of this more modern polity, which finally led to the breakdown of Ayub's political edifice.

8 / Introduction: the problem of national integration

And finally, side by side with the analysis of the Ayub regime's nation-building policies, it is essential to examine the gradual transformation of Bengali ferment, from a linguistic-cultural phenomenon into a much broader, economic-political one, and to trace the increasing radicalization of Bengali politics and the changing nature of Bengali political demands—from demands for participation in the national political system to demands for a totally autonomous system.

two / Background: east-west imbalance, 1947-58

Anatomy of the Pakistani nation

THE NEW STATES that have the best opportunity of success in the process of nation-building are, in the words of Joseph R. Strayer,

> ... those which correspond closely to old political units; those where the experience of living together for many generations within a continuing political framework has given the people some sense of identity; those where the political units concide roughly with a distinct cultural area; and those where there are indigenous institutions and habits of political thinking that can be connected to forms borrowed from outside.[1]

In the light of these preconditions, the task of nation-building in Pakistan seems difficult indeed, for, as Rupert Emerson has pointed out, "by the accepted criteria of nationhood there was in fact no such thing as a Pakistani nation."[2]

[1] Joseph R. Strayer, "The Historical Experience of Nation-building in Europe," p. 25.
[2] *From Empire to Nation*, p. 92.

Geography and population. Pakistan has appropriately been called a "double country."[3] Comprising a total area of 365,529 square miles, it is made up of two unequal regions (East Pakistan: 55,126 square miles; West Pakistan: 310,403 square miles) separated from each other by more than a thousand miles. West Pakistan is a largely arid land, with an average annual rainfall of less than twenty inches. Its western and northern parts have high mountains. While the Indus Basin in the east and south is a vast alluvial plain, huge areas to the southeast of the basin are arid desert. East Pakistan by contrast is situated in one of the largest and most heavily watered deltas of the world. It comprises alluvial plains with marginal hills in the east and southeast. Its monsoon climate gives East Pakistan an average annual rainfall of one hundred inches. The region's vast network of rivers undergoes extensive periodic flooding: every year nearly 30–40 percent of the land of East Pakistan is inundated by flood waters.

Geographical separation makes communication between the two wings difficult and expensive, resulting in little mobility of population and resources between them.[4] This lack of mobility makes common patterns of social mobilization between the two wings almost impossible. Under the economic conditions now prevailing, only a small elite can afford to have interwing contact—which means that the national elite tends to be narrowly oligarchic. Another result of the geographical separation of East and West Pakistan is that investment in socioeconomic overhead in one wing does not have a significant spread effect in the other wing; thus the logic of geography dictates that there be a dual economic and administrative apparatus. Given the importance of capital site and political clientele in the developing countries, geographical separation further means that the wing where the capital is not situated may be at an economic and administrative disadvantage. The disparity in geographical location of the two wings—West Pakistan being closer to the Middle East and East Pakistan being nearer to Southeast Asia— can also create different strategic interests.[5] Moreover, climatic and

[3] See Richard Weekes, *Pakistan*, p. 3.
[4] See Table 1 in the Appendix for interwing travel figures.
[5] See Charles Burton Marshall, "Testimony before the Committee on Foreign Affairs," U.S., Congress, House, Committee on Foreign Affairs, *Review of the Mutual Security Programs, Hearings*, p. 5. It should be noted, though, that India is the major strategic problem for both East and West Pakistan.

topographic differences often lead to divergent economic problems. While West Pakistan's problem is scarcity of water, that of East Pakistan is flood in the monsoon season and lack of water in the months (November to April) following the monsoon. Thus, while West Pakistan requires extensive irrigation facilities, East Pakistan needs both flood control measures and irrigation. Finally, climatic and geographic differences have resulted in different crops, patterns of housing settlement, food, and dress, all of which have effected different life styles in the two wings.[6]

East and West Pakistan also exhibit sharp differences in demography (see Table II.1). East Pakistan's population density is nearly seven

Table II.1 / Demographic differences between East and West Pakistan

	TOTAL POPULATION (MILLIONS)		POPULATION DENSITY (PERSONS/ SQ. MI.)		URBANIZATION (PERCENTAGE)		LITERACY (PERCENTAGE)	
	1951	1961	1951	1961	1951	1961	1951	1961
EAST PAKISTAN	41.9	50.8	701	922	4.3	5.2	21.1	21.5
WEST PAKISTAN	33.7	42.9	109	138	17.8	22.5	16.4	16.3

Source: Adapted from Pakistan, Ministry of Home and Kashmir Affairs, Home Affairs Division, *Population Census of Pakistan, 1961,* Vol. I, pt. ii, statements 2.3, 2.11, 2.14; pt. iv, statements 4.1, 4.4.

times that of West Pakistan.[7] The average density of population in the East Pakistani rural areas is 1,300 persons per square mile of cultivated land.[8] While the whole of East Pakistan is densely populated, there are five especially overcrowded districts—Dacca, Comilla, Chittagong, Noakhali, and Faridpur—where according to the 1961 census there were 2,700 persons per square mile of cultivated land.[9] These districts, which comprise approximately 35 percent of the province's total population, are also the food deficit areas. From 1960 to 1965 roughly 50 percent of their cereal consumption was imported from outside.[10]

Though East Pakistan has a higher density of population, its rate of

[6] See O. H. K. Spate, *India and Pakistan,* for a detailed discussion of the geography of South Asia.
[7] See Table 2 in the Appendix.
[8] Roger Revelle and Harold A. Thomas, "Population and Food in East Pakistan" (unpublished paper, Harvard Center for Population Studies), p. 2.
[9] *Ibid.,* p. 4.   [10] *Ibid.,* p. 5.

urbanization is lower (5.2 percent) than West Pakistan's (22.5 percent). This means that only a small percentage of the population is socially mobilized; the task of mobilizing the vast "underlying population"[11] — may create still further cleavages in the nation's society.

A distinct demographic feature of Pakistan as a whole is its large refugee population (6.5 million). East Pakistan, however, has fewer refugees (0.7 million, according to the 1951 census) than West Pakistan (7.2 million). The discrepancy in refugee settlement between the two wings has been partially responsible for East-West economic disparity in Pakistan. The influx of immigrants to West Pakistan contributed to West Pakistan's higher rate of urbanization (the rate of urbanization for the refugees alone was 39.9 percent according to the 1951 census) and economic development (the vast majority of private entrepreneurs in West Pakistan came from these immigrants). By contrast the vacuum created in the east wing by the departure of the Hindu elite was not filled by new immigrants.[12]

Language. Whereas East Pakistan "very closely approximates a linguistic unit," West Pakistan "presents a complex polyglot."[13] As Table

Table II.2 / *Frequency of languages commonly spoken as mother tongue in Pakistan (percentage of population)*

LANGUAGE	EAST PAKISTAN		WEST PAKISTAN		PAKISTAN	
	1951	1961	1951	1961	1951	1961
Bengali	98.16	98.42	0.02	0.11	56.40	55.48
Punjabi	0.02	0.02	67.08	66.39	28.55	29.02
Pushtu	—	0.01	8.16	8.47	3.48	3.70
Sindhi	0.01	0.01	12.85	12.59	5.47	5.51
Urdu	0.64	0.61	7.05	7.57	3.37	3.65
English	0.01	0.01	0.03	0.04	0.02	0.02
Baluchi	—	—	3.04	2.49	1.29	1.09

Source: Adapted from Pakistan, Ministry of Home and Kashmir Affairs, Home Affairs Division, *Population Census of Pakistan, 1961,* Vol. I, pt. iv, statement 5.3.

[11] Deutsch, *Nationalism,* p. 128.
[12] For a detailed discussion of the migration pattern and its role in widening the economic disparity between East and West Pakistan, see Hanna Papanek, "Entrepreneurs in East Pakistan." The departure of the Hindu elite, however, eased the process of land reform in East Pakistan and helped the rapid rise of a Bengali Muslim counterelite.
[13] Donald N. Wilber, *Pakistan,* p. 71.

II.2 reveals, the linguistic differences between the two wings are very great, making the development of a lingua franca between the wings difficult indeed. None of the languages has general acceptance in both wings. Most of the tongues are regionally based. Bengali, though the language of the majority, is virtually unknown in West Pakistan. Of the principal spoken languages of West Pakistan—Urdu, Punjabi, Sindhi, Pushtu—all are similarly unfamiliar in East Pakistan (although a small elite know Urdu); and do not even have general applicability in West Pakistan. Differences in script add to the difficulty of learning a second language from the other wing. The linguistic traditions in the two wings also differ. Bengali claims the distinction of having been in the vanguard of the literary renaissance in modern India. The Bengali are intensely attached to and proud of their language and often reveal a sense of linguistic nationalism. But though the Bengali language developed under the patronage of Muslim rulers and was greatly influenced by Islamic thought, albeit in the form of Sufi mysticism,[14] its secular renaissance in the nineteenth and twentieth centuries was very largely due to the contribution of Hindu authors. Arguing that Bengali was permeated with Hindu imagery, the Pakistani policy-makers initially rejected Bengali's claim for recognition as a national language and attempted to make Urdu—a minority language, but one closely associated with the Indian Muslim heritage and the Pakistan movement[15]—the only national language. The attempt was abandoned in 1954 after strong Bengali opposition, and both Bengali and Urdu were recognized as national languages. But neither tongue gained a substantial acceptance in both wings. Though English is the official language, it still remains very much the language of the elite. Table II.3 clearly reveals Pakistan's failure to develop a second language commonly understood in both wings. It is especially disturbing to note that the percentages for all the languages

---

[14] See Qazi Din Mohammad, *Bangla Sahityer Itihas* [History of Bengali literature], I, 170–79; II, 191–325; Dr. Mohammad Shahidullah, *Bangla Sahityer Katha* [History of Bengali literature], II; Mohammad Abdul Hai, *Sahitya o Sanskriti* [Literature and culture] pp. 1–114.

[15] Urdu first developed as a lingua franca in North India after the Muslim conquest. With the Hindu revival of the early twentieth century, the Urdu-Hindi controversy started. Since the Muslims of Uttar Pradesh were most sensitive to this issue and since the leadership of the Muslim League generally came from their ranks, Urdu came to be closely associated with the Pakistan movement. Also, Urdu literary figures like Sibli Nomani and Iqbal did much to foster Muslim nationalism in India.

Table II.3 / *Frequency of major languages spoken as additional tongues (percentage of population)*

LANGUAGE	EAST PAKISTAN		WEST PAKISTAN		PAKISTAN	
	1951	1961	1951	1961	1951	1961
Bengali	0.29	0.55	0.01	0.03	0.17	0.32
Punjabi	—	0.01	1.98	1.18	0.84	0.52
Pushtu	—	—	0.96	0.47	0.41	0.21
Sindhi	0.01	0.01	1.16	1.57	0.50	0.69
Urdu	0.46	0.72	8.85	7.28	4.03	3.59
English	1.31	0.83	2.63	2.07	1.87	1.38

Source: Adapted from Pakistan, Ministry of Home and Kashmir Affairs, Home Affairs Division, *Population Census of Pakistan, 1961*, Vol. I, pt. iv, statement 5.3.

except Bengali and Sindhi have declined over the years. Given the increased rate of urbanization (see Table II.1) in Pakistan, the number of "mobilized but differentiated"[16] groups in the country has increased — a trend not conducive to national integration.

Society and culture. Pakistan was established on the premise that Indian Muslims needed a separate state, where "they could rule according to their own code of life and according to their own cultural growth, tradition, and Islamic laws."[17] This argument presupposed the existence of one Indian Muslim society and culture and overlooked the very real regional variations in Indian Muslim society. It is true that society and culture in both East and West Pakistan are based on Islamic principles;[18] and Islam, to its followers, is not a mere set of beliefs, but a way of life which colors every aspect of the believer's daily existence. Within this broad common context of Islam, however, there are certain basic disparities between the society and culture of East and West Pakistan — disparities which are of special significance from the viewpoint of nation-building.

West Pakistani society is much more segmented than East Pakistani society. Tribalism is strong in the regions of the former North-West Frontier and Baluchistan provinces. Some of the tribes are spread over

[16] Deutsch, *Nationalism*, pp. 129–30.
[17] M. A. Jinnah, quoted in Sharif al-Mujahid, "National Integration," in East Pakistan, Bureau of National Reconstruction, *Pakistani Nationhood*, p. 148.
[18] See I. H. Qureshi, *The Pakistani Way of Life*; S. M. Ikram and P. Spear, eds., *The Cultural Heritage of Pakistan*.

the neighboring states of Iran and Afghanistan, and some pose a threat to national integration.[19]

The problem of subregionalism is also acute in West Pakistan. Though the four provinces (the Punjab, the North-West Frontier Province, Baluchistan, and Sind) and several former native states were merged into one administrative unit in 1956, intraregional conflict did not diminish. Rather the group identities of the various ethnic minorities — Pathans, Baluchis, and Sindhis — were heightened, and anti-Punjabi feeling spread among these groups.[20]

Feudal landlordism is widespread in West Pakistan. Especially in Sind, landownership is concentrated in a few hands (see Table II.4). A

Table II.4 / Distribution of landownership in West Pakistan

SIZE OF HOLDING (ACRES)	PERCENTAGE OF OWNERS	PERCENTAGE OF LAND OWNED
5 or less	64.5	15.0
5 to 25	28.5	31.7
25 to 100	5.7	22.4
100 to 500	1.1	15.9
500 or above	0.1	15.0

Source: Adapted from West Pakistan, *Land Reforms Commission Report, 1959*, Appendix I.

castelike system is prevalent, particularly in the Punjab; often endogamy is practiced and children follow the caste occupation. Some of the Muslim castes are synonymous with Hindu castes such as the Rajputs, Jats, and Arains. Because of a paucity of information, however, it is difficult to judge the extent and stability of the Muslim caste system.[21]

East Pakistani society, by comparison, is less stratified and more homogeneous. The overwhelming majority of the people belong to one

---

[19] For a detailed analysis of West Pakistan's tribes and tribal problems, see Sir Olaf Caroe, *The Pathans*; Khalid B. Sayeed, "Pathan Regionalism," *South Atlantic Quarterly*, LXIII (1964) 478–506; James W. Spain, *The Pathan Borderland*; *The People of the Khybar*; Wayne A. Wilcox, *Pakistan*; Robert N. Pehrson, *The Social Organization of the Marri Baluch*; Sylvia A. Matheson, *The Tigers of Baluchistan*.

[20] Talukdar Maniruzzaman, "Crises in Political Development and the Collapse of the Ayub Regime in Pakistan," *The Journal of Developing Areas* V (1971), 221-38.

[21] For a detailed discussion of the caste system among Muslims in West Pakistan, see Stanley Maron, ed., *Pakistan*; Zekiye Eglar, *A Punjabi Village in Pakistan*.

Table II.5 / Socioeconomic indices of East Pakistan's development

DISTRICT	TOTAL POPULATION (MILLIONS)	NONAGRICULTURAL LABOR FORCE (PERCENTAGE)	INCOME FROM AGRICULTURE AND LARGE-SCALE INDUSTRY (RS.)	PER CAPITA CONSUMPTION OF ELECTRICITY (KWH)	PAVED ROAD MILEAGE	NO. OF FACTORIES
NORTHERN AND SOUTHERN REGIONS						
Dinajpur	1.7	9.2	175.38	0.39	112.50	53
Rangpur	3.8	7.6	193.18	0.00	98.25	64
Bogra	1.6	10.8	177.57	0.00	39.50	28
Rajshahi	2.8	12.0	215.55	0.84	88.51	61
Pabna	2.0	20.3	213.86	1.64	109.06	86
Kushtia	1.2	23.1	168.16	0.26	88.33	99
Jessore	2.2	15.5	181.78	1.31	185.38	16
Khulna	2.4	20.3	326.81	17.20	60.72	82
Barisal	4.2	12.7	217.30	0.36	39.50	15
Faridpur	3.2	12.7	135.07	0.03	98.95	25
CENTRAL AND EASTERN REGIONS						
Mymensingh	7.0	8.8	170.52	0.01	166.37	55
Dacca	5.1	37.8	218.15	41.24	209.86	821
Sylhet	3.5	10.6	294.92	0.04	148.23	42
Comilla	4.4	7.1	139.90	1.23	151.25	33
Noakhali	2.4	9.6	131.27	0.00	84.75	46
Chittagong	3.0	33.1	193.24	28.54	250.75	253
Chittagong Hill Tracts	0.4	11.9	189.15	0.35	19.00	4

DISTRICT	URBAN POPULATION (PERCENTAGE)	LITERACY (PERCENTAGE)	SCHOOL ENROLLMENT (PERCENTAGE)	NO. OF POST OFFICES (PER 100 VILLAGES)	NO. OF DISPENSARIES (PER 100 VILLAGES)	NO. OF TELEPHONES
NORTHERN AND SOUTHERN REGIONS		6.0				
Dinajpur	4.2	25.9	6.42	3.17	0.55	306
Rangpur	4.2	18.9	5.10	4.19	2.11	555
Bogra	3.3	23.0	6.95	3.36	2.44	287
Rajshahi	4.3	20.0	6.32	2.90	2.50	419
Pabna	5.1	17.1	5.17	4.88	2.26	218
Kushtia	5.4	15.4	4.40	6.71	4.94	297
Jessore	3.4	20.8	5.81	6.67	2.42	261
Khulna	7.1	27.2	6.42	10.09	3.51	1,285
Barisal	2.8	24.8	6.29	11.07	0.70	328
Faridpur	2.5	17.8	4.81	8.23	3.18	201
CENTRAL AND EASTERN REGIONS						
Mymensingh	3.4	17.3	4.34	5.29	2.18	637
Dacca	14.8	23.0	5.98	5.96	1.99	9,734
Sylhet	2.0	20.0	5.80	1.90	0.78	497
Comilla	3.2	24.8	5.11	5.72	1.15	531
Noakhali	1.4	24.7	7.29	6.23	1.72	166
Chittagong	12.5	26.4	7.09	11.54	4.96	3,970
Chittagong Hill Tracts		15.3	2.58	4.67	2.95	25

Sources: Data on literacy, school enrollment, post offices, and dispensaries are taken from S. Wiqar Husain Zaidi, *An Analysis of the District Census Reports of East Pakistan*, Research Report No. 49 (Karachi: Pakistan Institute of Development Economics, 1966), pp. 42–57. Data on population, urbanization, road mileage, nonagricultural labor force, and telephones are taken from East Pakistan, Bureau of Statistics, *Statistical Digest of East Pakistan, 1966*, pp. 15–20, 26, 132, 158–59. Data on electricity consumption are from East Pakistan, Bureau of Statistics, *Handbook of Economic Indicators of East Pakistan, 1965*, p. 77. Data on factories are from East Pakistan, Commerce, Labour and Industries Dept. *Annual Report on the Administration of Factories Act in East Pakistan for the Year Ending 31st December 1959*, pp. 14–15. Income from agriculture and industry was compiled by adding the value of fourteen major agricultural products and that of large-scale industry.
Data on the agricultural products are from Haroun er-Rashid, *East Pakistan: A Systematic Regional Geography and Its Development Planning Aspects* (Karachi: Sh. Ghulam Ali, 1965), pp. 140–248. The values used are the 1959–60 annual average wholesale prices of East Pakistan.
Data on large-scale industry are from East Pakistan, Bureau of Statistics, *Handbook of Economic Indicators of East Pakistan, 1965*, p. 53.

ethnic group, the Bengalis.[22] There are some tribal peoples in the Chittagong Hill Tracts, Sylhet, Mymensingh, and Comilla; but since the total tribal population is only about 496,000, it does not pose any serious problem of integration.[23]

Interregional differences in East Pakistan are dependent mainly on socioeconomic factors, rather than on ethnic or cultural differences. East Pakistan is divided into four regions: north, south, center, and east.[24] The popularly held view in East Pakistan generally casts the north and south as underdeveloped; and indeed certain disparities between the north and south and the center and east can be discerned (see Table II.5). The center-east has most of the big urban centers. The capital, Dacca; the major port town, Chittagong; and the major industrial center, Narayanganj; all lie in this region.[25] The center and east have higher rates of urbanization (8.2 percent and 4.7 percent) than the north and south (4.2 percent and 3.8 percent). They have more people in nonagricultural labor (center, 18.1 percent; east, 13.8 percent; north, 11.1 percent; south, 16.5 percent), and a higher literacy rate (center, 16.3 percent; east, 19.3 percent; north, 16.7 percent; south, 17.7 percent).

While the center-east is more "modern," it also comprises most of the crowded districts and contains nearly half of the province's total population. There is more migration out of this region to the less crowded north and south. This internal migration creates some resentment of migrants in the north and south. The interregional conflicts in East Pakistan are still in a rudimentary stage, however.

Landownership is more dispersed in East Pakistan (see Table II.6) than in the west wing. Before independence, nearly 75 percent of the land, including all the biggest zamindari holdings, belonged to Hindu landlords. But after partition most of the landlords fled the country, or

---

[22] Racially, however, the Bengalis are a mixed group, comprising proto-Australoid, Mongoloid, and Caucasoid strains.

[23] This is generally true, though the Communist-led peasant movements in the early years after partition drew heavy support from some of the tribal population.

[24] The northern region consists of Dinajpur, Rangpur, Bogra, Rajshahi, and Pabna; the southern region, of Kushtia, Jessore, Faridpur, Khulna, and Barisal; the central region, of Dacca, and Mymensingh; and the eastern region consists of Sylhet, Comilla, Noakhali, Chittagong, and Chittagong Hill Tracts.

[25] For an elaboration of the thesis that early centers of modernization determine later development, see Peter Gould, "Tanzania, 1920-63," World Politics, XXII, (1970), 149-70.

Table II.6 / *Distribution of landownership in East Pakistan*

SIZE OF HOLDING (ACRES)	PERCENTAGE OF OWNERS	PERCENTAGE OF LAND OWNED
0 to 0.4	13	1
0.5 to 0.9	11	2
1.0 to 2.4	27	13
2.5 to 4.9	26	26
5.0 to 7.4	12	19
7.5 to 12.4	7	19
12.5 to 24.9	3	14
25.0 to 39.9	—	3
40.0 or over	—	2

Source: Pakistan, Ministry of Food and Agriculture, Agricultural Census Organization, *Pakistan Census of Agriculture, East Pakistan,* Vol. I, Table 3, p. 33.

were eased out of their holdings when feudal landlordism was abolished by the East Bengal Estates Acquisition and Tenancy Act of 1950, which fixed the ceiling of landholding at 33 acres per head. Moreover, since the economy is one of scarcity, landownership frequently changes hands.

The Muslim society of East Pakistan is relatively fluid. Some scholars attribute this to the former presence of a dominant agricultural caste and to the high population pressure on the deltaic land that resulted in little differentiation in occupational structure.[26] The traditional Muslim caste differences between the ashraf and the azlaf exist, as do the four common Muslim castes—Syed, Shaikh, Pathan, and Mughal— but it is the class differences based on economic status that have the greatest impact.[27] Since economic status depends on landholding, and landownership is highly mutable, class differences are not rigid.

Differences in social stratification in the two wings lead to differences in social and political organization. In rural West Pakistan the power structure and leadership patterns are relatively stable, whereas in rural East Pakistan society is loosely structured, with no permanent local leadership or institutions. Only when there is intravillage or multi-

[26] Peter J. Bertocci, "Patterns of Social Organizations in Rural East Bengal."
[27] For a detailed discussion of the caste system among Muslims in East Pakistan, see Nazmul Karim, *Changing Society in India and Pakistan;* Pierre Bessaignet, *Social Research in East Pakistan;* John Owen, ed., *Sociology in East Pakistan.*

village conflict do the local leaders (the sardars)[28] and the local council (the samaj)[29] meet to settle the dispute. Local leadership and institutions thus work only in crisis situations and not on a day-to-day basis. Power is highly localized, fragmented, and diffused. Historically, East Pakistan had been one of the areas least penetrated by governmental action. Its ecology made transportation and communication difficult. The relative isolation of rural areas gave rise to localized bases of power; and the absence of a well-knit social organization kept political power fragmented.

According to one observer of the Pakistani political scene, West Pakistan is "governmental," whereas East Pakistan is "political."[30] West Pakistan, especially the Punjab, has traditionally contributed heavily to the civil-military administration. The British called them the "martial races," and a tradition of military service grew there. The Bengalis, in contrast, have long been known as the most political people of the subcontinent. Bengalis gave the initial leadership to the Indian nationalist movement; and later, in the twenties and thirties, they eagerly took to the politics of violence. The terrorist movement, as well as the leftist movement, became popular in Bengal. With independence, Bengal was partitioned, but the three major traditions of Bengali politics—a demand for Bengali autonomy (or special treatment for Bengal), tactics of violence, and a leftist ideology—continued to flourish in both Bengals.[31] In the two decades following independence, the politics of both East and West Bengal remained volatile and turbulent.

History and tradition. Islamic history, especially the Muslim period of Indian history, is a common source of tradition for East and West Pakistan. This bond was emphasized by leaders of the Pakistan movement prior to the achievement of Pakistan; following independence

---

[28] Every village has a few influentials known as sardars, who belong to the dominant lineage. Sardars are not elected. Their power generally depends on their landholdings or family.

[29] A samaj is an intervillage organization of sardars. It works more or less like a council of elders. Recruitment to the samaj is generally by inheritance. That is, the eldest son of a sardar becomes a member of the samaj, though there are some exceptions. For a detailed discussion of rural social organization patterns in East Pakistan, see Bertocci.

[30] Charles Burton Marshall, "Reflections on a Revolution in Pakistan," *Foreign Affairs,* XXXVII (1959), 253.

[31] Though the three traditions appear in both Bengals, autonomy has been a more dominant issue in East Pakistan than in West Bengal, where leftist ideology is more important.

it was often used by Pakistani policy-makers to cement relations between the two wings.[32]

But there are differences between the historical traditions of East and West Pakistan. The region of West Pakistan, especially the Punjab, has been the gateway to India and passed through centuries of foreign domination by various races. It has truly been a melting pot of races and cultures. While East Pakistan too has been a melting pot, its historical tradition remained essentially separate from that of the central Gangetic plains. Only during the Mughal period were the regions now comprised by East Pakistan brought under central control for any extended length of time. The supporters of East Pakistani autonomy thus cite a long tradition of autonomy in their regions.

As for the recent past, the Pakistan movement was by no means a perfect bond between the two wings, for some prominent Muslim Leaguers from Bengal did not agree with Muslim Leaguers of the central and western provinces about the nature of Pakistan—whether there should be one, two, or more than two Pakistans—until 1946.[33] The

---

[32] Pakistani policy-makers from Mohammed Ali Jinnah and Liaquat Ali Khan to Ayub Khan have emphasized this common Islamic history and tradition. To emphasize the long tradition common to East and West Pakistan, Pakistani historians trace the origin of the Pakistan movement back to eighteenth-century Muslim resistance movements. See Hafeez Malik, *Moslem Nationalism in India and Pakistan;* Ishtiaq H. Qureshi, *The Muslim Community of the Indo-Pakistan Sub-continent.*

[33] When the concept of a separate Muslim nation was first put forward, there was no unanimous agreement as to the geographical composition of the new state. The first territorial demand was made on regions which at present correspond roughly to West Pakistan. Iqbal's famous 1930 Muslim League presidential address referred to only that territory; and Choudhury Rahmat Ali and his associates, who coined the name "Pakistan," thought of regions in northwestern India: P for the Punjab, A for Afghanistan (i.e., the North-West Frontier Province), K for Kashmir, S for Sind, and TAN for Baluchistan. Later demands were put forward for two more separate Muslim states—one in the northeast, comprising Bengal and Assam, to be called Bangastan; and one in the south, comprising Hyderabad, to be called Osmanistan. There were also demands for seven Muslim states in India. During the Lahore Conference of the Muslim League in 1940, where the Pakistan Resolution was adopted, several proposals were put before the drafting committee. The resolution which was finally adopted dropped the idea of a Muslim state in the south but called for "independent states" in the north-west and east. The idea of one Muslim state gained ground when it became evident that Bengal would be partitioned and that the eastern region would be territorially vulnerable as an independent state. Only in 1946 was the Lahore Resolution amended in favor of one Muslim state. For details on the development of the concept of a separate Muslim state, see Choudhury Rahmat Ali, *Pakistan;* S. Sharifuddin Pirzada, *The Pakistan Resolution and the Historic Lahore Session;* Choudhury Khaliquzzaman, *Pathway to Pakistan.*

Lahore Resolution of March 23, 1940, which formalized the Pakistan demand, stated the following:

> ... Resolved that it is the considered view of this session of the All-India Muslim League that no constitutional plan would be workable in this country or acceptable to Muslims unless it is designed on the following basic principles, viz., that geographically contiguous units are demarcated into regions which should be so constituted, with such territorial readjustments as may be necessary, that the areas in which the Muslims are numerically in a majority as in the North Western and Eastern zones of India should be grouped to constitute "Independent States" in which constituent units shall be autonomous and sovereign.[34]

Many prominent Bengali Muslim Leaguers emphasized the term "independent states," and interpreted the Lahore Resolution as a demand for two states. The subsequent attempt by the Muslim League central hierarchy to modify the Lahore Resolution in favor of one state met with opposition from some Bengali Muslim Leaguers, and although the resolution was finally amended in the Muslim League Council session in 1946, the amendment's validity has been questioned by many since then on the ground that the council had no power to amend a resolution passed in an open conference.[35] Thus the nationalist movement does not serve as a firm integrative bond between East and West Pakistan. The East Pakistani autonomists refer to the original Lahore Resolution in support of their demand for independence, while the "centrists" refer to the modified 1946 version to challenge this demand.

Religion. Though Islam is most often cited as the main basis of Pakistani nationhood, its validity as an integrating force is limited. The distribution of religious groups in the two wings is actually quite disproportionate. East Pakistan has a large percentage of Hindus, while West Pakistan's Hindu population is minimal (see Table II.7). Many Bengalis are reluctant to put too much emphasis on Islam, because that would immediately alienate nearly 20 percent of East Pakistan's population. Moreover, emphasis on Islam is no sure guarantee for uniting all the Muslims.

---

[34] Cited in G. Allana, *Pakistan Movement Historic Documents*, p. 172.
[35] For conflicting views on the amendment controversy, see Khaliquzzaman, *Pathway*; Kamruddin Ahmad, *A Social History of East Pakistan*; M. A. H. Ispahani, *Quaid-e-Azam Jinnah*; Pirzada, *The Pakistan Resolution*.

Table II.7 / *Religious distribution in Pakistan (percentage of total population)*

	EAST PAKISTAN		WEST PAKISTAN		PAKISTAN	
	1951	1961	1951	1961	1951	1961
Moslem	76.8	80.4	97.1	97.2	85.9	88.1
Hindu	22.0	18.4	1.6	1.5	12.9	10.7
Christian	0.3	0.3	1.3	1.3	0.7	0.8
Other	0.9	0.9	0.0	0.0	0.5	0.4

Source: Adapted from Pakistan, Ministry of Home and Kashmir Affairs, Home Affairs Division, *Population Census of Pakistan, 1961*, Vol. I, pt. i, statement 2.18, Table 5.

> The two provinces of Pakistan have a somewhat different way of looking at Islam. Some West Pakistanis . . . have a patronizing way of looking at East Pakistanis in this respect. They sometimes . . . air the idea that Bengali Muslims are . . . members of the faith who came into it to escape the rigors of being the low men on the totem pole under the caste system prevailing among the Hindus — whereas, in contrast, such West Pakistanis will point out that their own Muslim heritage dates back to the Arabian antecedents who brought the faith in from the area of its origin — so their common faith may set them apart in relation to India, but it does not necessarily pull them together as Pakistanis.[36]

Finally, too great an emphasis on Islam can aggravate sectarian conflicts, as happened during the Punjab riots of 1953, and it can inhibit the process of modernization by strengthening the hands of orthodox "ulema" or fundamentalist parties.

State-building vs. Nation-building, 1947–58

The inherent disparities between East and West Pakistan were undoubtedly deepened by the policies pursued by the ruling elite in the first decade of Pakistan's independence. In the early years of Pakistan's existence, the viability of the new state was so much in doubt that the nation's policy-makers were compelled to pursue policies maximizing the state's cohesion. However, emphasis on the development of governmental capabilities not only meant an unbalanced growth of the political sys-

[36] Charles Burton Marshall, "Testimony," pp. 4–5.

tem (i.e., the growth of output functions at the cost of input functions) but also led to an imbalance in the distribution of power among the various subnational groups. Emphasis on the output sector, the civil-military bureaucracy—which was dominated by West Pakistanis, especially the Punjabis, who had a long tradition of bureaucratic participation—automatically "limited the immediate Bengali participation in the government."[37] A demand for autonomy arose in the east wing in the early fifties when the Bengalis found that their representation in the power center of the state was virtually nil.

The power elite: The elite that came to power in Pakistan after independence was a small group of people having a narrow base of support in the society. The oligarchic nature of this elite was due partly to the rapid decline in support of the more popular "national" political elite which emerged before independence. The latter generally came from regions that were not part of Pakistan and lost their political constituencies after partition. They were reluctant either to broaden their ranks by including the regional leaders from within Pakistan or to risk an election, for fear of losing power. As the "national" political elite continued to avoid elections, their mandate grew stale and the ranks of the opposition (mainly regional leaders) swelled. In their bid to stay in power, the "national" political elite found an ally in the civil-military bureaucracy, whom they often used (or were used by) for political purposes.[38] The civil-military bureaucracy came to the aid of the political elite, partly because they were trained to carry out their political superiors' orders and partly because they also believed in the policy of centralization and "nationalization" that the elite was following. Thus, during the first decade, a close working alliance developed between the "national" political elite and the civil-military bureaucracy—an alliance that in later years, especially after 1954, was dominated by the latter.[39]

In the first decade following independence, Bengali participation in the national power elite was limited. Although the Bengalis had nearly 50 percent representation in the central political elite (Table II.8), they

---

[37] Wayne A. Wilcox, "Problems and Process of National Integration in Pakistan," *The Pakistan Student,* March–April 1967, p. 12.

[38] See Henry F. Goodnow, *The Civil Service of Pakistan,* pp. 51–103.

[39] Here, however, it should be remembered that the alliance was not so much an institutional one as a personal one among a few top civil servants and military personnel who were participants in key decision-making.

Table II.8 / Central political elite in Pakistan, 1947–58

	EAST	WEST
Heads of state	2	2
Prime ministers	3	4
Ministers, deputy ministers, state ministers*	27	27
Members of Constituent and National Assemblies	84	75

Sources: Compiled from data in Keith Callard, *Pakistan: A Political Study* (New York: The Macmillan Company, 1957), Appendix II; and Pakistan, Constituent Assembly, *List of Members of the Constituent Assembly of Pakistan, 1952*.
* The number of ministers, deputy ministers, and state ministers includes those up to 1957 and omits those in the two short-lived ministries from 1957 to 1958.

Table II.9 / Military elite in Pakistan, July 1955 (no. of officers)

SERVICE	EAST	WEST
Army	14	894
Navy	7	593
Air Force	60	640

Source: *Dawn* (Karachi), January 8, 1955.

had a bare 5 percent in the military elite (Table II.9), only about 30 percent in the civil bureaucratic elite (Tables II.10 and II.11) and 10 percent in the entrepreneurial class (Table II.12). This imbalance was due largely to historical factors. Before partition East Bengal was an underdeveloped hinterland of West Bengal. Bengali Muslims were generally poor peasants. At the time of partition, only one of the 133 Muslim Indian Civil Service/Indian Political Service (ICS/IPS) officers who opted for Pakistan was a Bengali Muslim.[40] Though postindependence recruitment policy was geared toward increasing Bengali representation in the higher Civil Service of Pakistan (CSP),[41] the initial lag resulted in a continuing gap between the participation of the two wings. (Table II.10). The British policy of army recruitment from the "martial races" of West Pakistan had the effect of almost completely excluding Bengalis from

[40] Ralph T. Braibanti, *Research on the Bureaucracy of Pakistan*, p. 49.
[41] After partition, the recruitment policy in the CSP included a quota system to increase the number of Bengalis. Thus, only 20 percent were selected purely on merit, while 40 percent had to be chosen from East and West Pakistan, respectively.

Table II.10 / East-West representation in CSP, 1948–58*

YEAR	TOTAL NO. OF OFFICERS	EAST PAKISTAN NO.	EAST PAKISTAN % OF TOTAL	WEST PAKISTAN NO.	WEST PAKISTAN % OF TOTAL
1948	18	2	11.1	16	88.9
1949	20	9	45.0	11	55.0
1950	20	6	30.0	14	70.0
1951	11	4	36.4	7	63.6
1952	17	5	29.4	12	70.6
1953	13	3	23.1	10	77.9
1954	25	7	28.0	18	72.0
1955	17	5	29.4	12	70.6
1956	21	11	52.4	10	47.6
1957	20	7	35.0	13	65.0
1958	24	10	41.7	14	58.3

Sources: Compiled from Pakistan, Establishment Division, *Civil List of Class I Officers Serving under the Government of Pakistan, 1st January, 1966*; and *Gradation List of the Civil Service of Pakistan, January 1, 1968*.
* Note: Figures are for the beginning of each year.

Table II.11 / East-West representation in the higher ranks of the Central Secretariat, 1955

RANK	EAST	WEST	EAST % OF TOTAL
Secretary	—	19	—
Joint secretary	3	38	7.3
Deputy secretary	10	123	7.5
Undersecretary	38	510	7.0

Source: Pakistan, Constituent Assembly, *Debates*, Vol. I, January 17, 1956, p. 1844.

the army. After independence, the military, unlike the civil service, did not adopt any conscious policy to counteract this imbalance. Similarly, the Bengali Muslims, by tradition, were not represented in the landed or entrepreneurial classes. In East Bengal, Hindus were generally the big landlords, and whatever private enterprise there was, was in Hindu and Marwari hands.

Even in the political elite, where the Bengalis had near parity of representation, real power always seemed to elude them:

Table II.12 / Industrial assets by "community" in Pakistan, 1959

COMMUNITY	PERCENTAGE OF PRIVATE MUSLIM FIRMS ASSETS	PERCENTAGE OF ALL FIRMS ASSETS	PERCENTAGE OF POPULATION
PRIVATE MUSLIM ENTERPRISES	100.0	67.0	88.0
Halali Memon	26.5	18.0	0.16
Chinioti	9.0	6.0	0.03
Dawoodi Bohra	5.0	3.5	0.02
Khoja Isnashari	5.5	4.0	0.02
Khoja Ismaili	5.0	3.5	0.06
Other Muslim trading communities	5.5	4.0	0.08
Syed and Shaikh	18.0	12.0	—
Pathan	8.0	5.5	7.00
Bengali Muslim	3.5	2.5	43.00
Other Muslim (including unknown)	14.0	8.5	37.50
PRIVATE HINDU AND FOREIGN ENTERPRISES		21.5	12.5
Bengali Hindu		8.5	10.00
Marwari		2.0	—
Other Hindu and Sikh		1.5	2.50
Parsi		1.0	0.01
British		7.5	—
American, other foreigners		1.0	—
PUBLIC ENTERPRISES		12.0	
Pakistan Industrial Development Corporation		7.0	—
Government		5.0	—

Source: Gustav F. Papanek, *Pakistan's Development: Social Goals and Private Incentives* (Cambridge; Harvard University Press, 1967), p. 42.
Note: Percentages are approximate.

Nazimuddin [Bengali] became Prime Minister, but lacked force of will, and was ultimately dismissed by the (Punjabi) Governor General. Mohammed Ali (Bogra) was brought in as Prime Minister but, although a Bengali, he remained the captive of the West Pakistan group that provided the main strength of his government. The Bengali members attempted to use their majority to diminish the power of the Governor-General, but as a result they found themselves out of their own jobs. The electorate of East Bengal had repudiated the Muslim League, but the outcome was a rule for more than a year by West Pakistan bureaucrats.[42]

Thus the power structure that Pakistan inherited had little effective Bengali participation, and the policy pursued by the "national elite" in the early years—a policy of one state, one government, one economy, one language, one culture—tended to perpetuate this imbalance; and was a significant factor in the growth of Bengali alienation in the first decade of Pakistan's existence.

Administrative and political centralization:"the viceregal system" and East Pakistan. The administrative-political policies pursued during the first decade were characterized by extreme centralization. They led to the establishment of an administrative-political system which has been termed "viceregal."[43] The Act of 1935, under which Pakistan was administered until 1956, provided for a strong central government; and the constitution of 1956 perpetuated the essentially strong position of the center vis-à-vis the provinces.

The office of the governor of each wing was often used as an instrument of centralization. Though under a parliamentary system of government the governor is supposed to be a figurehead, in Pakistan during the 1947-58 period the governor (like the governor-general at the center) was generally the effective head of the province; and, being the center's appointee, he always protected the center's interests in the province. Furthermore the governors were often powerful men who had close party contacts.[44]

Another often used instrument of centralization was governor's rule. Article 92A of the Government of India Act of 1935 (article 193 in the 1956 constitution) enabled the central government to dismiss the provincial government and impose direct central rule on the provinces.

[42] Keith Callard, *Pakistan*, p. 173.
[43] Khalid B. Sayeed, *Pakistan*, chap. 10.
[44] The five governors who succeeded the first English governor in East Bengal all remained active in politics. Firoz Khan Noon after his East Bengal governorship (1950-53) went on to become chief minister of the Punjab (1953-55) and prime minister (1958). Choudhury Khaliquzzaman (1953-54) later became president of the Muslim League. Iskandar Mirza (1954-55) was an IPS officer, and a secretary of defense, and went on to become interior minister (1954-55) and president (1955-58). Fazlul Huq (1956-57) was a former chief minister of Bengal and was still the unofficial head of his political party during his tenure of governorship.

The article was used to thwart any challenge to the position of the "national" political elite. Its more blatant imposition was in East Bengal in 1954, when the newly elected United Front was forced from office.[45] The center could also control individual provincial politicians through the Public and Representative Offices (Disqualification) Act (PRODA).

Though there were Muslim League governments in both the center and East Pakistan during the 1947–54 period, the party channel of control was seldom used and the East Bengal Muslim League only occasionally took stands differing from those of the central Muslim League.[46]

But the most effective instrument of centralization was the central services, especially the Civil Service of Pakistan, which manned most of the key decision-making posts in both the center and the provinces. And even when the CSP worked in the provinces, its ultimate coordination lay with the center. As was the case in preindependence India, the central services were the single stable bond between the center and the provinces.

The Bengali elite, especially the growing vernacular elite of East Bengal (see below), was unhappy with this policy of political-administrative centralization, for they found that not only were they not participants in the strong center that was being developed but they were not even masters of their own house, since centralization invariably diminished provincial autonomy. The demand for full provincial autonomy was put forth as early as 1950, when the first draft of the constitution was submitted. As the centralization process continued, the demand for autonomy drew growing public support. Autonomy became the main issue which swept the United Front to power in 1954. The summary dismissal of the United Front ministry and the continued imposition of governor's rule was interpreted by the Bengali counterelite as yet another illustra-

---

[45] Though the Adamjee industrial riots were given as the reason for the center's imposition of governor's rule, continuation of the rule for over a year, along with the "national" elite's attempt to portray the United Front leaders as traitors, secessionists, communists, etc., made it evident that the elite was unwilling to tolerate even legal opposition to its policies and position.

[46] Bengali Muslim League members fought for provincial autonomy in the subcommittee drafting the Basic Principles Committee (BPC) Report. After publication, the report was opposed by many Bengali Muslim Leaguers. Also, in 1952, the predominantly Muslim League provincial assembly passed a resolution urging the center to adopt Bengali as one of the state languages. See Callard, *Pakistan*, pp. 172–82; and G. W. Choudhury, *Constitutional Development in Pakistan*, pp. 108–9.

tion of the "national elite's" intolerance of any political opposition.[47] The demand for autonomy therefore intensified after 1954. But while the policy of administrative-political centralization first prompted the Bengalis to demand autonomy, it was the economic policies of the central government that lent material support to the demand.

Economic Policy: disparity between East and West Pakistan. As in the political-administrative sphere, so in the economic, the early policy was one of centralization and expediency. Bengalis attacked the economic policy of the ruling elite as a significant factor in the perpetuation and widening of economic disparity between East and West Pakistan. While the causes for this economic disparity are complex and debatable,[48] there is little question that during the first decade East Pakistan's economy was relatively stagnant compared to West Pakistan's. All the available data indicate a widening economic gap between East and West Pakistan in the first decade (see Tables II.13, II.14, and II.15). The economic gap which existed between the two wings in 1947–48 increased substantially by 1958. Per capita income increased in West Pakistan from Rs. 330 in 1949–50 to Rs. 373 in 1959–60; whereas in East Pakistan it declined from Rs. 305 to Rs. 288. Agriculture's contribution to regional income dropped in West Pakistan from 50 percent in 1951–52 to 46 percent in 1959–60, and that of industry rose from 8 percent to 15 percent; whereas in East Pakistan agriculture dropped from 68 percent to 65 percent and industry rose from 7 percent to 10 percent.[49] Infrastructure also developed more rapidly in the West. During the period 1947–58, enrollment in primary schools increased by 163 percent in West Pakistan and by 38 percent in the east; enrollment in secondary schools increased by 64 percent in the west but dropped by 6.6 percent in the east; university

---

[47] See Abul Mansur Ahmad, *Āmār Dekha Rajnitir Panchāsa Bachara* [Fifty years of politics as I saw it]; Ataur Rahman Khan, *Ojaratir Dui Bachar* [Two years of chief ministership]. These memoirs by two former Awami League ministers show that they looked upon the imposition of the center's rule as an attempt to keep them out of power.

[48] The economic disparity between East and West Pakistan has been a matter of controversy among Pakistani economists. Generally, West Pakistani economists attribute it to the east wing's low level of development in 1947, while Bengali economists attribute it to the central government's policies. For a detailed discussion of the question, see Md. Anisur Rahman, *East and West Pakistan;* Mahbub ul Haq, *The Strategy of Economic Planning;* Nurul Islam, "Some Aspects of Interwing Trade and Terms of Trade in Pakistan," *The Pakistan Development Review,* III (1963), Joseph J. Stern and Walter P. Falcon, *Growth and Development in Pakistan, 1955–1969.*

[49] Mahbub ul Haq, *Economic Planning,* p. 105.

Table II.13 / *Gross domestic product, population, and rates of growth (rupees in crores: 1959-60 prices)*

SECTOR	1949–1950		1954–1955		1959–1960	
	EAST	WEST	EAST	WEST	EAST	WEST
Agriculture	850	589	887	649	938	701
Manufacturing	12	18	31	79	50	142
Other	451	576	514	703	567	836
Total	1,313	1,183	1,432	1,431	1,555	1,679
Population (millions)	43.1	35.8	48.1	40.2	53.9	45.0
Per capita (rupees)	305	330	298	356	288	373

Annual rates of growth (percent)

	1949–50 TO 1954–55		1954–55 TO 1959–60	
	EAST	WEST	EAST	WEST
Agriculture	0.9	1.9	1.1	1.6
Manufacturing	21.0	34.0	10.0	12.4
Other	2.6	4.1	2.0	3.5
Total	1.7	3.9	1.7	3.2
Population	2.2	2.3	2.3	2.3
Per capita	−0.5	1.5	−0.6	0.9

Source: Gustav F. Papanek, *Pakistan's Development: Social Goals and Private Incentives* (Cambridge: Harvard University Press, 1967), p. 20.

enrollment increased by 38 percent in West Pakistan and by 11.2 percent in East Pakistan. Similarly, the transport system (measured in road and railway mileage and number of motor vehicles) and communications facilities developed more quickly in the west wing.[50]

A number of complex economic and noneconomic factors led to the widening interwing economic disparity in the first decade. No attempt will be made here to discuss these factors in detail.[51] Following independence two factors were important in helping West Pakistan widen its initial advantage. First, West Pakistan got the bulk of the migrant entrepreneurs, who played the principal role in West Pakistan's rapid industri-

[50] *Ibid.*, p. 104.
[51] For a more detailed analysis of the problem see chap. IV.

Table II.14 / *Average annual per capita consumption of selected commodities, 1951-52 to 1959-60*

COMMODITY	EAST	WEST	INDICES FOR WEST PAKISTAN (EAST =100)
FOODS			
Food grains (lbs.)	389.0	399.0	103
Raw sugar (lbs.)	16.1	46.9	291
Refined sugar (lbs.)	2.7	6.8	252
Tea (lbs.)	0.1	0.8	800
Fish (lbs.)	8.3	3.2	39
Salt (lbs.)	11.4	16.7	146
ESSENTIAL CONSUMER GOODS			
Cloth (yds.)	2.2	7.8	355
Matches (no.)	7.0	11.0	159
Cigarettes (no.)	21.0	121.0	576
Kerosene oil (gals.)	0.5	0.4	80
Paper (lbs.)	0.4	1.0	250
SELECTED PRODUCTION GOODS			
Coal (lbs.)	32.0	66.0	206
Electricity (kwt.)	1.0	18.8	1,880
Petrol (gals.)	0.1	0.8	800
LUXURIES			
Motor cars (no. per 10,000 persons)	1.0	9.8	980
Radios (no. per 10,000 persons)	6.4	46.5	727

Source: Mahbub ul Haq, *The Strategy of Economic Planning: A Case Study of Pakistan* (Lahore: Oxford University Press, 1963), p. 95.

al development.[52] The second factor, and this was the result of public policy, was the decision to set up the capital in Karachi.[53] The influx of migrant entrepreneurs and the location of the capital meant rapid industrial and infrastructure development in West Pakistan—which led to a higher absorption capacity and higher demand on the government for

[52] Gustav Papanek, *Pakistan's Development*, pp. 32-36. Papanek argues that West Pakistan's development was due largely to the "response" of private entrepreneurs to the early "economic" incentives.
[53] *Ibid.*, pp. 21-24.

Table II.15 / Regional development of selected economic and social overheads

	1947–48		1954–55		1957–58	
	EAST	WEST	EAST	WEST	EAST	WEST
Primary school enrollment	2,021,702	544,360	2,604,369	1,274,099	2,794,915	1,431,921
Secondary school enrollment	526,020	508,041	457,297	722,822	491,045	837,499
College enrollment	N.A.	N.A.	24,351	30,817	40,272	64,284
University enrollment	1,620	654	2,858	1,998	3,450	3,136
No. of doctors	211	1,014	3,175	3,571	4,580	5,034
No. of nurses	—	204	188	1,553	275	2,021
No. of hospital beds	2,825	14,117	3,902	19,197	4,237	21,021
No. of motor vehicles	3,528	21,209	8,662	71,577	11,368	89,277
Route mileage of railways	1,615	5,316	1,708	5,333	1,713	5,335
Road mileage	240	13,821	470	19,102	700	19,424
No. of radio licenses issued	5,376	45,426	13,719	120,322	27,147	183,550
No. of newspapers and periodicals	N.A.	N.A.	116	707	171	945

Source: Adapted from Pakistan, Ministry of Economic Affairs, Central Statistical Office, *Twenty Years of Pakistan in Statistics, 1947–67*, pp. 149–54, 157, 162–63, 170–86, 190.

resources. During the first decade, the central government allocated nearly two-thirds of its developmental and nondevelopmental funds to West Pakistan. There was a similar disparity in the allocation of foreign aid (see Tables II.16, II.17, and II.18). The central government also

Table II.16 / Distribution of central government's revenue expenditure, 1947-48 to 1960-61

	EAST PAKISTAN		WEST PAKISTAN		UNALLOCABLE	
	RS. IN CRORE	% OF TOTAL	RS. IN CRORE	% OF TOTAL	RS. IN CRORE	% OF TOTAL
Revenue expenditure including working expenses of commercial departments	269	12	995	45	952	43
Revenue expenditure excluding working expenses of commercial departments	86	5	616	34	1,138	61

Source: Adapted from East Pakistan, Planning Department, *Economic Disparities Between East and West Pakistan* (1963), p. 17.

Table II.17 / Central government development outlay, 1947-48 to 1960-61

	EAST PAKISTAN		WEST PAKISTAN	
	TOTAL (RS. IN CRORE)	PER CAPITA (RS.)	TOTAL (RS. IN CRORE)	PER CAPITA (RS.)
Investment	172	38	430	117
Loans	184	40	224	61
Grants-in-aid	76	15	101	28

Source: Adapted from East Pakistan, Planning Department, *Economic Disparities Between East and West Pakistan* (1963), p. 18.

did much to develop the private sector through its economic and fiscal policies and its control of foreign exchange, import licensing, and capital issues. Here again there was interwing disparity in allocation (see Table II.19). Disparity in the allocation of resources was defended by the central government on the economic grounds that there were greater

Table II.18 / Foreign aid and loans 1947–48 to June 30, 1960

	EAST PAKISTAN		WEST PAKISTAN		CENTER		TOTAL
	RS. IN CRORE	% OF TOTAL	RS. IN CRORE	% OF TOTAL	RS. IN CRORE	% OF TOTAL	RS. IN CRORE
Foreign development aid	93.89	17	335.22	62	113.03	21	542.14
U.S. commodity aid	129.00	30	262.00	64	18.00	6	409.00

Source: Adapted from East Pakistan, Planning Department, *Economic Disparities Between East and West Pakistan* (1963), p. 21.

demands in the western wing.[54] But governmental allocations were open for all to see; and the disparity, whatever its economic rationale, led to the charge of discrimination against the Bengalis and created a sense of distrust among the Bengalis toward the central government.[55] The Bengalis were particularly dissatisfied with the "one-economy" policy of the government, which failed to take into consideration the essential differences in economic patterns and the geographical separation between the two wings. The east wing's low starting point, lack of private entrepreneurs in industry, and high labor and political unrest,[56] which was one reason for the smaller influx of foreign private capital, meant that a deliberate and sustained effort on the part of the government was necessary for East Pakistan's development. In the absence of such an effort, resources tended to gravitate to the more developed region.[57]

But what irked the Bengalis most and gave special impetus to their demands for autonomy was the transfer of resources from East to West Pakistan. Through a surplus in international trade and a deficit in interwing trade, a sizable amount of East Pakistan's foreign exchange earning was diverted to the west wing (see Table II.20).

Though interwing economic disparity dates from 1947, it was not a

[54] Mahbub ul Haq, *Economic Planning*, p. 113.
[55] Many Bengali politicians, economists, and administrators look upon the central government's policies as the main reason for economic disparity. See the East Pakistan Planning Department's publication *Economic Disparities Between East and West Pakistan*, as an illustration of this.
[56] See Tables 3 and 4 in the Appendix for an east-west comparison of labor and political unrest.
[57] See Gunnar Myrdal, *Rich Lands and Poor: The Road to World Prosperity*, for an elaboration of this point.

Table II.19 / Value of import licenses allocated for raw materials and spare parts, 1951–58 (Rs. 1000)

	EAST	WEST		EAST	WEST
1951	52,400	88,981	1955	51,072	144,201
1952	42,579	137,468	1956	84,782	84,178
1953	45,525	82,242	1957	94,123	94,854
1954	43,227	104,608	1958	84,832	87,266

Source: Adapted from East Pakistan, Planning Department, *Economic Disparities Between East and West Pakistan* (1963), p. 20.

Table II.20 / Trade balances for East and West Pakistan, 1948–58 (rupees in crores)

	FOREIGN BALANCE		INTERWING BALANCE	OVERALL BALANCE	
	EAST	WEST	EAST (−) WEST (+)	EAST	WEST
1948–49	14.68	−64.83	12.05	2.63	−52.78
1949–50	24.41	−34.70	18.51	5.90	−16.19
1950–51	75.82	+17.54	20.85	74.97	+38.39
1951–52	32.31	−55.20	18.77	13.54	−36.43
1952–53	27.61	−14.99	6.92	20.69	−8.07
1953–54	35.19	−18.33	23.50	11.69	+5.17
1954–55	41.14	−29.16	10.68	30.46	−18.48
1955–56	68.06	−22.21	9.55	58.51	−12.66
1956–57	9.09	−81.78	19.77	−10.68	−52.01
1957–58	25.25	−88.07	43.29	−18.04	−44.78

Source: Muhammad Anisur Rahman, *East and West Pakistan: A Problem in the Political Economy of Regional Planning* (Cambridge: Center for International Affairs, Harvard University, 1968), p. 12.

significant factor in Bengali alienation in the first years of independence. Economics did not become a full-blown controversy until 1955. It did not figure prominently in either the 21-Points election manifesto of the United Front or the pre-1954 Constituent Assembly debates. But after 1954, especially after the Awami League became the opposition party in the National Assembly in the 1955–56 session, economic disparity became the focal point of controversy between the center and East Pakistan.[58] The East Pakistan Awami League published a pamphlet called *Why Autonomy?* which focused on economic reasons for provincial autonomy. Studies by Bengali economists were also published, for the first time giving a sophisticated economic analysis of the interwing economic disparity.[59] Even after the Awami League came to power at the center, economic issues remained the main point of controversy between the center and East Pakistan and constituted one of the major reasons for the Awami League's loss of governmental power.[60]

Cultural policy. While economic disparity was an issue that primarily affected the middle class in East Pakistan, the cultural policy of the "national" elite gave a wider emotional appeal to the demand for autonomy and helped to develop a linguistic nationalism among the other classes of Bengalis. The cultural policy of the ruling elite during the early years was assimilationist. It was thought that the two wings could be held together only if there were one language and one culture between them. Quaid-i-Azam Mohammad Ali Jinnah's famous Dacca speech of 1948 defending Urdu as the state language typifies this view:

> ... let me make it very clear to you that the State Language of Pakistan is going to be Urdu and no other language. Anyone who tries to mislead you is really the enemy of Pakistan. Without one State Language, no Nation can remain tied up solidly together and function.[61]

But from the beginning such assimilation was opposed by the Bengalis. Even before the Quaid-i-Azam's speech, which triggered demonstrations in Dacca University, Bengali members of the Constituent Assembly had demanded due recognition of Bengali. The policy-makers stuck to their assimilationist approach, however, and efforts were made to Islamicize Bengali. The first Basic Principles Committee Report (1950) recommended Urdu as the only state language. The BPC report was widely rejected by the Bengalis. By 1952, the controversy led to open

---

[58] See Pakistan, Constituent Assembly of Pakistan, *Debates,* Second Assembly, Vol. 1, January 9, 17 (speech by Abul Mansur Ahmad); January 27 (Ataur Rahman Khan); January 28 (Professor Muzaffar Ahmad).
[59] See A. Sadeque, *The Economic Emergence of Pakistan.*
[60] See Talukdar Maniruzzaman, "Group Interests in Pakistan Politics 1947–58," *Pacific Affairs,* XXXIX (1966), 83–98; and Abul Mansur Ahmad, *Rajnitir Pamachāsa Bachara,* pp. 376–93 on the Awami League's conflict with the entrepreneurial elite.
[61] Jamilud Din Ahmad, ed., *Speeches and Writings of Mr. Jinnah,* II, 490.

confrontation, when Dacca University students engaged in violent demonstrations on behalf of Bengali. Not only did the opposition political parties and the intelligentsia continue to demand recognition of Bengali, but now even the party in power in the East Bengal Legislative Assembly passed a unanimous resolution urging recognition of Bengali as one of the state languages. The central government persisted in its policy until 1956, however, when the consititution recognized both Urdu and Bengali as national languages.

The center's assimilationist cultural policy, therefore, rather than uniting the two wings, drove a wedge between them. It alienated the Bengali intelligentsia, the professionals, the students—in other words, the newly mobilized groups in the east wing. Yet more critical, the policy stimulated rapid development of vernacular elite in East Pakistan who supported policies and priorities very different from those pursued by the "national" elite.

The rise of a vernacular elite in East Pakistan

From the viewpoint of east-west integration, the most crucial development during the first decade was the rise of a vernacular elite in East Pakistan. Unlike the ruling elite at the center or in West Pakistan, which changed little over the years, the Bengali elite changed a great deal during this period. At the time of independence, the ruling elite in East Bengal, like the central ruling elite, was "national" and "nonvernacular," or bilingual. The Bengali Muslims entered the modern age at a relatively late stage. Before independence their leaders generally were landlords or Calcutta-based urban cosmopolitans who were either nonvernacular or bilingual. But in the years following independence, preexisting factional groups and new social forces gave rise to a Bengali counterelite which was mostly "vernacular" and regional[62] During its struggle

---

[62] The difference between the vernacular and the nonvernacular elite is not merely in the languages they speak; it also lies in their socioeconomic backgrounds, socialization processes, and their philosophies and policy priorities. The vernacular elite generally come from poor or lower-middle-class families in rural areas or small towns; while the nonvernacular elite come from economically well-off urban families (though their income might come from rural zamindari sources) who could afford to send their children to English-language

for supremacy (1947-54), the vernacular elite developed its own separate political party and platform and a distinct linguistic nationalism. The election of 1954 marked the loss of power of the old ruling elite.[63] The ascent of the vernacular elite to power within the relatively short period of seven years was due partly to preexisting factional opposition to the "national" elite and partly to the inept policies followed by that elite and its allies in the center.

Origins of the vernacular elite. The vernacular elite drew its strength from various groups and organizations. At the initial stage, Muslim League factions opposed to the ruling faction played a key role. Prior to independence, the Muslim League was divided into three major factions: the Dacca, or Nazimuddin, faction; the Fazlul Huq faction; and the Suhrawardy faction. The Dacca faction, led by men like Khawaja Nazimuddin and Akram Khan, was an essentially traditional, conservative faction that represented the landed interests. Its leadership was nonvernacular and had little popular support in the countryside. The Suhrawardy faction was mostly modernist and urban-based, primarily in Calcutta. Many of the members, including Suhrawardy himself, were nonvernacular. Their main strength lay in their organizational capability and in their hold over the mobilized urban literati groups, especially the students. The Fazlul Huq faction was vernacular and rural-based. It was organizationally weak but had mass support because it championed popular socioeconomic causes like the abolition of landlordism and the settlement of rural debt, as well as specifically Muslim causes.

Both the Huq and Suhrawardy factions fell out with the central Muslim League hierarchy, one of the reasons being their disagreement over the issue of Bengal's political autonomy.[64] After partition, the Nazimud-

---

schools and universities. After independence, with the introduction of universal adult franchise and the sudden increase in political participation, the vernacular elite found themselves in a position of strength because of their numerical superiority, and they successfully challenged the nonvernacular elite. For similar developments in other South Asian countries after independence, see Selig S. Harrison, *India,* Chap. III; Howard Wriggins, *Ceylon,* Chaps. VI and IX.

[63] In the 1954 East Bengal provincial election the ruling Muslim League party could secure only 10 seats in a house of 309.

[64] When Fazlul Huq broke with Jinnah on the question of membership in the Imperial Defense Council, he complained bitterly of Jinnah's interference in Bengal politics. See the Huq-Jinnah correspondence in S. Sharifuddin Pirzada, ed., *Qaid-e-Azam Jinnah's Correspondence,* pp. 55-84; and Fazlul Huq's letter of resignation, quoted in Ispahani, pp. 48-49. Similarly, one of the reasons for Suhrawardy's disagreement with the central Mus-

din faction came to power in East Pakistan with the help of the central Muslim League hierarchy.[65] Thus the early power elite in the east wing was essentially nonvernacular, organizationally weak, and opposed by the Huq and Suhrawardy factions. A few of the prominent supporters of these factions were accommodated by the ruling elite; but the majority, including Fazlul Huq and Suhrawardy themselves, remained outside the government. The inability of the ruling elite to incorporate these dissatisfied factions spurred the quick rise of the vernacular counterelite. The opposition factions, coupled with Maulana Bhasani's group, which had its main strength in Assam and Sylhet, laid the foundation of a separate political party and platform.[66] Unlike the other leaders, Bhasani believed in nonconstitutional methods and civil disobedience, and he was the only Pakistani leader who sought a rural base. His belief in socialism and anti-imperialism made him a catalyst for leftist forces in East Pakistan.

In addition to these Muslim League factions, the Congress and Communist parties helped shape the ideology and organization of the Bengali counterelite. At the time of partition, Congress was the only official opposition party in East Bengal and hence bore the main burden of criticizing the policies of the ruling elite. Congress, for example, undertook the championship of the Bengali language and principles of secularism.[67] The Communists also had considerable impact.[68] After indepen-

---

lim League was his support of the cause of greater Bengal. For a detailed analysis of the shifting fortunes of the Suhrawardy and Nazimuddin factions, and the central Muslim League hierarchy's role in these fortunes, see Abdul Mansur Ahmad, *Rajintir Panachāsa Bachara*, pp. 210-11; Kamruddin Ahmad, *East Pakistan*, pp. 86-96; Ispahani, pp. 114-17, 216-17.

[65] Interestingly enough, top Bengali leaders, both Congress and Muslim League, often had open conflict with the central hierarchies of their parties. After partition the factions that came to power in both West and East Bengal were the ones backed by the central hierarchies. For a detailed analysis of this phenomenon, see Leonard Gordon, "Bengal and the Indian National Movement."

[66] While in the more developed countries, where parties are well organized, factional disputes are usually settled within the party, in East Bengal politics, where party organization is weak, factional disputes often lead to party splits and the establishment of separate parties.

[67] See Pakistan, Constituent Assembly, *Debates,* February 25, 1948 (speeches by D. N. Dutta, Prem Hari Barma, B. K. Datt, Sris Chandra Chattopadhaya).

[68] On the role of the Communists in East Bengal politics, see Talukdar Maniruzzaman, "The Leftist Movement in East Pakistan — Leadership, Factionalism, Doctrinal and Tactical Dilemmas" (unpublished paper available from author).

dence, the Communists at first adopted the policy of working for an immediate revolution, and organized a peasant movement.[69] The quick suppression of the revolutionary movement, and a change in the policy of Cominform, led the Communists to work in other, non-Communist front organizations. They worked in the Youth League,[70] East Pakistan Students Union (EPSU),[71] Ganatantri Dal,[72] and the Awami League— organizations from which the vernacular elite drew substantial support. The Communists also aided the vernacular elite in the 1952 language movement and the election of 1954.

It was, however, the student organizations that proved to be the vernacular elite's major source of strength. Students continued their pre-independence tradition of political activism,[73] and provided leadership and support for the various political movements undertaken by the vernacular elite. After independence, the enrollment of Muslim students increased steadily. The majority of them went to vernacular language schools, and they were an ever-expanding base of support for the vernacular elite.

Foundation of the Awami League (1949). The foundation of the Awami League, the first Muslim opposition party in East Bengal, brought many dissatisfied factions under one platform. Soon the Awami League became the chief spokesman of the budding vernacular elite. An examination of the Awami League's leadership reveals some of the characteristics of the Bengali counterelite. The party president, Maulana Abdul

[69] Y. V. Gankovsky and L. R. Gordon Polonskaya, *A History of Pakistan,* pp. 143–45.

[70] The Youth League was established in 1951. It was the first noncommunal student organization and aimed at mobilizing popular support on a program of secularism, antiimperialism, antifeudalism, world peace, unfettered democracy, and employment opportunities for all people. The Youth Leaguers provided leadership to the various political parties that were later established. Ten top-ranking leaders of different underground Communist party factions are former Youth Leaguers. See Maniruzzaman, "The Leftist Movement."

[71] The East Pakistan Students Union was established in 1952, on the initiative of the leftists, to be a noncommunal student organization with an antiimperialist plank. Since 1952, the EPSU has become the major leftist student organization.

[72] Ganatantri Dal was established in January 1953 by the Youth Leaguers and other leftists to facilitate the left's participation in the 1954 election as members of a separate party.

[73] Like students in many other developing countries, East Pakistani students are highly politicized. According to one recent survey of university students, 77 percent can be classified as politicized and 80 percent appear to have medium to high political competence. See Talukdar Maniruzzaman, "Political Activism of the University Students in Pakistan" (unpublished).

Hamid Khan Bhasani, was a peasant leader, a former president of the Assam Muslim League, a maulana (religious leader) with little formal education, who had a long record of political imprisonment.[74] The three vice-presidents—Abul Mansur Ahmad, Ataur Rahman Khan, and Abdus Salam Khan—were all small-town lawyers with little active political experience. The general secretary, Shamsul Huq, was a young student leader who came to prominence during the 1948 language demonstrations. The assistant general secretary, Sheikh Mujibur Rahman, was another young student leader who came to light during the 1948 movement. Thus the Awami League's leadership was dominated by mofussil (small town) lawyers and students—vernacular professionals or potential professionals.

The Awami League provided a political organization for the rising vernacular elite, but they still lacked a coherent political platform. Early Awami League demands and demonstrations dealt with issues such as food shortages and the restoration of civil liberties. But the vernacular elite needed a political issue that would clearly set them apart from the ruling elite and would mobilize mass support behind them.

Anti-BPC Movement (1950). The anti–Basic Principles Committee Report (anti-BPC) movement supplied the vernacular elite with their major political dogma—full regional autonomy for East Bengal. The Basic Principles Committee Report, which was the first draft of the Pakistani constitution, drew sharp criticism from East Bengal. Bengalis feared that the BPC draft, if implemented, would reduce East Bengal's majority to a minority and would turn "East Bengal into a colony of Pakistan."[75]

A committee of action formed at a mass convention of opposition political workers in Dacca was entrusted with drafting an alternative proposal for the constitution. The conveners of the committee of action, Ataur Rahman Khan and Kamruddin Ahmad, were both Awami Leaguers. The committee toured East Bengal and agitated mass opposition to the BPC Report. Finally, in February 1950, a "Grand National Convention" was held which adopted alternative constitutional proposals. These proposals,

[74] As pointed out above, Maulana Bhasani is the only political leader in Pakistan who has attempted, though with limited success, to build a rural base of support.
[75] Pakistan, Constituent Assembly, *Debates,* Sess. 8, November 21, 1950 (speech by Nur Ahmad).

especially those dealing with East Bengal's autonomy, remained the sheet anchor of all subsequent demands for autonomy in East Pakistan. The proposals assign only defense and foreign affairs to the central government; and even this jurisdiction was subject to the limitations that there would be two regional foreign offices and two regional defense forces, manned by the people of the regions.[76] The federal government was entitled to levy taxes only on certain specified items and could add new items of taxation only with the consent of the region. The draft constitution also called for the establishment of "a sovereign socialist republic" and for the recognition of Bengali as a state language.

Language movement. While the anti-BPC movement gave the vernacular elite its political program, its mass appeal and group coherence was supplied by the language movement. The language movement was, in fact, crucial to the development of the vernacular elite. It helped foster a kind of linguistic nationalism in East Pakistan. It made the students a potent political force and set the pattern of student-literati-professional alliance which was used successfully in all subsequent movements. Above all, it supplied the vernacular elite with a universally popular issue, a cause under which all Bengalis could unite, a cause which helped bridge the elite-mass gap.[77]

The language movement started soon after independence. The Congress members of the Constituent Assembly had demanded equal recognition of Bengali and Urdu as early as February 1948. In that month Dacca University students went on strike, demanding that Bengali be recognized as one of the state languages of Pakistan. Though the movement was short-lived, it showed for the first time the strength of the students, the main spokesmen for the vernacular elite. In 1952 a second language movement occurred which was by far the most remembered. The events of February 21, 1952, left a deep imprint on East Pakistan's political development. Massive student demonstrations in Dacca in deliberate violation of a government ban on public meetings, the death of student demonstrators under police fire, the subsequent province-

---

[76] For a full text of the proposed constitution see Kamruddin Ahmad, *East Pakistan*, Appendix C.

[77] For an interesting analysis of the impact of the language movement in giving Bengali Muslims a sense of identity, see Badruddin Umar, "Mussalmanera Sawadesh Pratyabartana [The Muslim's return home]," in Badruddin Umar, *Sanskritik Sampradayikata* [Communalism in culture], pp. 8–11.

wide strike and protest, all changed the political complexion of East Pakistan.

The 1952 language movement created myths, symbols, and slogans that consolidated the vernacular elite. It gave them not only a popular common cause but also their first martyrs. A whole new literary and cultural tradition grew out of the events of February 21.[78] The day is now celebrated every year as a memorial day when mass meetings are held with renewed pledges to support the vernacular elite's ideals and causes. In fact, the celebration of February 21 often serves as a political barometer of the vernacular elite's moods. The bigger the processions and mass meetings and the more violent the clashes with police, the more frustrated and dissatisfied the vernacular elite.

The main driving force of the 1952 movement was the students, working in close cooperation with political party members. The students took the crucial step of breaking section 144 on February 21, and in so doing they courted arrest and some of them died.[79] They organized not only the massive strike and demonstrations in Dacca but also the later province-wide strike, and thus demonstrated the coherence and effectiveness of student organizations.

The language movement drew widespread sympathy and support from the rural areas, in part because the large majority of Bengali students came from these areas.[80] Though the peasants did not actively participate in the movement, their tacit support became manifest in the election returns of 1954, when the Muslim League government in East Bengal was defeated by a massive rural vote. The students' campaign on the language issue had greatly influenced the vote. And the language issue was the first point in the 21-Point Manifesto of the United Front (see below). Representative of the language movement's importance in the

[78] See Hasan Hafizur Rahman, ed., *Ekushe February* [21 February], for a collection of writings commemorating the day.

[79] On the eve of 21 February, when section 144 of the Criminal Procedure Code of Pakistan was imposed banning public meetings and processions, the All-Parties Action Committee favored obeying the government order. The students, however, favored confrontation by breaking section 144. Of the four persons known dead by police fire, three were students and one was a clerk of the East Bengal Secretariat.

[80] Alex Inkeles' data on East Pakistani students, based on interviews with 357 students from Dacca University and the Dacca Polytechnic Institute in the early sixties, show that the fathers of 55 percent of students are engaged in full- or part-time agriculture, and nearly 73.8 percent of the students come from villages, small towns, or small cities. Alex Inkeles, Mimeograph, Center for International Affairs, Harvard University, Cambridge, Mass.

overthrow of the ruling elite was the defeat of the Muslim League chief minister by a young student leader of the language movement who had no past political experience.

The 1954 election: overthrow of the "national" political elite in East Bengal. The 1954 election marked the rejection of the "national" elite by the Bengali electorate. The election strategy of the vernacular elite was to maximize popular support by closing their divided ranks and drawing up a program upon which there was general consensus. Before the election campaign the Bengali counterelite was fragmented into separate political parties. In addition to the Awami League, the major political party of the counterelite, there were several other parties to the left and right. There was the Nizam-i-Islam, founded in 1950, which stood for the establishment of an Islamic polity based on Quranic principles. The Nizam consisted mainly of orthodox religious leaders, and its socioeconomic program was to the right of the Awami League. To the left of the Awami League stood the Ganatantri Dal. In addition, there was the Krishak Sramik Party (KSP), founded in 1953, composed mainly of Fazlul Huq's personal followers and allies, and similar to the Awami League in its ideology and program. To strengthen their position vis-à-vis the ruling political elite, the opposition parties decided to form an electoral alliance. A united front comprising the Awami League, the KSP, the Nizam-i-Islam, and the Ganatantri Dal was formed in 1953; and a common election manifesto, the 21-Point formula, was drawn up.

The United Front and its 21-Point Manifesto foreshadowed later political trends in East Pakistan. The United Front was the first of a series of coalitions. United more against the Muslim League than for any positive policy, it consisted of various antagonistic forces, among whom factionalism was rife from the start.[81] The coalition manifesto comprised a number of conflicting goals. Still it was a significant document, insofar as it was accepted by all the opposition groups and it contained the salient points on which a consensus was reached by the Bengali counterelite. The major thrust of the 21-Point manifesto is the accommodation of the vernacular elite's interests.[82] Twelve of the points expressed their

[81] East Pakistani politics has been dominated by political movements which aim more at getting into power than at achieving specific policies. In a traditional society, where party organization and penetration is weak, political movements stressing opposition to the ruling elite can mobilize the masses more readily than can other issues.

[82] According to S. F. Levin, "The People's League Party," in A. M. D'yakov, ed., *Paki-*

demands. Thus point nineteen called for establishment of full regional autonomy for East Bengal on the basis of the Lahore Resolution, giving to the central government power over only three subjects: defense, foreign affairs, and currency. Even in these matters, regional safeguards were included. In defense, the headquarters of the navy would be in the east wing, and an armament factory would be established there in order to make East Bengal self-sufficient in defense. Other demands included recognition of Bengali as one of the national languages (point one); introduction of the vernacular as a medium of instruction (point ten); abolition of "reactionary" Dacca and Rajshahi University acts, to make the universities autonomous (point eleven); repeal of security acts for political imprisonments (point fourteen); separation of executive and judiciary functions (point fifteen); assurance of regular and free elections (points twenty and twenty-one); declaration of February 21 as an official memorial day (point eighteen); and erection of a memorial for the martyrs of the language movement (point seventeen).

While the 21 Points were essentially a program of the vernacular elite, they also included demands directed toward mobilizing support from workers and peasants. Thus it called for the introduction of economic and social rights for industrial workers, according to the principles of the International Labour Organisation. To the peasants, it pledged "nationalization of jute" and securing of fair prices (point two), support of cooperatives and cottage industry (point four), and construction of irrigation facilities for flood and famine control (point seven). To the urban white-collar workers, it promised reduction of income disparity between high- and low-salaried employees (point twelve). Thus a very broadly based program and alliance was formed to fight the incumbent Muslim League government.[83] The strategy proved a success. The Muslim League was swept out of office, and the vernacular elite came to power.

The vernacular elite in East Bengal vs. the "national" elite at the

---

stan, p. 86, the manifesto was "primarily the program of the Bengal nationalist movement." In addition to expressing "the interests of the Bengal nationalist bourgeoisie," the program was designed "to receive the support of the other strata of the population of East Pakistan." (Levin gives a Marxist interpretation of the rise of Awami League.)

[83] In this respect the United Front and its 21-Point manifesto were similar to the preindependence Muslim League and its program. Before independence, the Muslim League promised policies designed to get the support of divergent groups. But some of these policies were mutually conflicting and could not be implemented—which led to the defection of

center, 1954–58. With the coming to power of the vernacular elite in East Bengal, the east wing's relationship with the center underwent severe strain. Even prior to 1954, there had been conflicts between the central government and the province; but these had generally been solved within committees and the Muslim League organization, beyond the public gaze.[84] The center always managed to impose its will upon the East Bengal government without resorting to direct intervention by the governor-general's rule, which had been used in other provinces. Thus there was a stable Muslim League government in East Bengal from 1947 to 1954. The 21 Points, however, especially the demands for full regional autonomy for East Bengal, were anathema to the "national" elite. Within six weeks of its assumption of power, the United Front ministry was dismissed by the center, on the grounds that it was bringing about disintegration of the country.[85]

But the vernacular elite and the "national" elite were soon forced to work with each other, out of mutual need rather than any shared objectives. The "national" elite needed the vernacular elite's support to provide their rule in the east wing with a semblance of legitimacy. And the vernacular elite, after waiting in a political wilderness for more than a year, found they needed the center's support to return to power. A working relationship thus grew between them. The new spirit of compromise and cooperation was revealed in the signing of the Murree Pact.[86] The vernacular elite conceded that West Pakistan be considered as one administrative unit, thus submerging West Pakistan's ethnic dif-

---

various groups and factions from the Muslim League. The United Front in its 21 Points, also, formulated a broadly based program to incorporate different groups. But some of these groups and proposed policies were also mutually conflicting, and the United Front broke up within two years.

[84] The Muslim League government in East Bengal fought for greater power for their province in the subcommittee entrusted with drafting the BPC Report. But they were overwhelmingly outnumbered. See Callard, *Pakistan,* pp. 172–75. Also see the editorials in the East Bengal Muslim League's mouthpiece, *Azad* (Dacca), September 29, 30, October 2, 4, and 16, 1950, for the East Bengal Muslim League's opposition to the center.

[85] When he imposed the center's rule, the central prime minister accused the provincial chief minister Fazlul Huq of treason and of conspiring to bring about the secession of East Bengal. See Mohammad Ali (Bogra's) speech, *Dawn* (Karachi), May 31, 1954.

[86] The Murree Pact, signed by members of the Muslim League, the Awami League, and the United Front, was an attempt to bring about an east-west agreement on some controversial issues. See *Dawn* (Karachi) July 8, 1955. For a detailed description of the bargaining that preceded the signing of the Murree Pact, see Abul Mansur Ahmad, *Rajnitir Panachāsa Bachara,* pp. 286–99.

ferences under one administrative and political structure, limiting Bengali ability to form coalitions with anti-Punjabi elements in the west wing and giving parity of representation with East Pakistan. For its part, the "national" elite recognized Bengali as a national language along with Urdu, and accepted the principles of a joint electorate, regional autonomy for East Bengal, and parity of the two wings in all spheres. This alliance, however, based as it was on a mutual quid pro quo, was at best tenuous and was likely to break down whenever either partner felt it could make a better bargain. The fragility of the alliance is well illustrated by the extreme instability in both the center and East Pakistan: between 1954 and 1958, there were five governments at the center and three in East Pakistan (there was governor's rule for nearly two years in East Pakistan).

Though the vernacular elite advocated regional autonomy for East Bengal, it was quite eager to participate in the center and was willing to cultivate an alliance with the West Pakistani political forces. When the United Front was formed, it was understood that, of its three leaders, Bhasani would remain with the party organization, Huq would be in East Pakistan, and Suhrawardy would go to the center. Suhrawardy consistently tried to make the Awami League a national party and himself a national leader. His first attempt to do so had been made in 1952 by joining the East Bengal Awami League with several West Pakistani parties—Mamdot's Jinnah Muslim League in Punjab, Pir of Manki Sharif's Awami League in the North-West Frontier Province, and Awami Mahaz in Sind. Conflict soon arose between the East Bengal Awami League and the largest component of the West Pakistan Awami League, the Mamdot group, which consisted mostly of feudal landlords who did not share the East Bengal stand on land reforms, provincial autonomy, and foreign policy. The Mamdot group's departure in 1953 weakened the West Pakistan Awami League numerically, but left it ideologically more cohesive. Between 1953 and 1955, the Awami League gained the support of regional autonomists in both East and West Pakistan.

Suhrawardy's efforts to build himself up as a national leader required the delicate balancing of conflicting forces. While he was himself a member of the nonvernacular "national" elite, his constituency was the vernacular elite in East Pakistan. He had become a major political figure by cultivating this constituency, but he could not come to power at the center unless he played up his "national" image and toned down some of the demands of the Bengali vernacular elite. After coming to power he was thus caught in a dilemma. By softening his stand on regional autonomy (especially on autonomy for West Pakistan's provinces) and on foreign policy he lost the support of regional autonomists (especially those from West Pakistan) and leftists;[87] while his support of Bengali business interests alienated West Pakistani entrepreneurs.[88] These irreconcilable forces led to a new split in the Awami League and to the fall of Suhrawardy's ministry within thirteen months of its accession to power.

Despite Suhrawardy's fall from power and the split in the Awami League, the fragmented Bengali counterelite still tried to form all-Pakistan parties and alliances. As long as there was hope of a free political process, the vernacular elite was willing, indeed eager, to participate in national politics. They believed that their numerical superiority would give them an edge in the political process and would enable them to use their political power to redress the administrative-economic disparity from which the east wing had suffered in the past. The Awami League tried to pick up some right-wing industrial and business support in West Pakistan to fill the vacuum created by the departure of regional autonomists. Similarly, the East Pakistani leftists who had left the Awami League joined with other leftist parties and the West Pakistani regional autonomists to form the National Awami Party (NAP) in 1957. But the hopes of the Bengali counterelite for effective participation at the center were dashed when, within a few months of the long-awaited national elections, martial law was declared, the established political institutions were swept aside, and the civil-military bureaucracy, in which Bengali representation was minimal, assumed power in the country.

---

[87] Thus after Suhrawardy became prime minister he declared that 98 percent autonomy was granted to East Pakistan by the 1956 constitution, though the Awami League had previously refused to sign the constitution on the grounds that it did not grant enough autonomy. Suhrawardy also defended the SEATO and CENTO security alliances, though the Awami League had campaigned against the signing of these pacts. In addition, he defended one unit for West Pakistan, though the West Pakistan Awami League wanted repeal of one unit.

[88] The Suhrawardy ministry came under fire from West Pakistani businessmen, who alleged that the government was using import licensing as a means of political patronage. For a detailed discussion of the conflict, see Maniruzzaman, "Group Interest," pp. 89–91; Abul Mansur Ahmad, *Rajnitir Panachasa Bachara*, pp. 429–32.

men who were already participants in the existing political system and who had institutional bases of power within that system. Long before the coup, the military had been working as a silent partner in the civil-military bureaucratic coalition that held the key decision-making power in the country.

Though the civil-military bureaucracy Pakistan inherited from the British had been trained in a tradition of neutrality, it was also law-and-order oriented and was accustomed to viewing politicians as rabble-rousers. In postindependence India, political control over the civil-military bureaucracy was made possible by strong political organization and leadership. But in Pakistan, in the absence of such organization, the civil-military bureaucracy assumed de facto political power and dismissed the politicians as superfluous and as impediments to modernization.[5] The military's disillusionment with political leadership dated from Liaquat's affixing his signature to the cease fire of the Kashmir campaigns of 1948 — a blunder, in the eyes of the army, which cost them victory.[6] Some top military men long nursed a grudge against the politicians' handling of the war. The seriousness of the rift became evident with the Rawalpindi Conspiracy of 1951, when a few military leaders allegedly tried to overthrow the government.[7]

The military bureaucracy developed a close working alliance with the civil bureaucracy,[8] not merely out of institutional interests — the military's needs were always quickly met by the civil service[9] — but also because their views on the country's problems and solutions were similar. Like the civil bureaucracy, the military gave priority to state-building and government-building tasks and believed in a policy of centralization.

[5] On the civil servants' attitude toward the politicians, see Henry F. Goodnow, *The Civil Service of Pakistan,* pp. 91–96.

[6] Fazal Muqeem Khan, *The Story of the Pakistan Army,* pp. 117–18.

[7] Though a precise reason for the Rawalpindi Conspiracy was never made public, it was widely believed that the generals involved were those dissatisfied with the government's Kashmir policy.

[8] See J. C. Hurewitz, *Middle East Politics: The Military Dimension,* pp. 179–86; and Wayne Wilcox, "The Pakistan Coup d'Etat of 1958," *Pacific Affairs,* XXXVIII (1965), 27–30, for a detailed discussion of this point.

[9] The military's cultivation of the civil bureaucracy was partly due to the latter's capacity to deliver the goods. Thus, both Ayub in his autobiography and Colonel Mohammad Ahmed in *My Chief,* pp. 38-55, mention that it was difficult to establish a modern army because resources were scarce and because it was hard for Ayub to get a decision from the politicians. Ayub also mentions that Iskander Mirza, then defense secretary, was able to make decisions quickly (*Friends Not Masters,* pp. 75–76).

Both looked with suspicion on the political elite, especially on the rising vernacular elite in East Pakistan, whom they considered to be a disruptive force.[10] After 1954, when the vernacular elite gained ascendancy, the civil-military bureaucratic elite began to express doubts about the capability of the parliamentary system to provide for political stability and national integration. Iskander Mirza, spokesman for the civil bureaucracy, publicly advocated a controlled democracy.[11] Ayub Khan, spokesman for the military elite, in 1954 circulated his draft constitution urging the adoption of a "controlled form of democracy with checks and counterchecks."[12] He suggested that "certain preliminary steps will have to be taken" before such a constitution is adopted, and that the "taking of such preliminary steps . . . is the *immediate* aim of Pakistan."[13]

There was no immediate attempt to take direct control, however, even though the 1956 constitution did not satisfy the military. Ayub referred to it as a "document of despair."[14] But so long as Iskander Mirza was president, the civil-military bureaucratic elite was satisfied to remain in the background. Their decision to intervene directly came only after it became apparent that Mirza had exhausted all possible political alliances, and that the national elections scheduled for February 1959 would bring the vernacular political elite to power, not only in East Pakistan but also at the center. The civil-military bureaucratic elite looked upon the forthcoming election, and the prospect of the vernacular elite's coming to power, as a prelude to chaos and national disintegration.[15] The military seized power five months before the scheduled election, on the plea of saving the country from "complete disruption."[16]

The events surrounding the actual decision to seize power have not

[10] *Ibid.*, pp. 55–58.
[11] *Dawn* (Karachi), October 31, 1954.
[12] Ayub Khan, *Friends Not Masters*, p. 188.
[13] *Ibid.*, p. 187. He does not elaborate on what these preliminary steps should be, however.
[14] *Ibid.*, p. 54.
[15] The military coup of 1958 may be termed what Morris Janowitz calls "reactive militarism." The military was apprehensive about the worsening socioeconomic and political condition of the country under the civilian regime, and the coup came essentially as a reaction to it. See Ayub Khan, *Friends Not Masters*, pp. 51–59; and Mohammad Ahmed, *My Chief*, pp. 77–82, on the military's growing impatience with the civilian regime and their apprehension about the forthcoming election.
[16] *Dawn* (Karachi), October 8, 1958.

yet been made wholly public, but all accounts point to the fact that the military took the initiative in planning the coup. Ayub in his autobiography refers to the constant pressure put on him to intervene by his civilian and military friends.[17] And a Pakistani military historian reported that when the commander-in-chief asked for an operations plan, "a broad tactical outline was ready."[18] Rushbrook Williams, who interviewed the major participants in the coup, alludes to a preexisting plan;[19] and Ayub himself refers to the politicians' attempt to make contact with certain members of the armed forces and thus isolate the senior officers.[20]

In spite of the military's initiative in preparing the October 7 coup, they at first used President Iskander Mirza as a figurehead, thereby giving their takeover the appearance of a palace coup.[21] Mirza talked of an early withdrawal of martial law, and said that a committee of experts would be established to frame a new consitution.[22] But, following a brief and futile struggle for power, Mirza was forced to leave,[23] and Ayub took power on October 27, 1958, pledging that there would be no premature lifting of martial law until the all-around confusion was cleared up.

The new regime. But who were the people entrusted with the task of overcoming the political ineffectiveness? A look at the composition of the new power elite and dominant interest groups is instructive in understanding the policies pursued by the new regime. Additionally, since the regime was highly elitist in nature, and the crisis of Bengali participation was essentially a crisis of elite participation, an analysis of the national representativeness of the new power elite is useful to underscore one significant factor of Bengali alienation from the regime.

The military coup did not bring about any fundamental change in the elite structure, as it was a defensive maneuver on the part of the

---

[17] Ayub Khan, *Friends Not Masters*, pp. 58-68.
[18] Fazal Muqeem Khan, p. 194.
[19] L. F. Rushbrook Williams, *The State of Pakistan*, p. 182.
[20] Ayub Khan, *Friends Not Masters*, p. 57.
[21] *Ibid.*, pp. 70-71. Ayub relates in some detail that he went to great lengths to get letters of authority from Mirza, so that the latter "assumes full responsibility for his decisions." Mirza was used as a figurehead because the military probably hoped thereby to hasten foreign recognition of the regime.
[22] *Dawn* (Karachi), October 16, 1958.
[23] Ayub Khan, *Friends Not Masters*, pp. 70-76.

ruling elite to thwart the challenge of the vernacular elite.[24] Still the change of regime did somewhat alter the fortunes of the various interest groups. One obvious change—and this was of critical importance from the viewpoint of Bengali participation—was the virtual removal of the political elite from power. With the coup the constitution was abrogated, political parties were abolished, and the established political process was completely halted. For politicians the regime had only contempt and scorn. In his first broadcast to the nation as chief administrator of martial law, on October 8, 1958, Ayub had the following to say of politicians:

> Ever since the death of the Quaid-i-Azam and Mr. Liaquat Ali Khan, politicians started a free-for-all type of fighting in which no holds were barred. They waged a ceaseless and bitter war against each other regardless of the ill effects on the country, just to whet their appetites and satisfy their base motives. There has been no limit to the depth of their baseness, chicanery, deceit, and degradation. Having nothing constructive to offer, they used provincial feelings, sectarian, religious, and racial differences to set a Pakistani against a Pakistani. They could see no good in anybody else. All that mattered was self-interest. In this mad rush for power and acquisition, the country and people could go to the dogs as far as they were concerned.[25]

With such a dim view of politicians' motivations and capabilities, the new regime could hardly be expected to share power with the political elite. Indeed, some of the early measures of the regime were directed specifically against prominent political leaders, who were either arrested or politically disqualified under EBDO.[26] Freedom of the press, association, and assembly was curtailed. Noting the general ineffectiveness of the politicians, Ayub boasted: "The biggest weapon of a politician is his tongue, which we have controlled. I think things are going to be quiet for a while."[27]

The first cabinet of the Ayub regime did not include any prominent politicians,[28] nor did the subsequent cabinets during the martial law

[24] For a detailed discussion of the elite structure before the coup, see chap. II.
[25] Ayub Khan, *Speeches and Statements, 1958-1964.* I, 2.
[26] The Elective Bodies Disqualification Ordinance (EBDO) was promulgated shortly after martial law, and was used to disqualify politicians from participating in politics for a period of eight years.
[27] *The New York Times*, October 19, 1958.
[28] Abul Kasem Khan of East Pakistan was the only politician. But he had not been active in politics since 1954 and was mostly known not for his political exploits but rather as the leading Bengali industrialist.

period (1958-62). With the introduction of the 1962 constitution, the regime was obliged to come to terms with the political elite and to include politicians in the cabinet. But even after 1962, none of the important cabinet portfolios—defense, planning, finance, home—were given to politicians. Ayub's key advisers throughout his rule remained nonpolitical: Manzur Qadir, Shoaib, Q. A. Shahab, Altaf Gauhar, and Fida Hasan.[29] Even when the regime reluctantly allowed the renewal of limited political activity, it formed an alliance with the old nonvernacular "national" political elite. The vernacular political elite was still anathema to the regime. In its failure to come to an understanding with the vernacular elite the new political system was weakened, for it thereby lost the support of a significant proportion of newly mobilized groups. One of the dichotomies of the regime's political experiment was that the politicians with mass support and strong organizational backing—who, given participation in the system, could have been effective—were not allowed a share in the power, while those politicians who had a share in the power were without party or mass support and hence were ineffective vis-a-vis the bureaucracy and the entrepreneurial elite. Even for achieving such obviously political objectives as maintaining the stability of the political system the regime depended upon the civil-military bureaucracy rather than upon its political supporters.[30] The politicians' weight in the new power elite was therefore understandably minimal.

The other group that lost some of its power under the regime was the landed aristocracy. Before 1958, it was a dominant interest group. The big landlords of West Pakistan owned not only the villages but also the votes within them. They dominated the assemblies[31] and blocked the adoption of any land reform measures in West Pakistan before 1958. But after the military coup, with the abolition of the old electoral process, the landlords' control of the rural vote lessened in value and their influence waned. In addition, some early measures of the new regime were directed against the landed interest. A land reform commission was set up on October 31, 1958, and the regime made explicit that one rationale behind land reform was curtailment of the landed elite's political in-

[29] Of Ayub's close advisers, only Z. A. Bhutto later turned to politics seriously. Manzur Qadir was a lawyer; Shoaib, Shahab, Gauhar, and Fida Hasan were all civil servants.
[30] Khalid B. Sayeed, *The Political System of Pakisan,* pp. 225-27.
[31] See chap. VII, n. 7

57 / The decade of Ayub (1958-68): an overview

fluence.[32] The measures suggested by the land reform commission and adopted by the regime could hardly be called radical.[33] There was no attempt at thorough land redistribution. Measures were directed exclusively at very large landowners. Furthermore, there were enough loopholes to permit landholdings above the fixed ceiling,[34] and enforcement was lax. One estimate put the redistribution of land as not more than 2 percent of all cultivated land.[35] Still the 1959 land reform was the first serious attempt at land reform in West Pakistan; and according to at least one source the landlords may have surrendered as much as a third of the land they owned.[36] The first Basic Democracies election of 1959 indicated the declining influence of landlords in rural politics. The "average" West Pakistani Basic Democrat of 1959 was thirty-eight years of age, had had eight years of schooling, and claimed an annual income of Rs. 2,320, 59 percent of which was obtained from nonagricultural sources.[37] The declining influence of the landed elite was also visible in the 1962 national and provincial assemblies.[38]

As the Ayub regime politicized itself, it fell back to some extent upon the support of landlords. This was partly because the regime entered into a political alliance with the old "national" political elite, whose major source of support was the landed aristocracy. Also, the landed elite's ready acquiescence to mild land reforms and its accommodation of the civil-military bureaucracy as a middle landed interest[39] helped cement an alliance with the regime. On the whole, however, compared to the civil-military bureaucracy or the entrepreneurial elite, the old landed elite suffered a setback during the Ayub regime. Rather than the old landed aristocracy it was the rising kulaks who became the

---

[32] Ayub Khan, *Friends Not Masters,* p. 88.

[33] The ceiling on landholding was put at 500 acres of irrigated land or 1,000 acres of nonirrigated land, plus whatever additional area might be needed to give the equivalent of 36,000 produce index units.

[34] Since there was an option for making gifts or voluntary surrender, many landlords redistributed land among relatives and friends, and thus avoided exceeding the ceiling while effectively retaining control of the land. See Gunnar Myrdal, *Asian Drama,* p. 329.

[35] Joe R. Motheral, "The Effect of Government Policy and Programs on Agricultural Production in Pakistan."

[36] S. J. Burki, "Interest Group Involvement in West Pakistan's Rural Works Program."

[37] *Ibid.*

[38] See Table VII. 3.

[39] Most of the land that was redistributed went to retired civil-military personnel. These new landowners showed great initiative in mechanized farming and were partly responsible for West Pakistan's agricultural surplus in the 1960s.

dominant interest group during the decade.⁴⁰ The "green revolution" had created a new group of rich farmers who became the chief base of political support for the regime.

The coup brought the civil-military bureaucracy to the forefront. The military decided to remain in the background, however, while the civil bureaucracy was very visible. The civil servants were initially shaken up by Iskander Mirza's ouster and the accompanying screening of some higher civil servants. Ayub testified to early reservations on the part of the civil servants.⁴¹ But the regime soon took care to restore the civil bureaucracy's confidence. Within a few weeks the army was sent back to the barracks; and, following the initial shock, the screening procedure was substantially relaxed. Barely 5 percent of the 2,800 class I officers charged with corruption were found guilty, and of these less than half were actually punished.⁴² The civil servants' quick rehabilitation is indicated by the influential positions soon assigned to them by the Ayub regime. Of the 280 members of the thirty-three major commissions formed by the regime for the purpose of suggesting substantive policy changes, nearly 60 percent were members of the civil bureaucracy; only 6.4 percent were military; and 5 percent each were lawyers, judges, and scholars. Politicians comprised barely 1.4 percent of the commissions' membership.⁴³ The civil servants not only monopolized all the policy-making jobs in the central and provincial governments but also gradually took over the different corporations and autonomous bodies that had been established, ironically enough, to circumvent the slow bureaucratic procedures of government departments.⁴⁴

Soon after his assumption of power, Ayub realized the futility of his attempt to "make the country pure by whacking it with the flat of his

---

⁴⁰ The term "kulak" in the Pakistani context refers to the owners of large farms who became politically powerful through the Basic Democracies system. For a detailed description of the process, see chap. VI.

⁴¹ Ayub Khan, *Friends Not Masters*, p. 72.

⁴² Herbert Feldman, *Revolution in Pakistan*, pp. 77–79. The percentage punished among class II and class III officials was even lower. Of 5,500 class II officials charged with corruption, 4 percent were found guilty, of whom fewer than 1 percent were punished, while of the 87,000 class III officials charged only 1.5 percent were punished, p. 77.

⁴³ Ralph Braibanti, *Research on the Bureaucracy of Pakistan*, pp. 311–14.

⁴⁴ In 1968, members of the elite Civil Service of Pakistan (CSP) held not only most of the secretaryships at the center but also the following diverse and powerful posts: chief justiceship of the Pakistan Supreme Court, chairmanships of the East and the West Pakistan Water and Power Development Authority, the East and the West Pakistan Industrial Development Corporation, the Central Public Service Commission, the Tariff Commission,

broad sword."[45] The military's initial involvement in economic and administrative decision-making led to chaos,[46] and the military was more than ever frustrated by the slow rate of progress.[47] As the need to disengage the military from political decision-making became evident, Ayub turned to the civil bureaucracy.

The civil servants, on their part, followed a shrewd policy of self-preservation. First, the elitist CSP opened its ranks to the military by allowing a select group of army men to join. Of the fourteen military officers who joined the CSP between 1960 and 1963, eight had close connections with the top echelon of the military hierarchy.[48] Second, the whole civil service, especially the CSP, modernized its training program in order to compete effectively in the changed sociopolitical milieu. Realizing the regime's commitment to modernization and development, the CSP sent its younger members abroad for advanced training in such fields as economics, public administration, accounting, finance, and community development. By 1968, 67 officers of the CSP had spent a total of 79 man-years in seventeen American and British universities.[49] This expertise enabled the CSP to head the numerous corporations set up by the government.[50] Third, the civil service changed its former law-and-order outlook to an orientation favoring development, especially rural development. The quick rise of the entrepreneurial elite under the regime eroded the civil servants' hold on urban areas. Through the control of the Basic Democracies and the works program, the civil servants found a new base of power, the rural gentry.[51] Fourth, the civil service continued, and even improved, its policy of regional and ethnic repre-

---

the Atomic Energy Commission, the Export Promotion Bureau, the East and the West Pakistan Agricultural Development Bank; managing directorships of the Pakistan Insurance Corporation and Trading Corporation; directorships of Radio Pakistan and the National Institute of Public Administration; office of chief economist, the East Pakistan Planning Department, and chief controller, Imports and Exports. (Pakistan, Establishment Division, *Gradation List of the Civil Service of Pakistan, 1968.*)

[45] *The New York Times,* October 20, 1958.   [46] Feldman, *Revolution,* pp. 44–46.

[47] Ayub Khan, *Friends Not Masters,* pp. 78–79.

[48] S. J. Burki, "Twenty Years of the Civil Service in Pakistan," *Asian Survey,* IX (1969), 248.

[49] *Ibid.,* p. 249.

[50] In 1964, the CSP held 63 posts in the corporations. By 1967, the number had risen to 85. *Ibid.,* p. 254.

[51] According to Albert Gorvine, "The Civil Service Under the Revolutionary Government in Pakistan," *Middle East Journal,* XIX (1965), 332, in Baluchistan "the C.S.P. has been able to use the Basic Democracy system to replace the sardari system with the Deputy Commissioner as the new Sardar." See also S. J. Burki, "Civil Service," p. 250.

sentation; whereas East Pakistani representation in the CSP was 24.3 percent in 1957, by 1967 it had risen to 34.1 percent.[52] Thus the CSP, by becoming the only national institution with substantial Bengali participation, ensured its indispensability and permanence and bettered its position in the new power elite.

The entrepreneurial elite, who were emerging as a powerful interest group even before 1958,[53] also made significant gains under the Ayub regime. The regime's policy of economic development through private enterprise helped consolidate the power of this "new, able, ruthless group of industrial entrepreneurs."[54] The concentration of economic power became so great that by 1968, "66% of all industrial profits, 97% of the insurance funds, and 80% of the banks in the country were controlled by some twenty families."[55] While the participation and influence of these "robber barons" in the policy-making process was more informal than formal, and the methods they used were more covert than overt,[56] they did achieve economic and fiscal policies advantageous to their interests. They assiduously cultivated informal channels of influence.[57] Leading industrialists such as the Dawoods became active supporters of the regime and major donors to the Muslim League party fund.[58] They also welcomed to their fold ex-military personnel—men like General Habibullah and Captain Gauhar Ayub—who had close contact with the top echelon of the regime, and thus strengthened their ties with the military.[59] The growing ascendancy of the entrepreneurial elite was reflected

[52] Pakistan, Establishment Division, *Gradation List of the Civil Service of Pakistan,* 1957, 1967.

[53] Talukdar Maniruzzaman, "Group Interest in Pakistan Politics 1947-58," *Pacific Affairs,* XXXIX, (1966), 88-91.

[54] *Ibid.*, p. 89.

[55] Mahbub ul Haq, chief economist, Pakistan Planning Commission, quoted in editorial, *The Pakistan Observer* (Dacca), May 3, 1968.

[56] A. Lee Fritschler, "Business Participation in Administration," in Guthrie S. Birkhead, ed., *Administrative Problems in Pakistan,* pp. 77-88.

[57] The formal channels open to them were advisory councils in the ministries of finance, industries, and commerce, where industry and business had representatives. But the councils met infrequently and had limited say on overall commercial and industrial policies. See Fritschler, pp. 78-81.

[58] The Dawoods, who increased their wealth many fold in the sixties and were the main beneficiaries of the PIDC's disinvestment policy in East Pakistan, were loyal supporters of the regime. Siddiq Dawood became the treasurer of the Muslim League and was one of the staunch supporters of the regime in the National Assembly.

[59] Retired military men went into business and became industrial magnates almost overnight. The most prominent of the ex-military men turned industrialist was Ayub's own son Captain Gauhar Ayub, who was reportedly worth $2–$3 million. See *The New York Times,* March 9, 1969.

in their increased representation in the national and provincial assemblies during the decade of Ayub. Nearly 32 percent of the East Pakistani members and 19 percent of the West Pakistani members of the national and provincial assemblies of 1962 and 1965 were businessmen, industrialists, or contractors,[60] whereas in the constituent and national assemblies of 1947-58 only 4 percent of the East Pakistani members and 3 percent of the West Pakistani members had been from business or industry.[61]

It was the military that remained the main power base of the Ayub regime, however. When Ayub first came to power he did not hesitate to acknowledge that his authority lay ultimately in the power of the sword.[62] Even when the military was relegated to the background and other sources of legitimacy were established through the Basic Democracies and the constitution, Ayub repeatedly used the threat of "a bloody revolution" to counter serious challenges to his rule.[63] During periods of crisis, military men were brought into key positions to demonstrate their continued support of the regime. Ayub on his part continually shifted and balanced his potential rivals in the military.[64] Civilian control over the armed forces was abolished.[65] But the military was more the support base of the regime than an actual participant in public policy-making, which was left mainly to the civil bureaucracy.

The change in power structure brought about by the coup—especially the loss of power of the political elite—meant that the Bengalis had little representation. As discussed in Chapter II, it was only in the political elite that Bengali representation was substantial.[66] Even after years of a quota system Bengali representation in the higher civil services re-

---

[60] Talukdar Maniruzzaman, "'Crisis in Political Development' and the Collapse of the Ayub Regime in Pakistan," *The Journal of Developing Areas*, V (1971), 227.

[61] *Ibid.*

[62] See the regime's arguments and their ultimate acceptance by the Supreme Court in the *Pakistan* v *Dosso* case. The full judgement is reported in *Dawn* (Karachi), October 28, 1958.

[63] Before the presidential election of 1964-65, Ayub often threatened a military takeover less benign than his if he lost. Also, during the height of the Six-Point controversy, Ayub threatened to use the language of weapons. See *The Pakistan Observer* (Dacca), March 21, 1966.

[64] The cases of generals Sheikh and Azam Khan are illustrations of Ayub's policy of self-preservation.

[65] The constitution of 1962 stipulated that the minister of defense for the next twenty years had to be a general in the military.

[66] See Table II.8.

mained less than 40 percent. As late as 1966, Bengalis constituted less than 30 percent of the class I officers of the Central Secretariat.[67] In the military elite, in the absence of a quota system, Bengali representation was nearly as poor during the Ayub decade as during the fifties (see Table III.1).

Table III.1 / East Pakistani representation in the military establishment, 1963 (percentage of total)

	COMMISSIONED OFFICERS	JUNIOR COMMISSIONED OFFICERS	WARRANT OFFICERS	OTHER RANKS
Army	5%	7.4%		7.4%
Air Force	17%		13.2%	28.0%

	BRANCH OFFICERS	CHIEF PETTY OFFICERS	PETTY OFFICERS	LEADING SEAMEN AND BELOW
Navy	5%	10.4%	17.3%	28.8%

Source: Pakistan, National Assembly, *Debates*, March 8, 1963, pp. 30–31.

While Bengali representation in the entrepreneurial class increased during the decade, none of the top twenty or thirty families who probably benefited most from Ayub's economic policies were Bengali.[68] Table III.2 shows the relative weight of the two wings in the power structure in the first two decades of Pakistan's history. Clearly, the Bengalis were marginally represented in the policy-making and political support groups during the Ayub period. This nonrepresentation in the elite in a highly elitist system naturally deepened the Bengalis' sense of alienation. It meant that the regime needed to devise policies and institutions which would give the Bengalis a sense of participation in and identification with the system, to counterbalance their nonrepresentation in the policy and administrative elite.

The new nation-building policies. Like military regimes elsewhere, the Ayub regime cited national disintegration as the major rationale for its coup. Nation-building therefore was expected to have top priority under the new adminstration. Within two weeks of assuming power,

[67] See Table V.1.
[68] According to Hanna Papanek, "Entrepreneurs in East Pakistan," p. 6: among the "twenty-nine largest 'Houses' [of family-controlled enterprise groups] ranked in terms of net worth, there are two Bengalis near the bottom of the list."

Table III.2 / East-West representation among policy-makers and political support groups, 1947–58 and 1958–68.

	CIVILIAN REGIME (1947–58)	MILITARY REGIME (1958–68)
Policy-Makers	Political elite (W-E) Civil-military bureaucratic elite (W-e)	Civil-military bureaucratic elite (W-e)
Political Support Groups	Political parties, factions trade unions (W-E) Urban groups: students, intelligentsia, salaried employees (W-E) Landed aristocracy (W) Ulema (W-e) Entrepreneurial "community"* (W-e)	Surplus farmers (W-E) Entrepreneurial "community"* (W-e) Landed aristocracy (W) Political parties, factions (W-E)

Note: W-E refers to near parity in east-west representation; W-e refers to West Pakistani predominance, with marginal East Pakistani participation; and W refers to exclusive West Pakistani representation.
* The term "community" is used here, since private enterprise is still very much in the hands of business communities.

Ayub visited East Pakistan and promised a fresh start at nation-building.[69] And from this and subsequent statements by him it appeared that East Pakistan was to get a "new deal." The regime's ideology about the distribution of power, however, remained much the same as that of its predecessors. Its achievement lay primarily in seeking "fresh techniques and initiatives through the use of administrative devices."[70]

The nation-building policies of the regime reflected the dominance of the new bureaucratic elite. The "new deal" policies toward East Pakistan smacked of the paternalism of an enlightened colonial rule. Ayub looked upon the Bengalis as a downtrodden, backward people who must be treated as a "special burden"—a view very much in the tradition of the British colonial administration. The following description of the Bengalis, quoted from Ayub's autobiography, is reminiscent of the attitude of Macaulay and Kipling.

> East Bengalis . . . probably belong to the very original Indian races. It would be no exaggeration to say that up to the creation of Pakistan, they had not

[69] *Dawn* (Karachi), October 23, 1958.   [70] Gorvine, p. 334.

known any real freedom or sovereignty. They have been in turn ruled either by the caste Hindus, Moghuls, Pathans, or the British. In addition, they have been and still are under considerable Hindu cultural and linguistic influence. As such, they have all the inhibitions of downtrodden races and have not yet found it possible to adjust psychologically to the requirements of the new born freedom. Their popular complexes, exclusiveness, suspicion, and a sort of defensive aggressiveness probably emerge from this historical background. Prudence, therefore, demands that these factors should be recognized and catered for and they be helped so as to feel equal partners and prove an asset.[71]

The regime's attitude vacillated between romanticism and exasperation. Like the old British administrators, Ayub showed a romantic faith in the goodness of the simple village folk. He saw the rural people as "by nature patriotic and good people" who are "tolerant and patient and can rise to great heights when well led."[72] And programs such as the Basic Democracies and the works program reflected this attitude of bureaucratic guardianship toward the rural masses. But, also like the British administration, Ayub distrusted the urban middle class and the intelligentsia,[73] whom he characterized as people "fed on Western ideas . . . few among them have any real contact with the people and fewer have given any serious thought to the problem of the people."[74]

Ayub looked upon the task of nation-building as twofold.

> . . . I could not convince myself that we had become a nation in the real sense of the word; the whole spectacle was one of disunity and disintegration. We were divided in two halves, each half dominated by a distinct linguistic and cultural pattern. The geographical distance between the two halves was in itself a divisive factor which could be exploited to create all kinds of doubts and suspicions among the people. We had inherited a deep antagonism which separated the people in the countryside from the urban

---

[71] Ayub Khan, *Friends Not Masters*, p. 187. Macaulay, in his *Critical, Historical and Miscellenous Essays*, V, 19–20, describes the Bengalis as a "feeble" people who "during many ages . . . has been trampled upon by men of bolder and more hardy breeds," and whose "mind is weak . . . for purposes of manly resistance."

[72] Ayub Khan, *Speeches and Statements*, I, 2.

[73] In the late nineteenth century the rising Bengali middle class started demanding equal rights. This made the Bengali Babu, who had long been an ally of the British administration, an object of suspicion and distrust; and the British administration began discovering the good rural folk.

[74] Ayub Khan, *Friends Not Masters*, p. 208.

classes. The latter represented a small minority of the total population, but it was a vocal minority and the people in the villages suffered from a sense of domination and exploitation by the elite of the towns.[75]

In its attempt to bridge the two gaps of regional separatism and elite-mass division, the Ayub regime made economic development the major national goal, and the bureaucracy the main integrative instrument. In emphasizing economic development, the Ayub regime's nation-building policy was in sharp contrast with that of the previous, civilian regime, whose goal had been Islamic democracy. The military regime believed that the general poverty and backwardness of the country were being used by an "unscrupulous type of politicians" to stir up regional sentiment, and that rapid economic development and modernization were keys to the problem of integration. Economic development, it was thought, would mobilize the conflicting groups toward a common constructive purpose and would automatically solve the problem of integration.

The regime's commitment to economic development resulted in significant economic growth during the decade, but an emphasis on GNP growth rather than distribution created additional problems of integration; instead of bridging the twin gaps of class and region, it exacerbated them.[76] The emphasis on economic development and modernization also led the regime to neglect ideology as a useful instrument of integration. The regime was secular and was opposed to the involvement of religion and religious leaders in politics,[77] but it failed to provide an alternative to Islam, which had been the state ideology during the previous decade. Yet the social tensions created by the rapid economic development during the Ayub decade more than ever needed a cementing force like ideology.

The regime adopted a policy of planned political institution-building. The cornerstone of the new political structure was the centralization of

[75] *Ibid*, pp. 194-95. See detailed discussion in chap VI.
[76] See the detailed discussion in chap. IV.
[77] The regime at first tried to establish a secular state. The 1962 constitution initially referred to Pakistan as the Republic of Pakistan. But as the regime politicized itself Ayub increasingly used religious symbols and religious leaders for political purposes. A constitutional amendment changed the name of the republic to the Islamic Republic of Pakistan. During the 1964-65 elections religious leaders were enlisted for campaigning.

power, which according to Ayub was a basic precondition for national integration.[78] Ayub blamed the lack of a "focus of power" in the previous political system as the main cause of disintegration in Pakistan. His regime therefore tried to build political institutions which would focus all power in one office—the presidency. Ayub argued that centralization of power would create a strong, stable government capable not only of holding the two wings of Pakistan together but also of taking bold steps toward bridging the elite-mass gap. Ayub defended his centralization policy not just on political grounds but in terms of tradition as well: he claimed that a centralized political structure is indigenous to the "Islamic" peoples and is best suited to their genius.[79]

While stressing centralization, the regime recognized the people's need for a sense of participation in the system. But the participation was controlled. Urban areas were disfranchised, and the rural areas were mobilized as a counterweight.

So far as the accommodation of Bengali demands is concerned, Ayub's views seemed to undergo some changes over the years. In his 1954 memorandum, Ayub called for treating the Bengalis as "equal partners." This he thought could be done by giving the provinces "as much autonomy as possible and that means that in addition to the subjects already in their hands, communications, except inter-provincial, industries, commerce, health, etc. should be handed over to the provinces, leaving defense, foreign affairs, and currency in the hands of the centre."[80] But following his rise to power in 1958, Ayub started favoring a unitary government with a strong central rule. While in 1954 he had regarded autonomy for East Pakistan as the best policy for national integration after 1958 he looked upon this solution as "disruptive" and "secessionist" and advocated a strong central government, preferably unitary. This policy of centralization naturally met with opposition from East Pakistan, since the limitations of centralization had already been exposed during the parliamentary era.

[78] Ayub Khan, *Friends Not Masters*, pp. 204–5.   [79] *Ibid.*, p. 204.   [80] *Ibid.*, p. 190.

four / The regime's attempt at nation-building through economic development

AS WE HAVE SEEN, the Ayub regime made economic development its prime national goal, with the expectation that this would pull the different regions and groups together for a constructive national purpose.[1] But while the decade saw a significant increase in economic growth rate, the economic policies pursued by the regime created additional problems for national integration and intensified the east-west conflict. The emphasis on economic development and modernization as a means of national integration brought forth the old question of the economic disparity between East and West Pakistan, which became the focal point of east-west controversy during the Ayub period. Economic conflict now replaced political autonomy as the major issue, not only because the regime was preoccupied with economic development but also because the economic arena was the only one where dissent was permitted by the regime. Ultimately, however, the sophisticated economic analysis that

[1] In addition to the discussion in Chap. III, see Gunner Myrdal, *Asian Drama*, p. 328.

resulted from the economic controversy strengthened the hands of political autonomists. The Six-Point Movement in East Pakistan in the spring of 1966 was made possible by the previous six years' constant exposure of the problem of economic disparity.

Economic disparity between East and West Pakistan

Although economic disparity between East and West Pakistan had become a major factor in Bengali alienation after 1956, the Ayub regime did not take any immediate measures for East Pakistan's economic development. In the Second Five Year Plan (1960–65) regional allocations were said to be guided by the need "to maximize development in the less developed parts of the country without prejudicing national development"[2] But after mid-1961, as the Bengali socioeconomic and political demands were expressed in growing frequency and volume by the intelligentsia through the media of press, seminars, and professional organizations,[3] the regime began to respond with some policies for the economic development of East Pakistan. The first such response came in May 1961, when Ayub, in a press conference in East Pakistan, admitted the existence of economic disparity and pledged the regime's commitment to its removal.[4] As Bengali opposition to the forthcoming constitution became more articulate, the regime adopted a series of economic steps designed to improve the east-wing economy.[5] In December 1961, the National Finance Commission was established to recommend redistribution of resources between the center and the provinces. In January 1962, the Pakistan Industrial Development Corporation (PIDC) was bifurcated; this was followed by bifurcation of railways. And in March 1962, the new constitution was introduced which declared

[2] Pakistan, Planning Commission, *The Second Five Year Plan, 1960–65*, p. 398.
[3] See Edgar A. and Kathryn R. Schuler, *Public Opinion and Constitution Making in Pakistan, 1958–1962*, pp. 123–67, for a detailed account of East Pakistani public opinion during this period.
[4] *Ibid.*, pp. 125–26.
[5] The Ayub regime usually undertook economic, rather than political, measures in response to political demands.

the removal of economic disparity a constitutional obligation. According to article 145(4) of the constitution:

> A primary object . . . in formulating the plans . . . shall be to ensure that disparities between the provinces, and between different areas within a Province, in relation to income per capita, are removed, and that the resources of Pakistan (including resources in foreign exchange) are used and allocated in such a manner as to achieve that object in the shortest possible time, and it shall be the duty of each government to make the utmost endeavour to achieve that object.[6]

With growing Bengali opposition to the new constitution and the political system, the regime adopted still more responsive economic policies. The Twenty Year Perspective Plan (1965–85) made the removal of economic disparity one of its objectives; and the Third Five Year Plan for the first time allocated more funds to East than to West Pakistan. For economic development of the countryside, a vast rural works program was introduced in 1962–63.

The measures adopted by the regime for East Pakistan's economic development and the removal of economic disparity, generally fell into three categories: redistribution of resources between the center and the provinces; regional economic planning; and rural economic development through the works program.

Redistribution of resources between the center and the provinces. In the pre-Ayub era, one of the long-standing complaints of the provincial government in East Pakistan was the fiscal relationship between the center and the provinces.[7] In spite of the formula laid down by the Raisman Award of 1952 defining the distribution of tax revenues between the two wings, the provincial governments were left with few financial resources of their own. Most of the elastic sources of revenue were in the center's hands. The National Finance Commission, in its study of the allocation of resources between the center and the provinces, was sharply divided between its east- and west-wing members, who allegedly submitted two separate reports.[8] The East Pakistani members

[6] Pakistan, Ministry of Law, *The Constitution of the Republic of Pakistan, 1962*, p. 76.

[7] See East Bengal, *Memorandum on Allocation of Revenues Between the Central and the Provincial Governments of Pakistan for Presentation to the Export Committee*, passim.

[8] *Morning News* (Dacca), January 20, 1962.

urged distribution of resources on the basis of population. The recomendations of the National Finance Commission, however, rejected their plea. Under the 1962 arrangement, the percentages of the taxes and duties collected and administered by the central government and allocated to the provinces were as follows:

(i) 50 percent of the income tax including corporation tax (as compared to the 50 percent of the income tax, excluding corporation tax, under the previous arrangement).

(ii) 60 percent of the sales tax (as against 50 percent under the previous arrangement).

(iii) 60 percent of the excise duties on tea, tobacco, and betel nut (as compared to the previous 50 percent).

(iv) 100 percent of export duties on jute and cotton, to be shared by the two provinces (as compared to the previous 62.5 percent of jute duty allotted to East Pakistan alone).

(v) 100 percent of estates and succession duties on agricultural land, and 100 percent of the tax on capital value of immovable property.

The basis of east-west allocation was also changed. Under the previous arrangement, income tax and excise duties were distributed broadly in the ratio of 55 percent to West Pakistan and 45 percent to East Pakistan, and sales tax was distributed on the basis of collection. Under the 1962 arrangement, 30 percent of the sales tax was allocated on the basis of collection, and 70 percent on the basis of population (East Pakistan, 54 percent; West Pakistan, 46 percent). Estates and succession duties were allocated on the basis of collection. Other taxes and duties were distributed on the basis of population. As a further relief to the provincial governments, the new award wrote down by 50 percent outstanding debt liabilities of the provincial governments and converted them into one consolidated loan repayable over a period of twenty-five years.

The 1962 award fell far short of East Pakistani expectations.[9] So did the constitution of 1962, which granted most of the elastic sources of revenue to the center. A second National Finance Commission was

[9] Schuler and Schuler, pp. 146–47.

set up on March 31, 1964, to recommend, among other things, further changes in the distribution of resources between the center and the provinces. On the basis of its report,[10] a revised arrangement came into effect on June 12, 1965. Under this new arrangement, 65 percent of the sales tax and excise duties (as compared to 60 percent under the 1962 award), would go to the provinces. The 1965 arrangement reduced the provincial share of jute and cotton export duty from 100 percent to 65 percent, however. In all other respects, the basis of distribution under the 1965 arrangement remained the same as before.

The 1962 and 1965 redistributions did increase the east wing's revenue receipts (see Table 5 in the Statistical Appendix). But, as is indicated by Figure 1, the revenue receipts of the central government increased much more. The revenue resources at the disposal of the provincial government remained meager, and the Bengali counterelite gradually turned from demanding a greater share in central taxes to demanding an increase in the provincial government's power of taxation.[11]

Regional economic planning. In accordance with the regime's deliberate policy of regional economic planning—a policy long advocated by East Pakistani economists and politicians—regional development featured prominently in the Twenty Year Perspective Plan, which set a twenty-year limit for the complete removal of economic disparity between the two wings. The Third Five Year Plan (1965–70), the first program under the Perspective Plan, set as its goal the reduction of interregional disparity in per capita income by one-fifth. By its own account the regime took three steps to achieve that objective:

> (a) a higher level of public sector development expenditure in East Pakistan compared to West Pakistan and a corresponding provision of financial and economic resources to East Pakistan through the efforts of the public sector;
> (b) creation of adequate infrastructure by the government to stimulate and encourage accelerated development in East Pakistan; and
> (c) provision of adequate incentives and institutional framework for

---

[10] Pakistan, *National Finance Commission Report, 1964–65.*

[11] The Six-Point Program (see under Rahman, Sheikh Mujibur, in the Bibliography) of the East Pakistan Awami League in 1966 demanded that the center be divested of all taxation power. The provinces would collect all the taxes and give a fixed percentage to the center.

Figure 1 / Revenue receipts of East Pakistan and Center, 1948–65

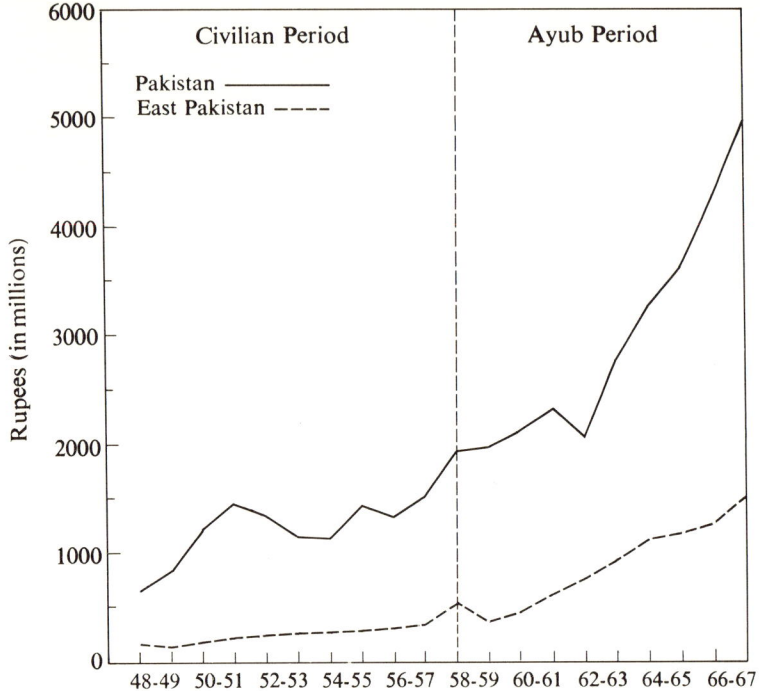

Source: Pakistan, Ministry of Economic Affairs, Central Statistical Office, *Twenty Years of Pakistan in Statistics, 1947–67*, pp. 276–77.

encouraging private investment in agriculture and industry in East Pakistan.[12]

The increase in the public sector allocation to East Pakistan had in fact been substantial over the years since 1960 (see Tables IV.1 and IV.2). The overall Third Five Year Plan public sector allocation for East Pakistan was larger (Rs. 14,390 million) than that for West Pakistan (Rs. 12,000 million). There was also a steady increase in the central government's developmental loans to East Pakistan. East Pakistan's share

[12] Pakistan, Planning Commission, *Socio-economic Objectives of the Fourth Five Year Plan, 1970–75*, p. 12.

Table IV.1 / Public sector allocation under the First Five Year Plan (1955-60) (rupees in crores)

	TOTAL	EAST	WEST
Original plan, 1955-60	935	400	535
Revised plan, 1957-58 to 1959-60	758	352	406
Actual development expenditures 1955-60	926	332	594

Source: Adapted from Muhammad Anisur Rahman, *East and West Pakistan: A Problem in the Political Economy of Regional Planning* (Cambridge: Center for International Affairs, Harvard University, 1968), p. 20.

Table IV.2 / Public sector allocation under the Second Five Year Plan (1960-65) and the first three years of the Third Five Year Plan

	MILLION RUPEES		PERCENTAGE OF TOTAL	
	EAST	WEST	EAST	WEST
1960-61	690	1,139	38	62
1961-62	930	1,437	39	61
1962-63	1,273	1,458	54	46
1963-64	1,640	1,676	49	51
1964-65	1,721	1,986	46	54
Annual average under Second Five Year Plan	1.251	1,539	45	55
1965-66	1,472	1,641	47	53
1966-67 (estimated actual)	2,190	1,960	53	47
1967-68 (estimates)	2,715	2,285	54	46
Annual average under Third Five Year Plan	2,125	1,962	52	48

Source: Pakistan, Planning Commission, *The Mid-Plan Review of the Third Five Year Plan 1965-70*, p. 35.

increased from 47 percent in 1960-61 to 71 percent in 1965-66 (see Table 7 in the Appendix). Similarly, East Pakistan's share of foreign project assistance was increased (see Table IV.3). However, West Pakistan continued to receive the bulk of the central government's grants-in-aid (see Table 8 in the Appendix).

Table IV.3 / Commitments and disbursements of project assistance by executing authorities (millions of dollars)

	COMMITMENTS		DISBURSEMENTS	
	EAST	WEST	EAST	WEST
1960-61	23	38	20	40
1961-62	30	23	21	45
1962-63	84	90	36	50
1963-64	150	116	48	47
1964-65	90	76	51	51
1965-66	109	115	63	66
Total (1960-66)	486	458	239	299

Source: Pakistan, Planning Commission, *The Mid-Plan Review of the Third Five Year Plan 1965-70*, p. 37.

While public sector allocation to East Pakistan showed a significant increase during Ayub's decade, the regime's efforts in the private sector lagged far behind. Among the few economic and fiscal policies adopted to spur the east wing's private sector were the relaxation of selective credit measures for East Pakistan, the extension of the tax holiday for East Pakistani industries, and the reduction of custom duties for imported machinery and spare parts in East Pakistan. But the allocation of resources in the private sector to East Pakistan, either in the five-year plans or by the developmental banks, remained much less than that to West Pakistan. The Second Five Year Plan estimate for the private sector investment for East Pakistan (Rs. 272 crores) was roughly half of West Pakistan's (Rs. 478 crores). And even in the Third Five Year Plan the projection for the two regions was equal in the private sector (Rs. 1,100 crores in each region). A recent study reveals that from 1963-64 to 1965-66 only 22 percent of the total private investment

Table IV.4 / *Private investment, in East and West Pakistan 1963–68*

	MILLION RUPEES		PERCENTAGE OF TOTAL	
	EAST	WEST	EAST	WEST
1963–64	547	2,091	21	79
1964–65	817	2,614	24	76
1965–66	681	2,397	22	78
1966–67	819	2,918	22	78
1967–68	1,038	3,647	22	78
Total	3,903	13,667	22	78

Source: Pakistan, Planning Commission, *The Mid-Plan Review of the Third Five Year Plan 1965–70*, p. 39.

took place in East Pakistan, as compared to 78 percent in West Pakistan (see Table IV.4).[13]

The distribution of loans by the central government's credit-giving agencies—the Industrial Development Bank of Pakistan (IDBP), the Pakistan Industrial Credit and Investment Corporation (PICIC), and the National Investment Trust (NIT)—shows a similar pattern of disparity. From 1961–62 to 1966–67 East Pakistan received 22 percent of the PICIC loans and 47 percent of the IDBP loans (see Tables 10 and 11 in the Appendix). The industrial sanctions granted by the Central Investment Promotion and Co-ordination Committee—the principal organ of the government for coordinating, planning, and implementing industrial programs in the private sector—likewise exhibit a continued disparity. During the second five-year plan period, the committee granted sanctions to 96 cases in East Pakistan and 385 cases in West Pakistan (Table 9 in the Appendix).

During the Ayub decade, then, as compared to 1947–58, the public sector allocations to East Pakistan increased significantly, while the private sector performance remained more or less static. From the First to the Second Five Year Plan, East Pakistan's share in public sector allocations increased by 128 percent, as compared to West Pakistan's increase of 55 percent; and from the Second to the Third Five Year

[13] Pakistan, Planning Commission, *The Mid-Plan Review of the Third Five Year Plan 1965–70*, p. 39.

Plan, East Pakistan's share increased by 150 percent, as against West Pakistan's increase of 90 percent.[14] But though allocation to East Pakistan increased relatively, until 1966–67 the east wing's allocation was not greater than the west wing's in absolute terms. Even during the second plan period East Pakistan received 38 percent less of the development funds.[15] And though the Third Five Year Plan showed a larger public sector allocation for East Pakistan, it did not include the multimillion dollar expenditure for the Indus Basin Project, funds which would be spent totally in West Pakistan, and which, if included in the plan, would make West Pakistan's gross investment much higher than East Pakistan's.[16] Similarly, the development expenditure on the new capital in Islamabad, whose economic benefits accrue to West Pakistan, was not included in the Third Five Year Plan. In addition to developmental expenditure, the central government's budget expenditure also devolved mostly on West Pakistan, since the major portion (more than 70 percent) of the budget went to defense and civil administration, which are centered in the west wing.

Rural development through the public works program. One of the most publicized projects undertaken by the Ayub regime for East Pakistan's economic development was the rural public works program, introduced in East Pakistan during 1962–63. The program was designed to serve economic, administrative, and political goals.[17] According to the regime's own account, the economic objectives of the program were:

> (a) to provide larger employment, by creating work opportunities in the rural areas on local projects not requiring large capital investment, the benefits of which can be easily recognized by the workers . . .
> (b) to create an infra-structure such as roads, bridges, irrigation channels, and the like in the rural areas, and
> (c) to raise additional financial and manpower resources for the implementation of local projects, through taxation or voluntary labour.[18]

---

[14] S. M. Akhtar, "The Problem of Regional Disparities in Economic Development," in Anwar I. Qureshi, ed., *The Third Five Year Plan and Other Papers,* p. 205.

[15] Muhammad Anisur Rahman, *East and West Pakistan,* p. 20.

[16] The Indus Basin Project was not included in the Third Five Year Plan, on the grounds that it is replacement work and is covered by a special treaty.

[17] The political and administrative role of the works program will be discussed in chap. VI.

[18] Pakistan, Planning Commission, *Final Evaluation of the Second Five Year Plan,* p. 129.

77 / Nation-building through economic development

The works program was designed to utilize the huge surplus of manpower in East Pakistan's rural areas by giving them gainful employment during the dry months, employment which, it was hoped, would pump extra purchasing power into the rural economy. The works created by the program, on the other hand, would improve the infrastructure of the rural economy and help to increase agricultural production and marketing facilities. From 1962-63 to 1966-67, Rs. 671.63 million was invested in the rural works program in East Pakistan,[19] and resulted in the creation of, among other things, 111,402 miles of "kutcha" (dirt) roads and 7,264 miles of "pucca" (surfaced) roads; 9,840 miles of drains and canals; and 8,874 miles of embankments[20] (see Tables 13 and 14 in the Appendix).

The impact of the works program on East Pakistan's rural economy has been a matter of controversy,[21] because of the uncertainty of available data. The program's impact on agricultural production is hard to measure. A government study claims that "the construction of roads, embankments and drainage canals under the works programme definitely helped increase agricultural production."[22] Another empirical study estimates that an annual increase of 364,123 tons of agricultural produce is due to works program drainage projects.[23] The overall effect of the works program on East Pakistan's agriculture seems to be negligible, however. Agricultural production still depends largely on weather (as is indicated by the drop in production during 1964-65, and 1966-67), and from 1963-64 to 1966-67 the growth rate in agriculture in East Pakistan was less than one percent per annum as against West Pakistan's growth rate of 3.1 percent.[24]

But the works program achieved a significant measure of success

[19] Pakistan, Planning Commission, *The Mid-Plan Review of the Third Five Year Plan 1965-70*, p. 267; and idem, *Final Evaluation of the Second Five Year Plan*, p. 130.
[20] *Final Evaluation*, p. 132; *Mid-Plan Review 1965-70* p. 262.
[21] For an unfavorable view see Rehman Sobhan, *Basic Democracies, Works Programme and Rural Development in East Pakistan*; for a favorable view see John Thomas, "Rural Public Works Program and East Pakistan's Development."
[22] East Pakistan, Basic Democracies and Local Government Department, *Works Programme for 1964-65 for East Pakistan*, p. 1.
[23] Thomas, "Works Program and East Pakistan's Development," p. 218.
[24] Pakistan, Planning Commission, *The Mid-Plan Review of the Third Five Year Plan 1965-70*, p. 41.

in building a rural infrastructure. Both John Thomas's and Rehman Sobhan's studies reveal that the development of rural infrastructure and marketing facilities has helped to monetize the rural economy. It has also created 173,200 man-years of employment annually, although that means a bare 3.4 percent decrease in the total annual agricultural unemployment.[25] On the whole, the economic benefits of the program have far exceeded its costs,[26] though the benefits have gone mostly to the rich farmer, as against the vast majority of landless labor.[27]

Impact of the new economic policies on interwing disparity. The effect of the regime's policies on interwing economic disparity has been much debated. Even the regime's own evaluation of its policies underwent a change, from buoyant optimism in the early years to a pessimistic realism later. In 1964, the National Finance Commission reported hopefully:

> The second five year plan basically laid the foundation for accelerated economic growth of East Pakistan . . . we . . . feel satisfied that there is enough evidence to warrant the conclusion that the economy of East Pakistan has registered a significant improvement for the first time.[28]

In 1965, the guidelines of the Third Five Year Plan asserted: "there is some reason to believe that the disparity is diminishing and it can be stated with confidence that it is not increasing."[29] The plan "confidently predicted," moreover, that "disparities in income can ultimately be eliminated . . . given a dedicated effort, it should be feasible . . . to eliminate disparities completely within the period of the perspective plan."[30] But by the time of the mid-plan review, however, it was admitted that "inter-regional disparity is much more complex and stubborn a problem than was originally conceived. It can be resolved only through sustained efforts over a period of time."[31]

---

[25] Thomas, "Works Program and East Pakistan's Development," p. 207.
[26] *Ibid.*, pp. 216-25.
[27] See Sobhan, *Basic Democracies,* for an elaboration of this point. Similarly unequal results in the rural sector can be discerned in the "green revolutions" of other Asian countries.
[28] Pakistan, *National Finance Commission Report, 1964-65,* pp. 9-10.
[29] Pakistan, Planning Commission, *The Guidelines for the Third Five Year Plan,* p. 42.
[30] Pakistan, Planning Commission, *The Third Five Year Plan, 1965-70,* p. 129.
[31] Pakistan, Planning Commission, *The Mid-Plan Review of the Third Five Year Plan 1965-70,* p. 43.

79 / Nation-building through economic development

The controversy over economic disparity partly stems from different ways of measuring it. Tables IV.5, IV.6, IV.7, and IV.8 and Figures 2, 3, and 4 give the disparity figures for some of the crucial indicators of economic development during the Ayub period. From these indicators, some conclusions can be drawn about economic disparity during the Ayub period and the regime's impact on it. First, disparity in per capita income continued to rise. While East Pakistan's per capita income rose from Rs. 269 in 1959–60 to Rs. 291.5 in 1968–69, West Pakistan's per capita income rose from Rs. 355 to Rs. 473.4.[32] The disparity index rose

Figure 2 / Per capita GNP and cost-of-living index, 1947–66

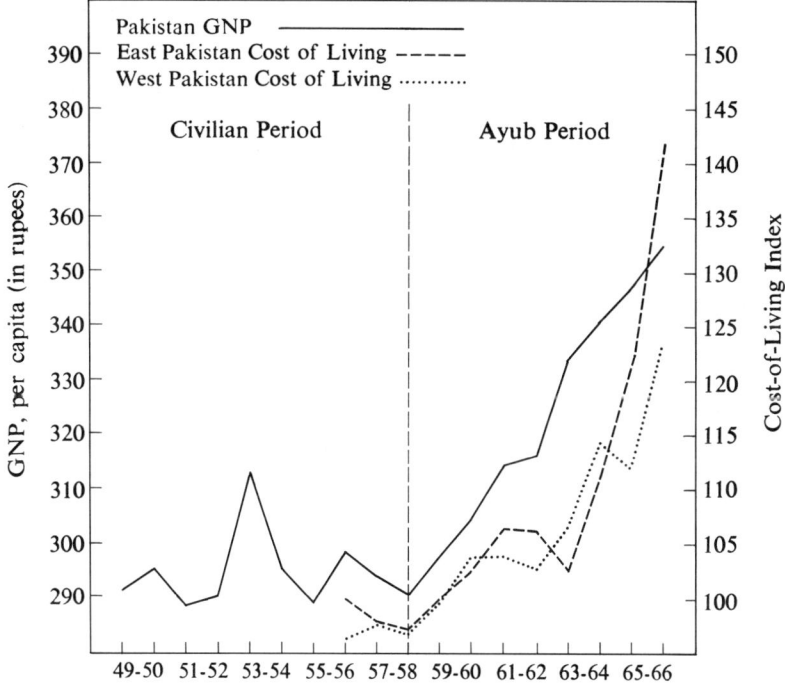

Source: Pakistan, Ministry of Economic Affairs, Central Statistical Office, *Twenty Years of Pakistan in Statistics, 1947–67*, pp. 3, 194.

[32] Azizur Rahman Khan, "A New Look at Disparity," *Forum* (Dacca), January 3, 1970.

80 / Nation-building through economic development

Table IV.5 / Per capita income (rupees in constant 1959–60 prices)

	1959–60	1960–61	1961–62	1962–63	1963–64
East Pakistan	269	278	278	280	305
West Pakistan	355	359	368	382	388
All Pakistan	318	325	334	336	353
Percentage of Interwing disparity (Pakistan = 100 +)	28	26	25	31	24

Source: Adapted from Pakistan, Planning Commission, *The Mid-Plan Review of the Third Five Year Plan 1965–70*, p. 34.

Table IV.6 / Gross domestic product, population and rates of growth (rupees in crores: 1959–69 prices)

	1959–60		1964–65	
SECTOR	EAST	WEST	EAST	WEST
Agriculture	938	701	1,151	849
Manufacturing	50	142	80	302
Other	567	836	768	1,228
Total	1,555	1,679	1,999	2,379
Population (millions)	53.9	45.0	61.2	51.3
Per capita (rupees)	288	373	327	464

Annual rate of growth (percent)

	1954–55 TO 1959–60		1959–60 TO 1964–65	
	EAST	WEST	EAST	WEST
Agriculture	1.1	1.6	4.2	3.9
Manufacturing	10.0	12.4	9.9	16.3
Other	2.0	3.5	6.3	8.0
Total	1.7	3.2	5.2	7.2
Population	2.3	2.3	2.6	2.7
Per capita	−0.6	0.9	2.6	4.4

Source: Gustav F. Papanek, *Pakistan's Development: Social Goals and Private Incentives* (Cambridge: Harvard University Press, 1967), p. 20.

from 28 percent in 1959–60 to 62 percent in 1968–69.[33] The cost-of-living index increased at a higher rate in the east than in the west (Figure 2), and the real wages in both urban and rural areas were much lower in the East.[34]

Second, though East Pakistan's economic growth rate registered a significant increase over the stagnation of the previous period, West Pakistan's economy continued to rise at a faster rate. East Pakistan's per capita economic growth rate went from —0.6 percent during 1954–60 to 2.6 percent during 1959–65. West Pakistan's corresponding increase was from 0.9 percent to 4.4 percent (Table IV.6). Third, East Pakistan continued to lag behind in economic structural development. In 1962–63 the share of manufacturing in overall regional income was 7.4 percent in East Pakistan and 12.7 percent in West Pakistan.

Fourth, the disparity in physical and social infrastructure showed no declining trend. While infrastructure development was generally neglected in both the wings during the decade, it was more so in East Pakistan. From 1959–60 to 1966–67, new roads increased by 1,548 miles in East Pakistan but by 2,824 miles in West Pakistan (Table 18 in the Appendix). During the same period the number of motor vehicles increased by 31,875 in East Pakistan and by 150,167 in West Pakistan. During the period 1959–66, the number of hospitals increased by 5 in East Pakistan, but by 55 in West Pakistan; the number of hospital beds, by 2,512 in East Pakistan and by 4,642 in West Pakistan (Table 16 in the Appendix). The increase in the number of doctors was 1,929 in East Pakistan and 4,873 in West Pakistan. The corresponding figures for nurses were 243 and 1,272, respectively. Development of the education sector in West Pakistan also far outstripped East Pakistan's growth during this period, though compared to the pre-1958 period, enrollment increased significantly in East Pakistan. (Figure 3). Enrollment in primary schools increased by 1,153 in East Pakistan and by 16,412 in West Pakistan. The increase in secondary school, college, and university en-

[33] *Ibid.*
[34] Azizur Rahman Khan, "What Has Been Happening to Real Wages in Pakistan?" *The Pakistan Development Review*, VII (1967) 317–47; S. R. Bose, "Trend of Real Income of the Rural Poor in East Pakistan, 1949–66," *The Pakistan Development Review*, VIII (1968), 452–88.

Figure 3 / Enrollment in schools and universities in East and West Pakistan, 1947–66

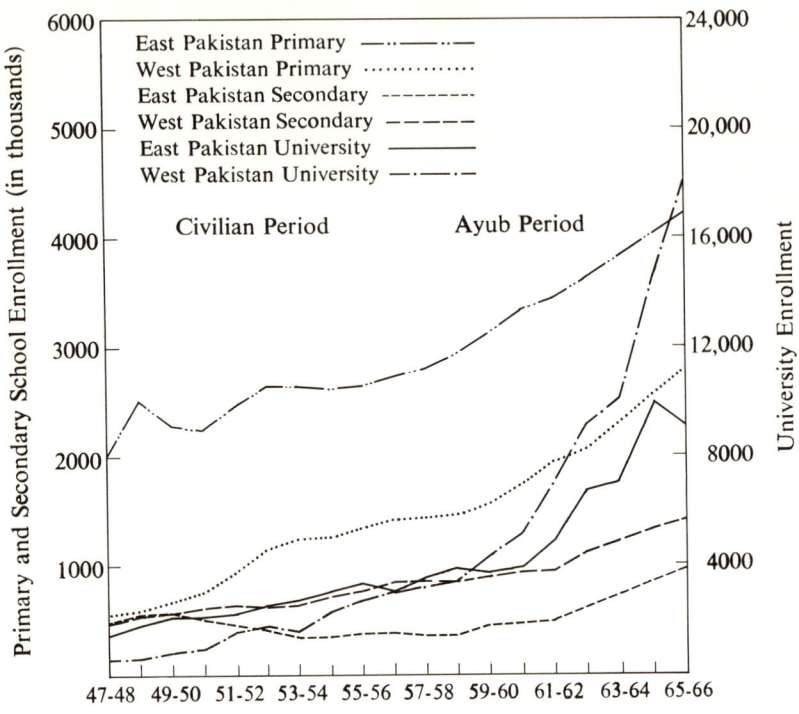

Source: Pakistan, Ministry of Economic Affairs, Central Statistical Office, *Twenty Years of Pakistan in Statistics, 1947–67*, pp. 166–86.

rollment was 419,001, 81,103 and 5,065, respectively, for East Pakistan, and by 568,711, 167,820, and 14,616, respectively for West Pakistan.

Trade patterns also showed no significant change, though the east wing's share of export earnings dropped sharply between 1962–63 and 1964–65. (Figure 4). East Pakistan continued to have a surplus in foreign trade and a deficit in interregional trade (Table IV.8).

It has been argued that the continued economic disparity between the two wings was due partly to West Pakistan's higher initial stage of development.[35] By 1959–60 West Pakistan was far ahead of East Paki-

[35] On this point, see the discussion of disparity in the pre-Ayub period (chap. II), and the article cited in chap. II, n. 25.

Figure 4 / Export earnings of East and West Pakistan, 1947–66

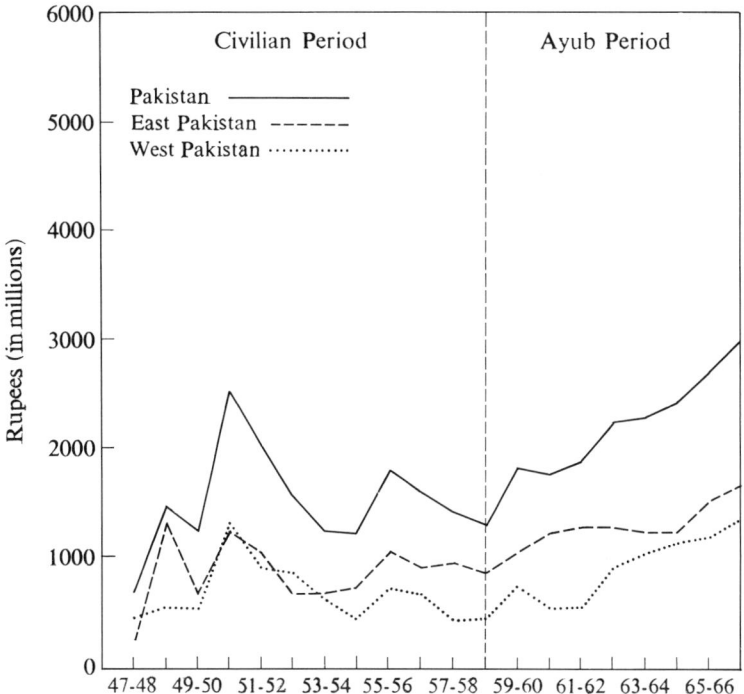

Source: Pakistan, Ministry of Economic Affairs, Central Statistical Office, *Twenty Years of Pakistan in Statistics, 1947–67,* p. 104.

stan, and its economy continued to grow at a faster rate in the sixties, making greater demands on national resources. But the lag in East Pakistan was also due to the inadequacy of government policy. The Third Five Year Plan set the reduction of interregional disparity by one-fifth as its goal; the resources it allocated were insufficient to achieve that objective.[36] Additionally, there was always a gap between the planned allocations and the actual developmental expenditures. In spite of higher allocations, the percentage distribution of expenditures under the Third Five Year Plan was not much different from that under the Second (see Table IV.9). Finally, the war with India in 1965, with the

[36] Muhammad Anisur Rahman, *East and West Pakistan,* pp. 33–36.

Table IV.7 / Sectoral contributions to regional income (percentage of total)

	1950-51		1962-63	
	WEST	EAST	WEST	EAST
Agriculture and mining	51.0	70.0	45.8	59.5
Manufacturing	16.0	9.0	12.7	7.4
Large scale	—	—	7.8	4.0
Small scale	—	—	4.9	3.4
Transport and storage	3.5	2.7	4.7	6.0
Trade, banking, insurance	9.5	6.7	14.7	12.4
Dwellings	—	—	3.8	4.7
Services	16.0	9.0	8.5	4.7
Construction, utilities, public administration	—	—	9.8	5.5

Source: Muhammad Anisur Rahman, *East and West Pakistan: A Problem in the Political Economy of Regional Planning*, (Cambridge: Center for International Affairs, Harvard University, 1968), p. 8.

Table IV.8 / Trade balances for East and West Pakistan, 1958-67 (crores of rupees at current prices)

	FOREIGN BALANCE		INTERWING BALANCE	OVERALL BALANCE	
	EAST	WEST	WEST (+) EAST (—)	EAST	WEST
1958-59	32.72	—58.02	39.71	—6.99	—18.31
1959-60	42.43	—104.26	20.10	22.33	—84.16
1960-61	24.48	—163.30	45.54	—21.06	—117.76
1961-62	42.78	—169.30	45.09	—2.31	—124.25
1962-63	23.06	—180.20	48.44	—25.38	—131.76
1963-64	—22.44	—190.66	38.40	—60.84	—152.26
1964-65	—43.37	—252.63	33.74	—77.11	—218.87
1965-66	18.61	—167.67	—	—	—
1966-67	10.04	—126.76	—	—	—
Total	+487.87	—1,804.57			

Source: Muhammad Anisur Rahman, *East and West Pakistan: A Problem in the Political Economy of Regional Planning* (Cambridge: Center for International Affairs, Harvard University, 1968), p. 8.

resulting diversion of funds to defense, had an adverse effect on Pakistan's economic development in general, and on East Pakistan's development in particular.

Table IV.9 / *Development expenditures in East and West Pakistan, 1959–70 (rupees in millions)*

	SECOND PLAN (1960–65)		THIRD PLAN (1965–70)	
	EAST	WEST	EAST	WEST
Public sector	6,700	10,800	11,300	13,700
Private sector	3,000	10,700	5,500	16,000
Total	9,700	21,500	16,800	29,700
Percentage of total	31	69	36	64

Source: Pakistan, Planning Commission, *An Outline of the Fourth Five Year Plan, 1970–75*, p. 26.

Whatever the reasons for the continuation of the interregional economic disparity may be, the Ayub regime's failure to remove the disparity, in spite of its public commitment to do so, created a crisis of communication with the east wing. While the central government went on publicizing that it was doing more for East Pakistan, the continued low investment in East Pakistan and that wing's low share in the country's overall economic growth (only about one-third of the total for the 1960s occurred in East Pakistan) led the Bengalis to discredit the regime. Bengali criticism ranged from doubts about the adequacy of the regime's policies[37] to charges of outright colonial exploitation.[38] The continuation of disparity thus led to demands for alternative strategies of economic development, most notably the two-economy thesis.

The two-economy thesis and East Pakistan's autonomy

The two-economy thesis was first propounded in 1956 at a special conference of economists meeting in Dacca to discuss the First Five Year Plan. These economists recommended that development in Pakistan be

---

[37] M. N. Huda, noted Bengali economist and finance minister of East Pakistan, representing the moderate Bengali reaction to the regime's economic policies, argued that "current government policies appear to be designed for this purpose [removal of disparity], although one may doubt their adequacy and boldness to meet the problem." See his "Planning for Regional Development," in A. I. Qureshi, *Third Five Year Plan*, p. 197.

[38] One oft-repeated Bengali complaint is that West Pakistan would "keep" East Pakistan only so long as it is economically exploitable.

planned as if the country consisted of two separate economies. The major arguments for the two-economy theory, which were greatly developed in the 1960s, focused on two main points: first, that because of its peculiar geography, Pakistan did in fact have two distinct economies; and second, that the one-economy policy pursued by the various Pakistani governments worked to East Pakistan's disadvantage and resulted in economic disparity between the two wings.[39] The two-economy theorists argued that the geographical separation of the two wings resulted in virtual immobility of the factors of production between East and West Pakistan, and meant that investment in one wing did not have a "spread effect" on the other. Moreover, the structural differences between the economies of the two wings—West Pakistan having a large share of manufacturing and private capital, and East Pakistan being predominantly agricultural with little private capital—required separate economic strategies in the two regions. Price differentials and trade imbalances between the two wings further separated the two economies. The pursuit of a one-economy norm, according to two-economy theorists, led to a transfer of resources from East to West Pakistan. The center controlled major revenue sources, the larger share of which initiated in East Pakistan, invested chiefly in West Pakistan. Thus money raised in East Pakistan was spent in the other wing. Additionally, East Pakistan's surplus in foreign trade was obliterated by its deficit in interwing trade: the foreign exchange earned by the east wing was surrendered to West Pakistan, which in turn used the surplus to import raw materials for west-wing manufacturing.

One-economy theorists have defended this policy of transferring resources from East to West Pakistan on the grounds of "economic efficiency":[40] that is, investments must be made where there is the greatest demand and absorption capacity. But the two-economy theorists contend that such a policy totally ignores Pakistan's geography and results in an economic drain on East Pakistan, since investment in West Pakistan does not have any significant impact on the east wing's economy. The policy of

---

[39] For detailed analyses of the two-economy thesis, see A. Sadeque, *The Economic Emergence of Pakistan; idem, Pakistan's First Five Year Plan in Theory and Operation*; Muhammad Anisur Rahman, *East and West Pakistan*.

[40] See Muhammad Anisur Rahman, *East and West Pakistan*, pp. 21–32, for some of the contradictions of the definition of economic efficiency.

avoiding duplicity—i.e., discouraging similar industries in the two wings, in order to make the regions interdependent—also brought criticism from two-economy theorists, who argued that East Pakistan's dependence on west-wing manufacturing made the east wing highly vulnerable, as interwing trade is subject to constant uncertainty and disruption.

Two-economy theorists have therefore demanded that the economy of the two regions be regarded as completely separate, and that separate economic policies be pursued in each wing. They suggest that most, if not all, revenue be controlled by the regions themselves, and that each region have control of its own foreign exchange earnings. Each should have the freedom to pursue separate foreign trade policies, to enter into trade pacts with foreign countries, and to adopt credit and fiscal policies best suited to the growth of its economy.

While East Pakistani economists, later joined by politicians, repeatedly pleaded for the adoption of a two-economy policy, the Ayub regime rejected it, branding it as a prelude to political disintegration. Though the Perspective Plan and the Third Five Year Plan accepted the concept of regional economic development, the regime still maintained that regional development would have to be coordinated under a single national economic goal and strategy. It therefore failed to satisfy the Bengali counterelite, who wanted a clear-cut two-economy strategy. They viewed the proposed steps as a mere "tokenism" which failed to accommodate their most crucial demands, such as a separate trade and foreign exchange policy.

The two-economy theory strengthened the hands of the radical autonomists in East Pakistan, for it lent a material foundation to their otherwise vague ideological and political demands, and helped mobilize the support of the various strata of Bengali society behind their cause.

To the budding Bengali industrialists and businessmen, the appeal of the two-economy theory was the elimination of competition from West Pakistani big business. Although the economic measures adopted by the regime to encourage the private sector had helped a small group of Bengali industrialists and businessmen, Bengali entrepreneurs were still hard pressed by competition from bigger, already well-established West Pakistani business houses.[41] The following excerpts from the

---

[41] See the editorials in *The Pakistan Observer* (Dacca), May 31, and June 22, 1968.

speech of a Bengali member of the National Assembly typifies the Bengali businessman's fear of West Pakistani competition:

> How can we, East Pakistanis, form capital? How can capital be formed in East Pakistan? Sir, when the government decided to give more and more to East Pakistan in the import trade—as you know in the import trade East Pakistanis are not categorized importers—they decided that there should be OGL [Open General License] importers and the OGL system was introduced and East Pakistanis were allowed to import and they were registered as importers. But as soon as the authorities found that East Pakistanis are coming and becoming importers and trying to form small capitals, they overnight abolished the system of OGL and brought free list. Sir, it is open to everybody that East Pakistanis have very small capital. They cannot compete in free list . . . They cannot compete with the big industrialists . . . In East Pakistan, you will find that not even a single Chamber will be able to come and stand for this system of free list because the system of free list has completely damaged the economic backing and background of the commercial community of East Pakistan. . . . You cannot have the same system for both East and West Pakistan. . . . If you want real national integration . . . treat us equally in the economic life of the country.[42]

In the two-economy thesis, Bengali businessmen found an excellent weapon to combat West Pakistani competition. Thus it is not surprising that they supported the Awami League which included the two-economy thesis in its Six-Point Program.[43]

The two-economy theory also attracted urban salaried employees to the autonomists' cause. The regime's emphasis on economic growth and the private sector led to a rising cost of living in East Pakistan (Figure 2). The rise in GNP apparently did not affect the salaried middle class,[44] who therefore preferred a separate economic policy for East Pakistan which would eliminate West Pakistani cartels, bring prices down, and start the process of redistribution.

Bengali bureaucrats favored the two-economy system because they found in it the key to their autonomy from the center's fiscal control.[45] The radical Bengali intelligentsia supported it because they felt that

---

[42] Speech by A. S. M. Sulaiman (who was, incidentally, a trade union leader). Pakistan, National Assembly, *Debates*, Vol. II, June 22, 1966, pp. 1281–82.

[43] See Sheikh Mujibur Rahman, *Six Points: Our Demand for Survival.*

[44] A mere twenty or thirty families reaped the main harvest of the economic growth. See Mahbub ul Haq, *The Pakistan Observer* (Dacca), May 3, 1968.

a socialist economy could be more easily established in an independent East Pakistan, since that wing has few indigenous capitalists.

The two-economy theory also appealed to urban labor. The low wages of industrial labor,[46] coupled with the fact that industrial employers were mostly West Pakistani, led to an intermingling of class and ethnic antagonism. By joining the ranks of the radical autonomists, industrial labor reckoned that they would be able to overthrow their West Pakistani capitalist employers.

The support of the rural poor was also won. As already discussed, agricultural growth in East Pakistan was less than one percent per annum, and the works program's impact on agricultural output was minimal. The development of an infrastructure benefited the "surplus farmer" more than the rural poor. And though there was a slight increase in the real wages of the rural poor in the 1960s, the level was still below that in 1949–50.[47]

Thus the economic policies of the Ayub regime, by deepening economic inequality and concentrating wealth in a few hands, led to the alienation of all the politically relevant strata of Bengali society.

---

[45] In interviews with Bengali administrators in Dacca in the summer of 1968, I found that financial control by the center was regarded by them as most irksome. Though they preferred being part of the central civil services, they wanted fiscal autonomy.

[46] A. R. Khan, "Real Wages in Pakistan," p. 332.

[47] Bose, "Trends of Real Income," pp. 471–73.

five / Bureaucracy and nation-building

DURING the Ayub period the civil bureaucracy became the main instrument for implementing the regime's nation-building policies. It was a role not unfamiliar to Pakistani bureaucrats. Nor indeed is it a role unusual for the bureaucracy in developing countries in general.[1] The civil bureaucracy has often been called to play a "critical role when the major need of a society is that of creating a sense of nationhood."[2] As Joseph La Palombara points out:

> ... the histories of Japan after the Meiji restoration, of Prussia in the eighteenth century, and of Germany and Italy in the nineteenth century clearly demonstrate that a centralized bureaucracy can be a vital factor in the

[1] See Joseph La Palombara, ed., *Bureaucracy and Political Development*; Fred Riggs, *Administration in Developing Countries*; J. D. Montgomery and William J. Siffin, eds., *Approaches to Development: Politics, Administration and Change* (New York: McGraw-Hill, 1966); Ralph Braibanti, *et al.*, *Asian Bureaucratic Systems Emergent from the British Imperial Tradition*; Ralph Braibanti and J. Spengler, eds., *Administration and Economic Development in India*.

[2] Joseph La Palombara, "An Overview of Bureaucracy and Political Development," in *Bureaucracy and Political Development*, p. 22.

molding of a national entity out of disparate ethnic, regional, feudal or otherwise atomistic groupings.[3]

And, in fact, in Pakistan, even before the Ayub regime's assumption of power, the bureaucracy had been credited with holding together the new state, which few observers had given a chance for survival.[4]

Under the Ayub regime, however, the bureaucracy did more than merely meet "the integrative needs of the society"; it was also asked to perform "goal gratification activity."[5] But the simultaneous pursuit of these two objectives (which, theoretically and historically, normally follow each other) often worked at cross purposes. The bureaucracy's assumption of goal-gratification activity brought it into the political limelight and subjected it to political pressures. And during Ayub's decade, in the absence of political channels of communication, "intra-bureaucratic struggles" became the "primary form of politics."[6]

In the pre-Ayub period the bureaucracy's major role was one of integration. The bureaucracy, especially the elitist CSP, succeeded in maintaining the unity of the state through a highly centralized administration. Ralph Braibanti persuasively argues that it was the CSP's generalist and elitist ethos that helped institutionalize the service and make it the main stabilizing force in an unstable sociopolitical system.[7] The British tradition of training a "guardian" class had no doubt created a breed of "denationalized" rulers,[8] but their aloofness from the social environment made the higher civil servants less susceptible to regional

[3] *Ibid.*, p. 13.   [4] Keith Callard, *Pakistan*, pp. 298–99.

[5] Bert F. Hoselitz, "Levels of Economic Performance and Bureaucratic Structures," in La Palombara, pp. 170–71. According to Hoselitz, bureaucracy performs four types of functions: pattern maintenance, integrative, goal gratification, and adaptive. He suggests that, while none of these needs are ever absent, at a certain stage of development certain needs predominate, and the requirements of goal gratification may destroy the integrative system.

[6] Fred Riggs, "Bureaucrats and Political Development: A Paradoxical View," in La Palombara, p. 120. Riggs puts forth the thesis that "premature or too rapid expansion of the bureaucracy when the political system lags behind tends to inhibit the development of effective politics" (p. 126). Riggs's thesis fits Pakistan, where political institutions with low organizational capabilities are pitted against a developed and rational bureaucratic structure.

[7] Ralph Braibanti, "Public Bureaucracy and Judiciary in Pakistan," in La Palombara, pp. 383–409 *idem*, "The Civil Service of Pakistan: A Theoretical Analysis, *South Atlantic Quarterly*, LVIII (1959); 258–304.

[8] Ayub Khan, cited in Ralph Braibanti, *Research on the Bureaucracy of Pakistan*, Appendix 3, p. 350; also see Masihuzzaman, "Public Service Tradition in Pakistan: A Case for Revision," in Inayatullah, ed., *Bureaucracy and Development in Pakistan*, pp. 285–98, for a critical analysis of the continuing British tradition of bureaucracy in Pakistan.

political pressures and enabled them to take over the task of administration smoothly whenever there was a political deadlock or a constitutional crisis. Being part of the nonvernacular elite they were also "national" in their outlook and served as a strong bulwark for concepts of one state, one nation, one government.

During the Ayub decade, an attempt was made to transform the bureaucracy from an agency of law and order to an agency of socioeconomic change. The regime, as we saw in Chapter IV, undertook economic development and modernization as its primary "national" objective, and the bureaucracy was entrusted with the task of attaining this goal. This shift from a merely integrative role to a "goal-gratification" role required a change in the bureaucracy's training and ethos. Ayub himself, early in his administration, called for such a change. At the inauguration of the Administrative Staff College, on December 25, 1960, he said:

> The system of stereotype administration which we inherited was devised over a 100 years ago to suit the purpose of a colonial Power. Its fundamental emphasis was on the maintenance of law and order and one of the many ways in which this object was fulfilled was to create a superior class of somewhat de-nationalized individuals who could maintain proper distances and rule with awe and disdain under the cover of public service . . . but the demands of an independent society are entirely different . . . with the growing involvement of government in many new spheres of social life, the role of administrators . . . has to assume fresh techniques and attitudes . . . in this context the essential prerequisites of a worthwhile administrator are a ceaseless urge to invent and organize new fields of development; ability to bridge the gulf between the Government and the people; and a genuine endeavor to stimulate the broad mass of our population and goad and guide them on the path of progress, enlightenment and responsibility.[9]

The regime was not satisfied with words alone; steps were taken to reform the administrative structure in order to decentralize the administration and make it more development-oriented. Within two months of the regime's assumption of power, the Administrative Reorganization Committee was set up, which was concerned mainly with recommending reforms of the central government's administrative structure. The committee's report[10] recommended greater decentrali-

---

[9] Ayub Khan, cited in Braibanti, *Bureaucracy of Pakistan*, pp. 350–51.
[10] Pakistan, Establishment Division, Efficiency and O. & M. Wing, *The Report of the Administrative Reorganization Committee*. The committee consisted of seven members,

zation of functions and delegation of power. It suggested the creation of a "section officer's scheme" which would delegate power for middle-level decision-making. The report also introduced the device of the "economic pool," which underlined the need for specialists even among the generalists.[11]

The provincial governments underwent similar decentralization and delegation of power. The Provincial Administration Commission (better known as the Akhtar Hussain Commission) recommended decentralization by delegation of power, transfer of functions, or reorganization of the financial system.[12] The main functions of most departments in East Pakistan were declared "transferred subjects"; only planning, procurement and divisional distribution of materials, training, research, evaluation, and coordination were "reserved" for the headquarter officers.[13]

Also, one of the declared objectives of the Basic Democracies scheme was to effect democratic decentralization by bringing the will of the people closer to government and the personnel of government closer to the people. The bureaucrats and the elected representatives of the people were expected to cooperate closely and to maintain reciprocal feedback in the Basic Democracies councils. It was thought that by increased contact with the people's representatives the officials would develop a less elitist attitude toward the people.

To suit the changed functions of the civil service, the training program was altered. In the pre-1958 period, young CSP probationers were sent abroad for a year to the United Kingdom or Australia to pursue general courses of studies. In the post-1959 period, they were instead sent to the Rural Academy at Comilla. Foreign training was not eliminated, but it was made more selective and was given in specialized fields such as economics, public administration, finance, accounting, management, etc., so that the generalist civil servants could perform the special-

---

none of whom were from East Pakistan. Of the seven, five were from CSP, one from the Police Service of Pakistan (PSP), and one from the Audit and Accounting Service (AAS).

[11] The economic pool consisted of experienced officers, drawn from all the superior services, who were to fill senior executive posts in certain specialized departments such as finance, industry, and commerce.

[12] Pakistan, *Report of the Provincial Administration Commission*.

[13] A. M. A. Muhith, "Political and Administrative Roles in East Pakistan's Districts," *Pacific Affairs*, XL (1967-68), 284.

ized functions required in their new responsibilities in the Planning Commission, the Institute of Public Administration, and the public corporations.

These efforts to make the civil service more "representative" of the people, to make them agents of change and development, subjected them to extreme political pressures, especially the pressures of regional politics. And, in the absence of a political elite, the regional conflicts which "had been tearing the country apart were diverted from the usual political channels of expression and deflected into the bureaucracy, and the bureaucracy hence became the arena for covert forms of political struggle."[14] Regional conflict came to dominate the bureaucracy, not only because the civil service had assumed a quasi-political role,[15] but also because there was an increase in the number of Bengali civil servants. Pakistani civil servants are often influenced by regional considerations in decision-making,[16] and the increase of Bengalis in the civil service created a vociferous, influential pressure group within the central bureaucracy. Furthermore, the limitations put on the political process, and the absence of Bengali representation in the military elite, meant that the Bengali civil servants were the only substantial Bengali group participating in national affairs; hence, by default, they became the chief spokesmen for Bengali interests in national decision-making.

The regional conflict within the bureaucracy was heightened by differences in socioeconomic background between the East and West Pakistani civil servants. While West Pakistani civil servants generally came from upper-middle-class families, the Bengali civil servants generally came from comparatively lower-middle-class families.[17] Also, the

[14] Albert Gorvine, "The Civil Service Under the Revolutionary Government in Pakistan," *Middle East Journal,* XIX, (1965) 335.

[15] A. M. A. Muhith, a member of the Pakistani civil service, argues (p. 292) that the deputy commissioner has "combined the functions of a political leader and those of an administrator." The bureaucracy's role in system maintenance and political recruitment is discussed in chaps. VI and VII.

[16] Muneer Ahmad, *The Civil Servant in Pakistan,* pp. 112–13; 49.1 percent of the civil servants interviewed by him agreed that regional considerations greatly influence administrative decision-making; 14.4 percent agreed that regional considerations have some influence. Only 22.9 percent denied the existence of any such influence.

[17] *Ibid.,* pp. 52–56. Muneer Ahmad's findings on the socioeconomic background of members of the CSP (his sample is mostly West Pakistan–based) were that of the 31 members he interviewed 22 came from families with "high occupational status," four from those

overwhelming majority of West Pakistani civil servants were urban members of the nonvernacular elite.[18] The majority of Bengali civil servants, on the other hand, were post–language movement products of Dacca University. Many of them either actively participated in or sympathized with the language movement and other popular political movements. They had close ties of friendship and kinship with the vernacular political elite or the intelligentsia. The West Pakistani civil servants were mostly nonvernacular and had close ties with the civil-military bureaucracy and the landed elite.[19]

The east-west conflict in the bureaucracy, like that in the political sphere, revolved around two issues: participation at the center, and administrative autonomy for East Pakistan.

East Pakistani participation at the center. During the Ayub period, policy-making became highly centralized, for the regime believed in a strong center capable of maintaining uniformity of policy throughout the country. Though Ayub's rule was highly personal his commitment to modernization led to the rationalization of the administrative decision-making process and the rise of a corporate device in policy-making.[20] Even during the martial-law period, when the constitutional process was

---

with "intermediate status," and four from those with "low status." There is no published study on the socioeconomic background of East Pakistani civil servants, but from my own interviews with East Pakistani civil servants, it appears that few (only 4 out of the 25 I interviewed) are from families with higher economic status. The Central Public Service Commission's report shows that candidates from agricultural or lower-income families have lower rates of success in the Central Superior Services (CSS) examinations—which may partially explain the East Pakistani candidates' relatively poorer performance in the CSS examinations. (See Pakistan, Central Public Service Commission, *Annual Report for the Year 1965,* Tables 5, 6, 10).

[18] In the Muneer Ahmad study (pp. 68–69), of the 31 civil servants interviewed only 22.6 percent were not westernized, 25.8 percent were highly westernized, and 51.6 percent were semiwesternized. East Pakistani civil servants, in comparison, are "vernacular"; of the 25 CSP members interviewed by me only 16 percent could be called highly westernized; that is, all but 4 of the 25 were part of the Bengali vernacular elite.

[19] Khalid B. Sayeed, *The Political System of Pakistan,* pp. 156–57, reports that some of the senior members of the CSP are related to one another by marriage and by birth. He notes: ". . . two brothers-in-law of the Secretary of External Affairs are the Secretary of Economic Affairs and Secretary of Home and Kashmir Affairs. In addition the brother of the Secretary of External Affairs is Pakistan's Ambassador in Washington".

[20] The corporate device was used in noncontroversial, routine matters. Key political decisions were often made by Ayub against the advice of the commissions he had set up for policy suggestions.

suspended, the major reforms were the result of the "combined deliberation of thirty-three major commissions of inquiry involving the active participation of 280 persons who were either government officials, nonofficial experts, or leading citizens."[21] These commissions were entrusted with recommending policy innovations over a wide range of subjects. No doubt the commissions owed their origin to the will of the president, and their recommendations were merely advisory; indeed, at times, when the recommendations were against his known wishes, Ayub did not act upon them.[22] But the consensus of those in key policy posts in the government appears to be that action was taken on most of the commissions' reports, and that the government concurred in most of the recommendations.[23]

The commissions were, however, only temporary devices for policy-making. The permanent agency of central policy-making under the regime remained, as before, the Central Secretariat. One significant difference from the pre-1958 era was that under the Ayub regime the Planning Commission attained a dominant position in the central policy-making process.[24] It set priorities and objectives for all "nation-building" departments. The National Economic Council (NEC) became the supreme decision-making body in the economic sector and was entrusted with reviewing the overall economic position of the country. It was composed of the president, who was the chairman of the council; the two governors; all the central ministers except those of law, foreign affairs, and home and Kashmir affairs; the deputy chairman of the Planning Commission; and the provincial ministers in charge of finance and planning and the development departments.

One administrative innovation of the regime was the Governor's Conference—established immediately following the imposition of martial law in 1958—which became the highest decision-making body in the country. It was composed of the president and the two governors and such other ministers and officers as might be required. All adminis-

---

[21] Braibanti, *Bureaucracy of Pakistan,* p. 310.
[22] The commissions whose reports Ayub did not act upon were the Law Reform Commission, the Press Commission, and the Constitution Commission. Later he also rejected the Franchise Commission's report.
[23] Braibanti, *Bureaucracy of Pakistan,* p. 311.
[24] See Albert Waterston, *Planning in Pakistan,* pp. 73–129.

98 / *Bureaucracy and nation-building*

trative-political policy decisions were made in the Governor's Conference.[25]

Apart from the secretariat, the central public corporations also shared in central policy-making. These autonomous bodies had a near monopoly of control over a wide range of subjects.[26]

Bengali participation in these three types of central policy-making institutions—commissions of inquiry, the Central Secretariat, and public corporations—was marginal. Of the 280 members of the commissions of inquiry, only 75 were from East Pakistan—that is, a bare 27 percent.[27] Table V.1 reveals similarly low Bengali representation in the Central Secretariat.

As Table V.1 indicates, there was a significant increase in Bengali representation at the center over the years 1963–66, but despite the increase, overall representation remained generally less than 30 percent. And Bengali representation in the CSP increased by only 10 percent in the ten years between 1957 and 1967. Similarly, members of the boards of directors of the thirteen central corporations were overwhelmingly West Pakistani (87 from West Pakistan, as opposed to 17 from East Pakistan).[28]

Aside from inequitable numerical representation, another longstanding Bengali complaint has been that important central posts or departments were denied them, that whatever Bengali representation existed in the center was in the lower echelons or in departments which did not have much influence on vital areas of national concern.[29] For example, Bengali representation in the Central Secretariat during the Ayub regime was mainly at the section-officer or deputy-secretary level. In 1964, there were only two East Pakistani secretaries at the center (one in the National Assembly Secretariat, the other acting secretary in

---

[25] The Governor's Conference's minutes are not available for research purposes. Hence it is difficult to analyze East Pakistan's participation in this highest policy-making body.

[26] The central public corporations under the Ayub regime included Pakistan International Airlines, the Industrial Development Bank, the Atomic Energy Commission, the Agricultural Development Bank, the Industrial Credit Investment Corporation, the Security Printing Corporation, the House Building Finance Corporation, the Oil and Gas Development Corporation, the Capital Development Authority, the National Bank, and the Refugee Rehabilitation Finance Corporation.

[27] Braibanti, *Bureaucracy of Pakistan,* Table 10.   [28] *Ibid.,* Table 5.

[29] This was the most common complaint of the Bengali civil servants interviewed by me in Pakistan in the summer of 1968.

Table V.1 / Regional representation among class I officers in divisions of the Central Secretariat

DIVISION	JANUARY 1, 1963			JANUARY 1, 1964			JANUARY 1, 1966		
	EAST	WEST	% OF EAST IN TOTAL	EAST	WEST	% OF EAST IN TOTAL	EAST	WEST	% OF EAST IN TOTAL
Cabinet	3	23	11.5	4	20	16.6	5	21	19.2
Establishment									
Main	8	28	22.2	9	27	25.0	10	27	27.0
O&M Wing	6	18	25.0	4	19	17.3	2	19	9.5
Planning	13	44	22.8	17	46	26.9	19	61	23.7
Economic Affairs	6	39	13.3	9	40	18.3	11	36	23.4
Defense	1	38	2.5	6	35	14.6	4	38	9.5
Industries	4	22	15.3	7	19	26.9	8	14	36.3
Home	4	32	11.1	3	30	9.0	3	26	10.0
Education	5	25	16.6	6	22	21.4	8	21	27.5
Information and Broadcasting	3	16	15.7	2	24	7.5	2	19	9.5
Health	3	16	15.7	5	10	33.3	8	16	33.3
Labor and Social Welfare	5	16	23.8	3	17	15.0	4	14	28.5
Foreign Affairs	13	83	13.5	14	94	12.9	18	50	26.4
Communications	2	22	8.3	1	22	4.3	4	23	14.8
Finance									
Secretariat	21	91	18.7	20	106	15.8	27	107	20.1
Finance division (military)	—	—	—	1	37	2.6	3	34	8.1
Food and Agriculture									
Food Wing	3	19	13.6	3	20	13.0	2	12	14.2
Agriculture Wing	6	50	10.7	4	37	9.7	5	35	12.5
Commerce	12	40	23.0	11	42	20.7	22	34	39.2
Rehabilitation and Work	3	31	8.8	3	32	8.5	5	24	17.2

Source: Compiled from Pakistan, Establishment Division, *Civil List of Class I Officers Serving under the Government of Pakistan*, 1st January, 1963; 1964; 1966.

Planning). There were five East Pakistani joint secretaries: two in Law, one in the National Assembly, one in Food, and one in Health.[30] In 1966, there were four East Pakistani secretaries (one in Education, one in Law, one in the National Assembly, and one acting secretary in Planning) and seven joint secretaries (one each in Finance, Food, Law, the National Assembly, Health, and Natural Resources; and the chief controller of Imports and Exports, who was given the status of a central joint secretary).[31] Such key posts as the secretaryships for Establishment, Finance, Economic Affairs, Defense, Home, Commerce and Industries, and the deputy chairmanship of the Planning Commission always went to West Pakistanis. Similarly, of the thirteen public corporation presidents in 1966 only one was from East Pakistan.[32]

No doubt the Ayub regime made some efforts to increase East Pakistani participation. Thus the office of the chief controller of Imports and Exports has since 1963 consistently gone to East Pakistanis; and deputy secretaries in the Cabinet and Establishment divisions after 1962 were invariably East Pakistanis. East Pakistanis were also appointed to head the IDBP and the State Bank of Pakistan. Still these steps failed to satisfy the Bengali counterelite, who regarded the pace of change as too slow. They demanded that immediate parity in senior posts be achieved by the ad hoc appointment of East Pakistanis.[33]

And then there was the complaint, common to underprivileged groups, that participation was granted only to those who were "acceptable" to the "establishment"; that those chosen were more "official show boys" than effective wielders of power; that those who failed to be "acceptable" were squeezed out or removed to "penal" posts.[34]

---

[30] Pakistan, Establishment Division, *Civil List of Class I Officers, Serving under the Government of Pakistan, 1st January, 1964.* The Bengalis' complaints that they are not posted in important departments appear to be justified from the above appointments. Furthermore, of the two East Pakistani secretaries, one was ethnically non-Bengali.

[31] Pakistan, Establishment Division, *Civil List of Class I Officers, 1966.*   [32] *Ibid.*

[33] Editorial, *The Pakistan Observer* (Dacca), August 30, 1962. A Bengali member of the National Assembly who typified these sentiments suggested that Bengalis be raised, by accelerated promotion or by ad hoc appointment, to the posts of central secretaries and joint secretaries. See the speech by Md. Mukhlesuzzaman Khan in the National Assembly (*Debates,* Sess. 21, June 23, 1966).

[34] This view was widely held among the Bengali civil servants interviewed by me. The three CSP officers who were implicated in the Agartala conspiracy case (see chap. 7, 91) claimed that they were falsely accused because they had been active in calling attention to East Pakistani interests. See the full report of their testimonies in *The Pakistan Observer* (Dacca), February 2–6, 1969.

Administrative autonomy for East Pakistan. When the Ayub regime came to power, administrative autonomy for East Pakistan had been a long-standing Bengali demand. In the early days of independence, the east-west conflict had been exacerbated by the presence of West Pakistani civil servants in East Pakistan who gave the bureaucracy the appearance of a colonial rule.[35] Even as late as 1954, there was a complaint in the Constituent Assembly of Pakistan that one would not "find a single Bengali secretary in the whole of the Bengal Secretariat."[36]

The Bengali demand was not merely for more numerous representation at the center, but for a greater decentralization of power to make the east wing administratively autonomous. The Bengalis argued—and their arguments were substantiated by public administration experts—that the Pakistani administration was "over centralized and over coordinated" to a degree that resulted in "complete congestion at the center and paralysis at the extremities."[37]

The Ayub regime, partly because it was dominated by the civil bureaucracy, and partly because of its desire to steal some of the thunder from the Bengali demands for political autonomy, moved quickly with policies responsive to the Bengali demands for administrative autonomy. In June 1961, a policy was adopted to post only East Pakistani civil servants in East Pakistan so that the Bengalis might have a sense of self-government. This policy, which was continued till 1967,[38] resulted in great increases in the number of Bengali civil servants in the East Pakistan Secretariat and district administration. Thus, while in 1960 in the East Pakistan Secretariat, the chief secretary, and the secretaries of planning and development, food and agriculture, works and housing had been from West Pakistan,[39] in 1967–68 only the chief secretary and the secretary of agriculture were from West Pakistan.[40] Similarly,

---

[35] Ayub Khan in his autobiography (p. 27) refers obliquely to West Pakistani "mannerisms" that might have "irritated the East Pakistani" in the early days of independence.

[36] Pakistan, Constituent Assembly, *Debates,* Vol. 1 No. 26, July 17, 1954, p. 1474.

[37] Rowland E. Eggar, "Ministerial and Departmental Organization and Management in the Government of Pakistan," in Inayatullah, *Bureaucracy and Development,* pp. 133-34.

[38] The policy was revoked in 1967, chiefly at the request of the East Pakistan government, which felt that rotation of civil servants between the wings was necessary for national integration. All the East Pakistani members of the CSP interviewed by me were theoretically in favor of this exchange, though the large majority of them preferred to serve in East Pakistan for "personal" reasons.

[39] East Pakistan, S. & G. A. Department, *The East Pakistan Civil List, 1960.*

[40] Information gathered by me in personal interviews with CSP members in the summer of 1968.

in the district administration, by 1964, 53 of the 61 commissioners, additional commissioners, deputy commissioners, and additional deputy commissioners were East Pakistanis.[41]

Soon after assuming power, the regime also pledged decentralization of administration. The 1962 constitution granted more powers to the provinces than did the 1956 constitution. Important subjects such as industries and railways were handed over to the provinces. However, the provinces were not in total control of the subjects assigned to them. The post-1962 administrative relationships between the center and the provinces were spelled out more clearly by the report of the Standing Organization Committee,[42] which was formed to recommend reorganization of the central administrative structure necessitated by the transfer of subjects from the center to the provinces under the new constitution. The report defined the central government's jurisdiction under the 1962 constitution in the following way:

> ... in order to discharge its responsibilities satisfactorily, the Central Government has in all matters: (a) To keep in close touch with broad policy and planning on a national scale; (b) to secure co-ordinations and (c) to deal with international aspects even of such matters as fall wholly within the Provincial sphere.[43]

The committee report therefore recommended that "it would be necessary to maintain appropriate but small administrative units in the Central Government to deal with education, health, food and agriculture, labour, social welfare, railways, industries and fuel and power"[44] even though these had been made provincial subjects under the 1962 constitution. The purpose of the "administrative units" was to

> (i) perform duties in connection with international aspects of these subjects.
> (ii) look after the "Central agencies and Central institutions for the promotion of special studies and special research" which is a Central responsibility. . . . and
> (iii) keep in touch with the conduct of affairs in the provinces in their

---

[41] Sayeed, *Political System*, pp. 154–55.
[42] Pakistan, Establishment Division, Efficiency and O. & M. Wing, *Report of the Standing Organization Committee on the Reorganization of the Functions and Structure of the Central Government in the Light of the New Constitution.*
[43] *Ibid.,* cited in Braibanti, *Bureaucracy of Pakistan,* p. 442.
[44] *Ibid.*

respective fields, especially in regard to broad policy and planning, in order to assess the need for Central legislation or Presidential intervention.[45]

The underlying principle of the new administrative relationship between the center and the provinces was "to maintain in essence the strong character of the Central Government . . . by vesting the centre with broad policy functions, as opposed to operational or executive functions," which were made "the sole responsibility of the Provincial Governments."[46] The report recommended certain organizational changes which would increase the provincial government's autonomy. It suggested the abolition of the Progressing Wing of the Planning Commission, since the implementation of development programs was made a provincial responsibility. The additional chief secretary for development was entrusted with the task of overseeing the implementation of the provincial development programs. The report also recommended that the provincial programs be submitted directly to the Central Development Working Party (CDWP), and not to the central ministries as had been the case in the past. The administrative units concerned with the central government would be represented at the highest level in the CDWP. The report cautioned, however, that "the Central Government should not . . . undertake a detailed scrutiny of these projects."[47]

The report also recommended the reorganization of some agencies of the central Planning Commission so as to increase provincial, especially East Pakistani, participation. Thus the National Economic Council was reconstituted to include the provincial finance ministers. And the Committee for Co-ordination of Economic Policies was asked to coopt the services of "a Secretary having experiences of East Pakistan problems in case none of the members of the Committee is acquainted with the special problems of that Wing."[48] The report further recommended that the status of the provincial secretaries be raised (to be not lower than deputy secretary but not higher than joint secretary of the Central Secretariat), so that the provincial secretaries would feel more secure vis-à-vis the center.

As a result of the constitutional provisions and administrative reorganization, the provincial governments were indeed entrusted with

[45] Ibid.   [46] Ibid., pp. 443-44.   [47] Ibid., p. 460.   [48] Ibid., p. 459.

many more functions and greater power than before[49] In addition, there was more financial security, because the red tape of getting central sanctions was reduced, as the meetings of the Executive Council of the NEC and the CDWP rotated at regular intervals between Dacca, Lahore, and Islamabad. However, the post-1962 administrative arrangement did not bring about a true decentralization of power, since the provincial governments were not given exclusive jurisdiction over any subject. Power was still delegated from the center; and the center could intervene in all subjects in the name of coordination and uniformity of policy.[50] In fact, as far as policy-making and financial planning were concerned there was a greater centralization in the post-1962 period. This was due largely to the "nationalization" of the planning process. The East Pakistan Planning Board, which in the pre-1958 period was entrusted with formulating separate regional plans for East Pakistan, became moribund. In the post-1958 period, the national Planning Commission drew up "national" plans. No doubt East Pakistani views were represented in the planning process, but East Pakistani participation was in the central agencies—the Governor's Conference, the NEC, and the CDWP. There were regional conflicts but these conflicts were generally within the central agencies rather than between the central and provincial governments as had been the case in the pre-1958 period. Though the East Pakistan government often disagreed with the central government—as is evident from the East Pakistan Planning Department's comments on the five-year plans[51]—it did not articulate its differences publicly, unlike most provincial governments in a federation.

---

[49] The majority of East Pakistani civil servants interviewed by me in the summer of 1968 agreed with the regime's claims that more powers were granted to the provinces than before, and that there was little delay by the central government in approving East Pakistani programs.

[50] Most of the civil servants interviewed by me pointed out that coordination and uniformity of policy were the most effective instruments used by the center to control the provincial government. Thus, though education was a provincial subject, such decisions as the provincialization of colleges in East Pakistan and the taking over of the Textbook Board were made by the center on the plea of uniformity of policy and coordination. Ralph Braibanti also finds that of the fourteen acts and ordinances enacted and promulgated by the center under the authority of article 131 (2) from 1962 until the proclamation of a state of emergency in 1965, twelve were invoked under the "achievement of uniformity clause," the remaining two on the "economic and financial stability" provisions. See Braibanti, "The High Bureaucracy of Pakistan," in *Asian Bureaucratic System,* pp. 213–20.

[51] See East Pakistan, Planning Department, *Comments on Planning Commission Paper on Guidelines for the Third Five Year Plan,* and *Economic Disparities Between East and West Pakistan.*

Finance was another weapon of centralization. The provincial government was heavily dependent on the central government for development funds, since provincial sources of revenue were limited. Any provincial plan costing more than Rs. 5 million in foreign exchange required the center's approval. This meant that all but very minor programs had to be submitted to the center. While the central government generally approved provincial plans, the mere possibility of rejection worked as a limiting factor and led to the adoption of uneconomic schemes.[52] And of course the center controlled foreign exchange, economic and fiscal policy, and trade and loan policy, all of which vitally affected the provincial government's development programs.

The central services, especially the CSP, were also an instrument of centralization. As both provincial and central secretaries were recruited from the CSP, with the central secretaries being taken from among the senior CSP members, the provincial secretaries as a rule felt obliged to accept the center's views in the case of a serious disagreement between the two. However, as mentioned earlier, with the increase of relatively senior CSP personnel in the provincial government, the latter's position vis-à-vis the center was strengthened.

Another important factor that influenced the center-province relationship was the political balance between the center and East Pakistan. The fact that Ayub had a near monopoly on political power meant that the provincial administration could not take any determined and effective stand against the center's wishes, for it had no political power to support its position. On the other hand, Bengali political demands expressed outside the government helped strengthen the hands of the East Pakistani civil servants. Quite often, the position of the East Pakistan government on controversial projects and issues was leaked to the press, and the subsequent furor helped the East Pakistan administration to win its demands.[53]

In sum, then, the civil bureaucracy, which in the pre-1958 era had been a mainly neutral force holding the state together by arbitrating

---

[52] My interviews with East Pakistani civil servants gave me the impression that they were still working under the influence of the old fear that the center would turn down any expensive East Pakistani program (though they agreed, in answer to a separate question, that the center's sanction of development money became more routine in the post-1962 era).

[53] The issues of the Farakka Barrage and the Rooppur Atomic Energy Center were kept alive for more than five years in part because of press publicity incouraged for such purposes.

among the feuding political factions, was transformed by the Ayub regime into an "integrative" institution in which the different feuding groups were given participation. One hopeful observer has concluded that the "fabric of the nation state was never imperilled" by this transformation, because the Pakistani bureaucracy was "highly resilient."[54] But the question remains: How long will it remain resilient in the crosscurrents of regional pressure? The bureaucracy can be an effective instrument of national integration only as long as the East Pakistani bureaucrats retain the leadership and confidence of the Bengali vernacular elite. But the East Pakistani civil servants are already encountering strong opposition from the technical services, the intelligentsia, and the political elite, especially the leftists.[55] The crucial determinant will be whether the civil servants, in an effort to retain their supremacy, turn to the center or to the Bengali counterelite. The East Pakistani civil servants' staunch defense of central control of the CSP points to the first course,[56] while the Agartala conspiracy case points to the second.[57]

One limitation of the bureaucracy as an "integrative" force during the Ayub period was its narrowly oligarchic nature. Recruitment to the CSP was extremely limited and selective. In 1963 in East Pakistan of 3905 students receiving a B.A. degree in liberal arts (the vast majority of whom undoubtedly wished to enter the CSP) only 503 were admitted to the qualifying examination, 127 qualified, and 13 were taken into the CSP.[58] During the period 1957-67, college enrollment in East Pakistan increased by 162 percent, whereas the Bengali percentage in the CSP increased by only 10 percent. The civil service could thus accommodate

---

[54] Gorvine, p. 335.

[55] During the 1968-69 uprising, especially in its later stage, the higher Bengali civil servants felt threatened when the class nature of the movement became more manifest.

[56] The CSP generalist has long been pitted against the technical services and has managed to thwart all efforts to upgrade the technical services. The civil service looks upon central control as the most important factor contributing to its higher status. Thus, even the Bengalis I interviewed, while they wanted greater administrative decentralization, were in favor of maintaining their service as a central service.

[57] Though the three Bengali civil servants charged in the Agartala Conspiracy case denied involvement in the conspiracy, their testimony showed a remarkable similarity of views with the vernacular political elite. See *The Pakistan Observer* (Dacca), January 29-30, and February 2-6, 1969, and chap. 7, n. 91.

[58] East Pakistan, Bureau of Statistics, *Statistical Digest of East Pakistan, 1964*, Table 7.6; Pakistan, Central Public Service Commission, *Annual Report for the Year 1965*, Table 10.

Table V.2 / *East and West Pakistani representation in CSP, 1959–67*

	TOTAL NO. OF OFFICERS	WEST PAKISTAN		EAST PAKISTAN	
		NO.	% OF TOTAL	NO.	% OF TOTAL
1959	24	12	50.0	12	50.0
1960	31	19	67.7	10	32.3
1961	27	17	63.0	10	37.0
1962	27	15	55.5	12	44.5
1963	31	18	58.1	13	41.9
1964	33	19	57.8	14	42.2
1965	30	15	50.0	15	50.0
1966	30	16	53.4	14	46.6
1967	30	17	56.7	13	43.3

Sources: Compiled from Pakistan, Establishment Division, *Civil List of Class I Officers Serving under the Government of Pakistan, 1st January, 1965;* and *Gradation List of the Civil Service of Pakistan, July 1, 1967.*

only a fraction of the Bengali vernacular elite, and hence could hardly be regarded as an adequate substitute for an "integrative" political institution like a political party, where recruitment is broader, more rapid, and less selective. The Ayub regime's attempt to make the bureaucracy an integrative institution was a shrewd policy, but similar efforts were required in the political sector.

six / **The Basic Democracies
and political parties**

ONE OF THE remarkable features of the Ayub regime which set it apart from many other military regimes was its willingness to undertake the task of political institution-building. When the regime took power it blamed the politicians and the political system alike for the disintegration of the country. But its general scorn of politicians aside, the regime was convinced that a mere change of personnel was not enough, that the whole political system needed to be changed. Ayub, in an article in *Foreign Affairs,* wrote:

> Yes they [Politicians] were guilty of many misdeeds of omission and commission, but there is one fundamental point in which I have a feeling that they were rather sinned against than sinning. They were given a system of government totally unsuited to the temper and climate of the country.[1]

To make Pakistan "a sound, solid and cohesive nation" a new political system would have to be built. This system would have to be a "homegrown plant" and not an "imported herb," it would have to suit "the

[1] Ayub Khan, "Pakistan Perspectives," *Foreign Affairs,* XXXVIII (1960), 550.

genius of the people." According to the Ayub regime, the previous political institutions had "failed" in Pakistan because they were alien institutions borrowed from the West and superimposed on a traditional society. Soon after its seizure of power, therefore, the regime started building new political institutions. Within six months of the coup, the army was sent back to the barracks, the administration was civilianized, and the task of political institution-building began. Force was not discarded totally, but new political institutions were developed to legitimize the regime and recruit support for its policies.

The political institution-building efforts of the regime are analyzed here with particular emphasis on their role in "integrating" the Bengalis. The integrative capability of the regime's political institutions is evaluated according to the three criteria spelled out in Chapter I, namely, their structures, functions, and legitimacy. Several questions should be asked: How national were these institutions structurally? How participatory and/or mobilizational were they? Did they gain any evident legitimacy and/or support among the various groups in the country?

The regime developed three major political institutions, two of which—the Basic Democracies and the 1962 constitution—were parts of a deliberate political plan,[2] while the third, the political party, was the result of the exigencies of politics.[3] Discussions in the present chapter are devoted to the two institutions—the Basic Democracies and the political party—aimed at recruiting support for the regime. The next chapter will deal with the constitution, which aimed at maximizing compliance with the new political system.

The Basic Democracies

The Ayub regime's first attempt at political institution-building was the establishment of the system of local bodies known as the Basic Democracies. The Basic Democracies were established exactly one year after the regime's seizure of power, and soon came to be regarded as the mainstay of the new political system. The Basic Democracies program

[2] Samuel P. Huntington, *Political Order in Changing Societies*, pp. 250-51; Karl von Vorys, *Political Development in Pakistan*. Both Von Vorys and Huntington argue that Ayub's institutions were in large part the "result of conscious political planning."

was "variously hailed as the ultimate in political wisdom on the one hand and on the other as a mere sop to democratic sentiment."[3] Some looked upon the program as a new method of political institution-building for developing states—one which would foster change and modernization without creating political instability and would channel popular participation in a constructive manner without leading to the breakdown of the existing system.[4] Others looked upon it as a scantily veiled measure to perpetuate the power of the regime.[5] Ayub himself gave the following rationale behind the program:

> We have . . . kept the following factors in view in determining the system of Basic Democracies for our country.
> First, this type of democracy will not be foisted upon the people from above. Instead it will work from below gradually going to the top. Second, the people will not have to go far from their neighborhood to elect their representatives. It is highly difficult for an electorate in the rural areas where literacy does not prevail to elect their representatives from forty to one hundred thousand persons in a constituency . . . The third factor which is of considerable significance is that the council which will be formed will be free from the curse of party intrigues, political pressures and tub-thumping politicians that characterized the Assemblies in our country in the past.[6]

The Basic Democracies system was designed to accomplish multiple political objectives. It was expected both to mobilize the mass of the people, especially in rural areas, for development activities, and to give them a sense of active participation in local affairs. Mobilization and

---

[3] Herbert Feldman, *Revolution in Pakistan*, p. 103.

[4] According to Samuel P. Huntington: "The Basic Democracies . . . brought politics to the rural areas and created a class of rural activists with a role to play in both local and national politics. For the first time political activity was dispersed outward from the cities and spread over the countryside. Political participation was thus broadened, a new source of support created for the government and a major step made toward creating the institutional link between government and countryside which is the pre-requisite of political stability in a modernizing country" (*Political Order in Changing Societies*, p. 252). Also see Lawrence Ziring, "The Administration of Basic Democracies," in Gutherie S. Birkhead, ed., *Administrative Problems in Pakistan*; and Harry J. Friedman, "Pakistan's Experiment in Basic Democracies," *Pacific Affairs*, XXXIII (1960), 107–25, on the Basic Democracies' positive role in the political development of the country.

[5] My interviews with prominent political leaders in Pakistan in the summer of 1968 revealed that most of them branded the Basic Democracies system as an instrument created by the regime to remain in power. This was also the view of the vast majority of the intellectuals and civil servants I interviewed.

[6] Ayub Khan, *Speeches and Statements*, II, 24–25.

participation would be limited, controlled, and guided, however, so as not to put an unbearable pressure on the new political system. On the one hand, people would be given a more vigorous participation than before in their local affairs, through the expansion of the local councils' functions;[7] on the other, popular participation in national politics would be limited, through the granting of electoral rights only to the Basic Democrats. By localizing and fragmenting political conflicts, the regime hoped to prevent the polarization of opinion on national issues. It was also contemplated that the Basic Democracies would train local leaders and create a new cadre of responsible leadership from the bottom up, leaders who would gradually be given a greater degree of participation in the political system.

A major rationale behind the Basic Democracies was that they would help to legitimize the Ayub regime. As a first step toward civilianization, the regime needed a support base separate from the military. It was hoped that the new cadre of rural leadership created by the Basic Democracies would be imbued with the regime's ideals and would mobilize and recruit mass support for the regime's policies and programs. The Basic Democracies would also act to bridge the elite-mass gap. The Basic Democrats (as the local councilors were called) would work in cooperation with the government officials in the local councils and would thus help to create a link between the urban areas and the countryside.[8] Thus the Basic Democracies were expected to do what political parties normally do in other political systems.

As local bodies, the Basic Democracies were by no means a novelty in East Pakistan. Many of their features were borrowed from the old panchayats of traditional India and the local bodies introduced by the British in prepartition Bengal. In one respect, however, they differed from all past experiments in that "for the first time local bodies . . . were integrated from bottom to top into the provincial government apparatus."[9] The Basic Democracies had multiple functions: administrative,

[7] The functions entrusted to local councils under the Basic Democracies scheme, as compared to the previous system, included a greater role in development activities. For a comparative analysis, see Elliot Tepper, *Changing Patterns of Administration in Rural East Pakistan*.

[8] Linking the cities with the countryside is an important aspect of national integration, and Ayub himself looked upon it as a crucial task (see the speech quoted in chap. III, p. 64–65).

[9] Tepper, p. 111.

developmental, local self-government, and constitutional. They were intended to decentralize administration, to provide for collaboration between the elected representatives of the people and the appointed higher government officials. They were to decentralize the planning and coordination of developmental activities at different levels of administration. They were entrusted with a wide variety of local environmental and social service functions. And finally, they were to work as the electoral college for the presidential and assembly elections. Over time, however, the political role of the Basic Democracies assumed greater importance than their administrative and local government functions.

The works program. The Basic Democracies system was launched with high hopes and amidst unprecedented publicity.[10] But there was a great deal of skepticism in East Pakistan about the scheme. The Bengali intelligentsia was especially critical of what they considered to be official domination of the nomination procedure and they looked upon the program as "putting the clock back politically for East Pakistan."[11] The first public murmur of dissent against the Ayub regime arose in East Pakistan after the introduction of the scheme.[12] To make things worse, the functioning of the Basic Democracies during the first few years of their existence was less than satisfactory.[13] The Democracies, like their predecessors, seemed to be plagued by a shortage of funds. To breathe new life into the Basic Democracies—in fact, to breathe new life into the East Pakistani rural areas as a whole—the regime introduced a vast rural public works program, first as a pilot project in Comilla Thana in 1961–62 and then as a province-wide scheme in 1962–63. Though the works program was mainly economic, it was expected to play a political role as well—a role clearly spelled out in Akhter Hameed Khan's memorandum to the president and the members of the Economic Coun-

---

[10] The publicity campaign for the Basic Democracies was unprecedented in the history of Pakistan. Thousands of copies of the program were distributed, seminars were arranged, and special newspaper supplements were published. Ayub himself made a tour through the two wings to explain the program to the people. For details, see Rushbrook Williams, *The State of Pakistan*, pp. 202–6.

[11] *The Statesman* (Calcutta), October 27, 1959.

[12] This can be seen from the Bengali journalists' pointed questions to Ayub regarding the nomination provisions of the program, during his electoral tour of East Pakistan.

[13] Two empirical studies done on the early years of the Basic Democracies testify to this. See A. T. R. Rahmon, *An Analysis of the Working of Basic Democracy Institutions in East Pakistan* and *Basic Democracies at the Grass Roots*.

cil of the Planning Commission.[14] Akhter Hameed Khan linked the economic distress of rural East Pakistan with the political instability of the region and its alienation from the previous ruling elite; and he warned the regime of serious political consequences unless steps were taken for the economic development of the area. He argued:

> ... Economic distress in the rural areas is the main cause of political instability:
> 1. 86% of the population is rural and even the trade and professional people depend to a large extent on rural customers. 90% of the students come from village homes and are intensely sensitive to rural distress.
> 2. Unemployment, loss of crops, low incomes, exploitation by the middlemen, money lenders, etc. have made the rural masses and their leaders bitter, they feel helpless, persecuted and hopeless ...
> 3. Therefore, the rural people respond readily and eagerly to agitators like Bhasani and other angry young and old leaders. Any dispassionate analysis would show that Muslim League government in East Pakistan was overthrown by the rural vote in 1953, and the Awami League and other governments would have been similarly dismissed unless they could find a suitable rural program.[15]

Akhter Hameed Khan foresaw many political benefits from the rural works program:

> a) Frustration, bitterness, cynicism will disappear ... as millions of low income rural people go to work in the slack farm season ...
> b) the protective works ... will be omnipresent symbols of a good government, as well as of a busy and constructively organized people ...
> c) Local institutions will be vitalised, for institutions are nourished by resources and programmes. The Public Works Programme will make Basic Democracies pulsate with life and energy; and
> d) Under the stress of constructive efforts, local leadership and managerial ability will grow ... with the growth of responsible leadership will come political stability and popular support.[16]

It was hoped, then, that the works program would bolster the Basic Democracies and help East Pakistan's rural people to participate in a constructive and meaningful manner in the administration and develop-

---

[14] Akhter Hameed Khan, "The Public Works Programme and a Developmental Proposal for East Pakistan," in Pakistan Academy for Rural Development, *An Evaluation of the Rural Public Works Programme, East Pakistan, 1962–63.* Akhter Hameed Khan and Richard Gilbert were the two moving spirits of the works program.

[15] *Ibid.,* pp. 131–32.   [16] *Ibid.,* pp. 133–34.

ment of their local area. Under the scheme, the local councils, called Union Councils, were entrusted with both the planning and implementation of local projects. The manual for the rural public works program[17] called for each member of the Union Council, in consultation with the people of his ward, to plan different projects, which would later be consolidated into a single plan for the whole union. The manual also called for publicity of the plan and public discussion on it in a village meeting. The implementation of the projects was entrusted to projects committees consisting of leading villagers and headed by a member of the Union Council.

The regime claimed success for the Basic Democracies and the works program. The evaluation reports published by the Basic Democracies Department, and other government-sponsored studies, gave highly favorable accounts of the institutions' workings. Few empirical studies have been done, however; and the few which exist express either extreme praise or extreme criticism. Still, on the basis of the scanty data available, certain conclusions about the integrative capabilities of the programs can be drawn.

Structure. Structurally, the Basic Democracies were pyramidal, as is evident from Table VI.1. It was a four-tiered institution.[18] At the

Table VI.1 / Structure of the Basic Democracies

	CHAIRMAN	MEMBERS
Divisional Council	Commissioner (Govt. official)	Half elected, half officials
District Council	Deputy commissioner (official)	Half elected, half officials
Thana Council or Municipal Committee	Subdivisional officer (official)	Half union council chairmen, half officials
Union Council or Union Committee	Elected by members	Elected by universal adult franchise

---

[17] Pakistan Academy for Rural Development, Comilla, *A Manual for Rural Public Works.*
[18] Originally, it was a five-tiered system, but the highest tier, the provincial development advisory council, was soon abolished.

116 / *The Basic Democracies and political parties*

bottom of the structure was the Union Council (called "Union Committee" or "Town Committee" in the towns and cities). Its members were elected on the basis of universal adult franchise, the ratio of representatives to electors being roughly one to a thousand. Originally, one-third of its members were nominated by an officer of the administration, the subdivisional officer, but this procedure was abolished after the introduction of the 1962 constitution. The members elected a chairman from amongst themselves.

Above the Union Council level was the Thana Council. Its membership consisted of all the chairmen of the Union Councils in the Thana and an equal number of government officials appointed by the deputy commissioner. The subdivisional officer was the ex-officio chairman of the Thana Council. The circle officer was an ex-officio member and acted as chairman in the subdivisional officer's absence. The next highest tier was the District Council, in which one half of the members were government officials and the other half were nonofficials appointed by the deputy commissioner. The deputy commissioner was the chairman of the District Council. Above the District Council was the Divisional Council, in which membership followed the same ratio as in the District Council. The commissioner was the ex-officio chairman of the Divisional Council. Basic Democrats were elected for a five-year term, and parity was maintained in their number in the two wings (forty thousand in each wing).

But though the Basic Democrats were recruited equally from East and West Pakistan and the Basic Democracies were nationally organized, the system failed to become the "grand national assembly" Ayub had hoped for.[19] In spite of their similarity in structure in the two wings, the Basic Democracies did not form a national body as national political parties or other national organizations do in other countries. There were no horizontal links between the Basic Democracies in the two wings. There was no built-in mechanism to develop a consensus on national issues or to train and promote national leaders. The separate pyramidal structures in the two wings were united only at the top in the will of Ayub. National conventions of Basic Democrats from the two wings

---

[19] Ayub Khan, *Friends Not Masters*, p. 214.

were held from time to time, but such temporary meetings often, instead of resolving, accentuated differences.[20]

In the Basic Democracies, as in other "national" institutions, regional differences were paralleled by socioeconomic differences. The average East Pakistani Basic Democrat was more literate and less wealthy than his West Pakistani counterpart. A 1962 study found 97 percent literacy among East Pakistani Basic Democrats, as against 69.7 percent in West Pakistan (with the exception of Karachi).[21] The average West Pakistani Basic Democrat elected in 1964 owned 30 acres of land, while in East Pakistan only around 19 percent of the Basic Democrats owned more than 25 acres of land.

Participatory and mobilizational functions. Though the existing empirical studies on the workings of the Basic Democracies are sharply divided,[22] it appears that the Democracies, especially after the introduction of the rural works program, did succeed in some ways in giving a more active and constructive participation to the rural areas. According to one long-time observer of the Basic Democracies system in East Pakistan, its major contribution lay in:

> . . . developing a pattern of official and rural leaders jointly working in productive operation e.g., the public works program and thus diverting the energy of a vast number of rural leaders from traditional political activities e.g. petitioning, civil disobedience, and strikes to modern leadership roles such as organizing programs, mobilizing rural masses, and working out local problems.[23]

The Basic Democrats were more directly involved than their predecessors in the development affairs of their local areas. They participated in the preparation and execution of local plans, and kept records and accounts of local development projects. And there was increased attendance at local council meetings.[24]

---

[20] Karl von Vorys, *Political Development in Pakistan,* pp. 154–55.
[21] Mushtaq Ahmad, *Government and Politics in Pakistan,* p. 203.
[22] See John Thomas, "Rural Public Works Program and East Pakistan's Development"; Rehman Sobhan, *Basic Democracies, Works Programme and Rural Development in East Pakistan;* M. Rashiduzzaman, *Politics and Administration in the Local Councils;* A. T. R. Rahman, *An Analysis of the Workings of Basic Democracy Institutions in East Pakistan* and *Basic Democracies.*
[23] A. T. R. Rahman, "Rural Institutions in India and Pakistan," *Asian Survey,* VIII (1968), 800.
[24] PARD, *An Evaluation of the Rural Public Works Programme,* p. 41.

There was, however, a twofold limitation on local participation through the Basic Democracies. First, the Basic Democracies were dominated by the government officials and the council chairmen. In all but the lowest tier, government officials and nominated members outnumbered the elected members. An early report on the Basic Democracies found that "85 percent of the items on the agenda for discussion at the Union Council meetings were initiated by letters and visits from government officials."[25] Most of the council resolutions were taken as a "face saving device to show compliance with the government directive,"[26] and very few of them were carried out. Councilors were also dominated to some extent by the council chairmen, whose position was buttressed by a close working relationship with the government officials.[27] Councilors frequently complained that during their visits and in their letters, government officials recognized only the chairmen.[28] One study found, however, that the council chairmen did indeed consult their colleagues in making decisions, though they generally depended on a small faction within the council.[29]

Second, popular participation, as distinct from participation by the Basic Democrats, was perhaps even more restricted. One study of the workings of the Basic Democracies and the works programs during 1963-64 found an actual decline in popular participation. According to the report:

> ... officers and union councillors agreed to dispense with the villagers and to take the total burdens of the works programme on their own shoulders. In many unions, no meetings were held in the project areas to discuss the audit reports ... In some thanas only one meeting was held.[30]

Printed booklets publicizing the audit reports were published in insufficient numbers. Each Union Council published, on an average, 200 booklets (a union has 1,500 to 2,000 families). Each Thana Council

---

[25] A. T. R. Rahman, *Basic Democracies*, p. 95.   [26] *Ibid.*, p. 59.
[27] See S. J. Burki, "West Pakistan's Rural Works Program: A Study in Political and Administrative Response," *Middle East Journal*, XXIII (1969), 331-42, for a discussion of the motivations leading to this working relationship.
[28] A. T. R. Rahman, *Basic Democracies*, p. 72.
[29] Rashiduzzaman, *Politics and Administration*, pp. 45-49.
[30] A. T. R. Rahman, *An Evaluation of the Rural Works Programme, East Pakistan, 1963-64*, pp. 18-19.

published, on an average, 500 booklets (a thana has 15,000 to 20,000 families).[31] The publicity on the projects was also inadequate. "In most cases no village meetings were held to select union council schemes . . . Project committees were seldom elected in meetings at the project site . . . Most of the project committees did not hold any regular meetings . . . and the office of the secretary as well as chairman tended to be monopolized by Union Councillors."[32] (One study, on the other hand, indicated an improved picture of participation. John Thomas found that 71 percent of the respondents in a random survey knew about open meetings on works program projects, and that 66 percent felt that they could attend and participate if they had a desire to do so.[33])

Finally, even if the works program did enable the Basic Democracies to mobilize the people in the rural areas, the mobilization was purely economic, rather than political. But the most crucial and controversial aspect of the Basic Democracies was their use as the electoral college for presidential and assembly elections, because, in the absence of a clear mandate, the Democracies were open to government pressure and manipulation.[34]

Legitimacy through the Basic Democracies. One major rationale behind the Basic Democracies was to help create legitimacy for the Ayub regime by establishing a new cadre of rural political leaders who would recruit support for the regime. The available socioeconomic background data on the Basic Democrats indeed indicate some changes in rural leadership. As Tables VI.2, VI.3, VI.4, and VI.5 show, there appears to have been a trend toward younger and more literate members. Additionally, whereas the lower income group seems to have been heavily represented in the 1960 Basic Democracies election,[35] there was a swing back to the higher income group in the 1964 election, (though, as we shall see, this group differed from the pre-Ayub rural elite). A similar pattern was discernible in the West Pakistani Basic Democracies, where younger, less wealthy representatives had been

---

[31] *Ibid.*, p. 19. [32] *Ibid.*, pp. 16–17.

[33] John Thomas, "Rural Public Works Program in East Pakistan."

[34] The opposition accused the regime of unfair practices in the 1965 presidential election. See *The Pakistan Times* (Lahore), January 4, 1965.

[35] The PARD study data about the very low economic background of the 1961 members have been questioned by Rehman Sobhan, *Basic Democracies*, pp. 244–58.

Table VI.2 / Age of union councilors (percentage)

	BELOW 30	30–44	45–59	60 OR ABOVE
1957 (survey of 129 councilors)	6.0	43.6	39.9	10.4
1961				
members	10.8	43.5	36.4	9.3
chairmen	7.3	41.4	41.5	9.7
1964				
members	7.7	45.7	33.2	9.1
chairmen	4.3	54.9	34.4	6.3

Sources: Compiled from data in Pakistan Academy for Rural Development, Comilla; and Bureau of National Reconstruction, *An Analysis of the Working of Basic Democracy Institutions in East Pakistan*, pp. 25–29; Rehman Sobhan, *Basic Democracies Works Programme and Rural Development in East Pakistan* (Dacca: Oxford University Press, 1968), pp. 77–100; M. Rashiduzzaman, "Pakistan's Local Bodies and Social Change: The Emerging Pattern of Local Leadership," *Orient*, IX (1968), 125–28.

Table VI.3 / Educational level of union councilors (percentage)

	1957 (SURVEY)	1961 MEMBERS	1961 CHAIRMEN	1964 MEMBERS
Illiterate	5.7	3.3	—	1.0
Primary school	36.7	40.2	13.4	28.2
Secondary school	44.6	48.6	67.1	64.1
College	12.8	5.6	12.2	4.2
College graduates		2.3	7.3	2.3

Sources: Compiled from data in Pakistan Academy for Rural Development, Comilla; and Bureau of National Reconstruction, *An Analysis of the Working of Basic Democracy Institutions in East Pakistan*, pp. 25–29; Rehman Sobhan, *Basic Democracies Works Programme and Rural Development in East Pakistan* (Dacca: Oxford University Press, 1968), pp. 77–100; M. Rashiduzzaman, "Pakistan's Local Bodies and Social Change: The Emerging Pattern of Local Leadership," *Orient*, IX (1968), 125–28.

elected in 1960.[36] This shift from middle-income farmers to wealthier farmers was due mainly to the exigencies of politics. The Basic Democracies system was planned by the regime to work in a society without politics. In fact, Ayub thought that the Basic Democracies would prevent the reappearance of the politics which he detested so much. But after

[36] Burki, "West Pakistan's Rural Works Program," pp. 232–33.

Table VI.4 / Occupations of union councilors (percentage)

	1957 (SURVEY)	1961	1964
Farmers	77.3	82.4	77.7
Businessmen including contractors	10.7	15.6	16.9
Lawyers, teachers, doctors	10.1	0.6	2.7
Others	1.8	1.2	2.4

Sources: Compiled from data in Pakistan Academy for Rural Development, Comilla; and Bureau of National Reconstruction, *An Analysis of the Working of Basic Democracy Institutions in East Pakistan*, pp. 25-29; Rehman Sobhan, *Basic Democracies Works Programme and Rural Development in East Pakistan* (Dacca: Oxford University Press, 1968), pp. 77-100; M. Rashiduzzaman, "Pakistan's Local Bodies and Social Change: The Emerging Pattern of Local Leadership," *Orient*, IX (1968), 125-28.

Table VI.5 / Annual income of union councilors

	BELOW RS. 1000	RS. 1,000–2,000	RS. 2,000–3,000	RS. 3,000–4,000	RS. 4000 OR ABOVE
1957 (survey)	3.7	15.7	26.6	—	34.8
1961 chairman*	76.0	12.2	7.3	1.2	2.4
1961 members*	89.2	7.0	3.8	—	—
1964	10.1	21.2	21.3	16.7	30.4

Sources: Compiled from data in Pakistan Academy for Rural Development, Comilla; and Bureau of National Reconstruction, *An Analysis of the Working of Basic Democracy Institutions in East Pakistan*, pp. 25-29; Rehman Sobhan, *Basic Democracies Works Programme and Rural Development in East Pakistan* (Dacca: Oxford University Press, 1968), pp. 77-100; M. Rashiduzzaman, "Pakistan's Local Bodies and Social Change: The Emerging Pattern of Local Leadership," *Orient*, IX (1968), 125-28.
* The 1961 figures are controversial.

the reintroduction of limited political processes in the postconstitution years, the Basic Democracies were highly politicized. Since the rich farmers were the local influentials, they managed to win in the 1964 election in large numbers; and the regime had to fall back on the time-tested, traditional alliance with them.

The reemergence of wealthy farmers was also due to an increased interest in the Basic Democracies system. In 1959, the scheme was still a novelty, and it evoked little popular interest. About 25 percent of the seats were uncontested, and voter turnout in East Pakistan was a mere 52 percent.[37] Of the elected Basic Democrats, only 7 percent in East Pakistan had previous party affiliations.[38] By 1964, however, the situation had changed. The tremendous economic and political patronage of the Basic Democracies had been clearly domonstrated. Elections in 1964 were, therefore, keenly contested,[39] and traditional political alliances and methods were involved.

Though the 1964 election saw the return to power of a higher income group, the new rural elite was different from the past elite in one significant way. While the old elite had been the landed aristocracy — the zamindars (landlords) and talukdars (petty landlords) — the Basic Democrats were generally from nontraditional, nouveau riche families.[40] They were rich farmers, not landlords. In addition, as Table VI.4 indicates, the Basic Democracies saw a rise in the participation of a new moneyed class — businessmen and contractors — and a decline in the participation of the old rural elite of the literati, the teachers, doctors, and lawyers. The regime was thus partially successful in fostering the growth of a new rural elite whose economic and political power was largely dependent on the regime's policies.[41]

How far was this new elite successful in recruiting political support for the regime? Most observers of Pakistani politics have maintained that the Basic Democracies and the works program succeeded in recruiting at least rural East Pakistani support for the regime. The results of the 1965 presidential elections are cited by them in support

---

[37] Von Vorys, *Political Development*, p. 201. Official estimate for the whole country was 60%.

[38] *Ibid.*

[39] In the 1964 elections, fewer than 6 percent of the Basic Democrats were elected uncontested in East Pakistan, and withdrawals amounted to 4.73 percent. See Pakistan, Election Commission, *Report on General Elections in Pakistan, 1964-65*, I, 42.

[40] Rashiduzzaman, *Politics and Administration*, pp. 42-44, in his study of 129 Union Councils, found that in as many as 112 Union Councils, candidates from nontraditional families broke the decades-long hold of traditional families on the Union Councils; 37 percent of the Basic Democrats belonged to the new class.

[41] Both the rich farmers and the businessmen and contractors benefited economically from the regime's policies. As already discussed in chap. IV, the works program and the regime's agricultural development policies helped rich farmers more than landless labor.

of their view; "massive" rural support is said to have helped Ayub to counterbalance his negative urban returns.[42]

This view is highly questionable, however, as a more careful analysis of the 1965 voting pattern will show. First, all but one of the four major cities in East Pakistan (Dacca, Chittagong, Khulna, and Narayanganj) went to Ayub. Second, since the percentage of urbanization in East Pakistan is low,[43] the vote in the district headquarters (which are always the biggest cities in the districts) should be considered part of the "urban vote." Here, too, we find (see Table VI.6) that, contrary to common opinion, the vote generally went to Ayub rather than to his opponent, Miss Jinnah. It is true that Ayub lost the district headquarters of Mymensingh and Faridpur, even though he carried these two districts; however, he won Sylhet and Comilla, while losing both their districts. In fact, out of seventeen district towns, he lost only five. A more rigorous analysis of the relationship between urbanization and voting also shows an insig-

Table VI.6 / Distribution of vote in the major towns and cities of East Pakistan in the 1965 presidential election

	AYUB	MISS JINNAH		AYUB	MISS JINNAH
Jessore	170	106	Dacca	336	544
Barisal	202	114	Mymensingh	122	168
Kushtia	112	99	Faridpur	129	133
Rangpur	162	119	Sylhet	145	121
Khulna	167	113	Comilla	156	128
Dinajpur	133	131	Noakhali	68	126
Rajshahi	117	72	Chittagong	181	151
Pabna	148	106	Rangamati	29	44
Bogra	102	80	Narayanganj*	131	112

Source: Pakistan, Election Commission, *Presidential Election Results, 1965.*
*Narayanganj is the only town in the list which is not a district headquarters.

[42] Khalid B. Sayeed, *The Political System of Pakistan,* pp. 221-22. Also *idem,* "1965 — An Epoch Making Year in Pakistan," *Asian Survey,* VI (1966), 79: "The common impression, particularly among the opposition circles was that East Pakistan like a solid bloc would turn against Ayub. The government circles, on the other hand, knew that Ayub's regime had poured money into the rural areas through the rural public works."

[43] According to the 1961 census, East Pakistan is only 5 percent urban.

nificant impact of urbanization on voting in the 1965 presidential election.[44]

Thus the theory that Ayub gained rural, as opposed to urban, support in East Pakistan is not substantiated by the election returns. Furthermore, whatever "rural support" the regime did muster probably depended more on the Basic Democrats than on the rural populace as a whole. There are indications that during the 1964–65 election campaign the regime addressed itself primarily to the Basic Democrats rather than to the people.[45]

Even in recruiting support through the Basic Democracies, the regime depended more on government officials than on the Basic Democrats. The different tiers of the Basic Democracies were linked not through their own political hierachy but through the administrative hierachy. Works program money was channeled through the administrators, and not through the politicians; instead of being the base of a political hierarchy, the Basic Democracies were thus more like a government agency. And, while the Basic Democracies system did help the regime to survive one presidential and two assembly elections, in the process it created more enemies than friends for itself and the regime.

The Basic Democracies system alienated nearly every powerful interest group in East Pakistan. First, it alienated the urban groups (the intelligentsia, the students, and the urban salaried workers) which prior to 1958 had played a leading role in East Pakistani political movements. Making the Basic Democracies the electoral college meant limiting the political participation of these groups. The Basic Democrats who were elected from East Pakistani urban areas did not come from these groups, but mostly from the rising middle class of businessmen and contractors. In the 1964 elections, 73.61 percent of the urban Basic Democrats were businessmen and contractors.[46] The old middle class therefore felt threatened and isolated under the Basic Democracies system. Election through the Basic Democracies was also antithetical

[44] See chap. VII for a more detailed analysis of the voting behavior in East Pakistan in the 1965 presidential election.

[45] Von Vorys, *Political Development,* Table 16, p. 285, notes that from the conclusion of the Basic Democracies elections to the end of the presidential election campaign, Ayub addressed 11 Basic Democrats' meetings and 2 public rallies; as opposed to Miss Jinnah's 4 and 26, respectively.

[46] Rehman Sobhan, *Basic Democracies,* p. 82.

to the urban intelligentsia's cherished faith in the liberal democratic ideal of universal adult franchise and direct election. But, above all, the urban groups were enraged because the Basic Democracies put an effective check on the Bengali counterelite's aspiration of sharing political power in the national system. The Basic Democracies system, devised to recruit a base of popular Bengali political support for the regime, and not to make the Bengalis equal sharers of power in the central decision-making process, deliberately isolated and disfranchised the Bengali counterelite and its most active group of supporters.

The Basic Democracies introduced a new kind of politics, to which the Bengali counterelite was unaccustomed. The old tactic of galvanizing mass support by holding mammoth public meetings and rallies, and issuing party manifestos on a wide variety of regional, national, and international issues, was no longer applicable. The new politics minimized the importance of party affiliations and national politics. As the number of electors was small, face-to-face contact, local issues, and money were important factors.[47] The existing empirical studies indicate that the Basic Democrats were elected more on the basis of personal characteristics than on party affiliations or philosophies.[48] The Bengali intelligentsia and the other urban groups looked upon this emphasizing of local issues and minimizing of party ideology as a backward political step for East Pakistan.

If urban groups were antagonized by the Basic Democracies, what of the rural population which the system was ostensibly addressing? The available studies show that the vast majority of rural people were theoretically in favor of the Basic Democracies and the works program,

---

[47] Sayeed, *Political System,* chap. 9. My interviews with National Assembly members substantiated this view: Mr. Farid Ahmad listed money and official backing as the two important factors influencing local elections. Mr. A. B. M. Nurul Islam cited personal popularity, money, and party affiliation as the three main factors, in that order. The importance of local, as opposed to national, issues is testified to by Rehman Sobhan, *Basic Democracies* and M. Rashiduzzaman, *Politics and Administration.*

[48] In the studies by Rehman Sobhan, *Basic Democracies* and John Thomas, "Rural Public Works Program in East Pakistan" party affiliation as a factor influencing election returns was low. Rehman Sobhan's study found party affiliations to be a major consideration in only 33.0 percent of responses; while 73.5 percent named personal abilities and 82.0 percent named honesty and sincerity as major considerations. John Thomas's study found 45.1 percent listed ability to serve the community as the major criterion, 4.4 percent listed age, 33.0 percent listed money, and 14.6 percent family connections.

but had serious reservations about the way both were run.[49] There were widespread charges of corruption, nepotism, inefficiency, and misappropriation of funds. The growing concentration of economic and political power in the hands of the Basic Democrats exacerbated economic inequality in the rural areas and heightened the rural poor's sense of deprivation[50] — a factor which undoubtedly contributed to the widely publicized "rural mob slayings" in East Pakistan in the popular uprising of 1968–69.[51]

Thus, the Basic Democracies system achieved only limited success in its goal of closing the elite-mass gap. As a device for overhauling the political structure of the country, it succeeded in limiting urban participation, but failed to fully mobilize the rural areas. In contrast to the rural areas' expanded participation in local affairs, their participation in national affairs was quite restricted. The new rural elite created by the Basic Democracies had a narrow social base and limited capability in recruiting mass support for the regime. It is true that through the Basic Democracies and the works program the rural areas for the first time pulled a greater weight in national affairs. The rural poor were probably better off in absolute terms. But they were not won to the regime, since rich farmers, businessmen, and contractors made more visible and, relatively speaking, much greater gains. Thus, by disfranchising the urban areas, the Basic Democracies alienated the previously mobilized and semimobilized groups, and the groups it enfranchised were neither mobilized nor large enough to counteract this urban dissatisfaction. And, finally, by monopolizing electoral rights the Basic Democracies system became the most visible target for the discontent of all alienated groups, who looked upon it as the mechanism by which the regime perpetuated itself. Ultimately, therefore, the Basic Democracies not only failed to legitimize the regime but in fact lost their own legitimacy, though local bodies had had a long tradition in the region.

---

[49] Rehman Sobhan, *Basic Democracies,* pp. 120–23, 234; A. T. R. Rahman, *Rural Works Programme,* p. 15.
[50] For similar developments in rural India, see Francine Frankel, "India's New Strategy of Agricultural Development: Political Costs of Agrarian Modernization," *Journal of Asian Studies,* XXVIII (1969), 693–710.
[51] *The New York Times,* March 20, 1969.

Political parties

Political parties were not legalized by the Ayub regime until quite late in its administration, and even then they were not part of a deliberate plan as were the Basic Democracies and the constitution. Rather political parties were introduced into the political system with great reluctance and their reentry was necessitated by the revival of the political process.

The Pakistan Muslim League. When Ayub took power in 1958, he was not favorably disposed toward political parties. Like many other military leaders, he failed to realize the crucial role political parties play in national integration. Embittered by his past experiences with politicians and political parties,[52] Ayub at first tried to construct a partyless polity. Political parties remained banned even after the constitution of 1962 was introduced.

The regime's initial decision neither to revive the political parties which were active at the time of the coup nor to organize a party of its own had a far-reaching impact on future political developments. First, it prevented the emergence of a new cadre of political leadership. Since party activity was frozen after the coup, and since the regime did not organize a new party, the electors were left with the same brand of politicians as had existed before 1958. The election campaigns in 1962 indicated that "old style" politics was back,[53] and the new group alliances of "like-minded" people in the National Assembly of 1962 tallied closely with pre-1958 party lines.[54] Second, the regime's denial of participation to the top political leadership made its political system less representative, particularly since the regime's political restrictions affected some parties more than others. Awami League and National

---

[52] For Ayub's views on politicians, see his *Friends Not Masters*, pp. 28–30, 48–57.

[53] Saleem M. M. Qureshi, "Party Politics in the Second Republic of Pakistan," *Middle East Journal,* XX (1966), 457.

[54] The initial alliance groups in the 1962 National Assembly were as follows: (a) *Democratic group:* mostly former Muslim Leaguers from East Pakistan, led by Mohammad Ali of Bogra; (b) *Progressive group:* mostly former Republicans, led by Mian Abdul Bari; (c) *Pak People's group:* mostly former United Front members from East Pakistan, led by Farid Ahmad (Nizam-i-Islam) and Mashiur Rahman (NAP); (d) *Independent group:* mostly former Muslim Leaguers from West Pakistan, led by Sardar Bahadur Khan; (e) *Independent neutrals:* led by Qamrul Ahsan (5 Members of the National Assembly); and (f) one undefined independent group from East Pakistan, led by Maulana Mushahid.

128 / *The Basic Democracies and political parties*

Awami Party members were imprisoned and disqualified under the EBDO more than were the Muslim Leaguers; hence, they had fewer representatives in the National Assembly, even though their popular support in East Pakistan was much broader.[55] Third, since the regime did not have a party of its own in the assembly, it had to resort to buying the support of assembly members, as had been done by all other governments prior to 1958. This led the regime into some unhappy alliances — mainly with the "old guard" Muslim League in East Pakistan. These Muslim Leaguers were to the Bengali counterelite a group of politicians who repeatedly betrayed the Bengali cause.[56] By aligning itself with this unpopular group, the regime alienated much of the east wing.

It soon became apparent that political patronage was not enough to hold the disparate groups in the assembly together, and Ayub's own supporters in the assembly put strong pressure on the regime for the revival of political parties. The pressure of the opposition outside the assembly was mounting, and the regime's supporters thought that by reviving political parties they could break the unity of the opposition. Additionally, they were afraid that the opposition in the assembly might carry through a political parties bill which would do away with EBDO and other party restrictions. All these considerations led the regime to introduce a political parties bill in the assembly, a bill which retained EBDO and other party restrictions.

Though Ayub allowed the revival of political parties, he did so with great reluctance; and he was not yet ready to join any existing party or to start a new one. Instead he assumed the role of a supraparty leader, and left it to his supporters to organize a party for him. His supporters, rather than build a party from the bottom up as he had suggested,[57] decided to take over the Muslim League. Since the League was a well-known national party which had been associated with the Pakistan

---

[55] In the National Assembly the strength of former Muslim Leaguers from East Pakistan was 40 as opposed to the combined opposition parties' strength of 36. This is surprising, considering the fact that in the direct election in 1954 the Muslim League was able to get only 10 seats in a house of 309, while the opposition got 228 (the rest being minority seats).

[56] Because of their association with the unpopular policies of the central government during the period 1947–54, the Muslim Leaguers were regarded by the Bengali counterelite as "betrayers" of Bengali interests.

[57] The day the political parties act was passed Ayub in a press conference suggested the reorganization of the parties on a national, programmatic, grass-roots basis. See his speech cited in Rais Ahmad Jafri, ed., *Ayub Soldier and Statesman*, pp. 124–25.

movement, Ayub's supporters felt that they would automatically inherit a "national organization" whose past glory would gain them some sort of legitimacy in the popular eye. Most of Ayub's political supporters were former Muslim Leaguers. And, because the League was greatly weakened after the election defeat in East Pakistan in 1954, it was relatively easy for the Ayub group to oust the old leadership and capture the party. The fact that the regime had already recruited the support of the second echelon Muslim Leaguers only made the task easier. Failing to revive the party through the old Muslim League Council, the "ministerialists"[58] revived it in a convention held in September 1962 at Karachi, and a constitution for reorganization of the Muslim League was adopted.[59]

But even though a party was formed—or, to be more precise, a section of an old party was captured—hardly any attempt was made to reorganize the party on a mass basis in both wings. Factional conflicts arose even before the convention ended its meetings, and a party manifesto was very slow in forthcoming. Ayub's own efforts were limited to occasional suggestions in his public statements. Even when he finally joined the Pakistan Muslim League in May 1963 and was elected its president, he did not try to reorganize the party. He still regarded the Basic Democracies and the bureaucracy as his main base of support. Although he ran on the PML ticket in the 1965 presidential election, it was obvious that he managed the campaign on his own. He issued his own election manifesto, which the party later adopted. He waged the campaign mainly on his personal record and performance, and not on the party's record.[60] For recruiting support from the Basic Democrats and from the mass of the people, he depended more on the civil bureaucracy than on his political party. It is true that the governor, the ministers,

[58] The term "ministerialists," coined by *Dawn,* is used here to depict those Pakistani politicians whose major objective was always to gain office, regardless of party loyalties.

[59] *Dawn* (Karachi), September 5, 1962. The official title of the reorganized party was the Pakistan Muslim League (PML).

[60] According to Von Vorys, *Political Development,* p. 280, the relative weights given by Ayub, in his major campaign speeches, and the PML manifesto to different issues were different. The PML manifesto gave 21.7 percent weightage to the political system, 51.0 percent to economic and social problems, 5.4 percent to Islamic ideology, 11.0 percent to foreign policy, and 11.9 percent to miscellaneous issues. Ayub's statements gave 58.0 percent weightage to the political system, 9.1 percent to economic and social problems, 11.9 percent to Islamic ideology, 11.0 percent to foreign policy, and 10.0 percent to miscellaneous issues.

130 / *The Basic Democracies and political parties*

and the parliamentary secretaries did a lot of campaigning; but whatever pressure they exerted on the Basic Democrats was due to their connection with the administration, rather than to their party affiliation. That the PML was not organized on a mass basis was made evident by its refusal to give party nominations in the Basic Democracies election of 1964. Also, the fact that Ayub polled a greater percentage of votes than did the Muslim League candidates in the assembly elections indicates that his election campaign was mainly personal.[61]

After the election, Ayub's supporters, especially in East Pakistan, tried to reorganize the Pakistan Muslim League party with greater vigor, though Ayub himself remained generally aloof. Characteristically, however, he took the initiative in defining the broad outlines for reorganizing the party on a mass basis. In a circular issued on May 13, 1965, to the members of the Working Committee of the party, Ayub urged that the PML reorganization parallel the Basic Democracies structure and link the two whenever possible.[62] A new constitution of the PML was soon adopted providing for the necessary reforms. PML conventions were regularly held, and party workers were employed to "get out the crowds" for party meetings and presidential appearances.[63] Party headquarters were established in Karachi, Islamabad, Lahore, and Dacca, and party literature was published. But in spite of these efforts, the Muslim League failed to gain mass support and remained a "national" party mostly on paper.

The PML's program was nationalistic, pragmatic, and policy-oriented. It stood for a strong central government, rapid economic growth, and Islamic ideology—in other words, the policies the Ayub regime was pursuing. But some parts of the PML program—namely, its emphasis on a strong center and on economic growth rather than distri-

---

[61] Ayub got 52.9 percent of the vote in East Pakistan and 73.3 percent in West Pakistan. PML candidates polled 49.64 percent (East) and 61.31 percent (West) in the National Assembly elections; and 38 percent (East) and 48.78 percent (West) in the Provincial Assembly elections.

[62] For details, see *The Pakistan Times* (Rawalpindi), May 14, 1965.

[63] Between 1958 and 1964, civil servants were generally used to get out the crowds for Ayub; but after the 1965 election, party workers were used to arrange "enthusiastic" receptions. East Pakistani Governor Monem Khan's zeal went so far that he temporarily introduced, following the Chinese cultural revolution, a "green book" of Ayub's quotes, which PML party workers waved when Ayub visited Dacca.

bution—were unpopular in East Pakistan, where programs for regional autonomy and socialism always had more appeal.

Organizationally, the PML was weak in both wings of the country. Like the other institutions Ayub created, the PML was heavily dominated by the president. Members of the key central bodies of the party were not elected, but were nominated by him. The members of the Central Working Committee, which was the "principal executive of the League," were nominated by the president, as were the members of the Finance Committee and the Central Parliamentary Board.[64] Because the central control of the party was thus concentrated in the person of the president, the East Pakistan Muslim League and West Pakistan Muslim League were linked only by their common allegiance to him. The party organization was further weakened by intraregional factionalism. In East Pakistan, the party was divided into two factions—one led by the governor, Abdul Monem Khan; the other led by his opponents: Sabur Khan, Kaji Kader, and Wahiduzzaman.[65] Intraparty feuds often made the PML ineffective in local elections.

In spite of factionalism, the PML remained united, mainly because of the party members' patronage relationship to Ayub. The PML's claim to national leadership rested only with Ayub, however. Apart from him, the PML did not have any nationally known leaders. Ayub's refusal to share key decision-making power with his party men prevented the growth of a broader leadership. In fact all care was taken to thwart and squeeze out potential rivals from the party—Z. A. Bhutto being the most notable case.

The PML's social support base was weak, especially in East Pakistan. It recruited some of the relative newcomers to politics, the rich farmers and the businessmen-contractors. But these groups were small and were not mobilized enough to give the PML a firm foundation. Moreover, their support was based not on ideological principles but on the personal gain they could derive from the regime. As for the old Muslim Leaguers, the PML got the support of only the second string, who had virtually no local or national power base. Of the eleven East Pakistani Muslim Leaguers who became Ayub's ministers, eight ran and

[64] See Pakistan Muslim League, *Constitution of the Pakistan Muslim League*, arts. 68, 70, 74.

[65] In the post-Ayub era, these factions formed two separate parties.

lost in the provincial assembly election of 1954. Most of the prominent Muslim Leaguers—Nazimuddin, Daulatana, Qayyum—remained in the opposition. Additionally, the Muslim League had been thoroughly discredited in East Pakistan. Though the PML won the overwhelming majority of seats in the assembly elections of 1965, that election can hardly be regarded as a true indicator of the PML's support in the country.[66]

The PML failed to gain ground because it was not established to carry out any ideology or programs of its own. Rather it was used as the regime's handmaiden. The PML never set goals for the regime; it merely echoed whatever programs the regime pursued. The party had been created almost overnight out of a disparate group of people whose only common interest was to share in political patronage. The PML's unity and claim to national character depended on Ayub. Without him, "it would crumble," as one observer noted, "like a pack of cards."[67] And indeed, following Ayub's downfall, the PML was split into three factions.

What of the other political parties which were revived or established after 1962? Even a cursory analysis reveals that during the Ayub decade all political parties underwent rift and schism, became organizationally weak, and could hardly claim to be mass-based national political parties. All available indicators show that the parties were gradually becoming more and more regional in their programs, leadership, and support base.

The Jama'at-i-Islami. The Jama'at-i-Islami was the first political party to be revived after the passage of the political parties act. The Jama'at claims to be a "national party": it has a "national" ideology, and it has party organizations in both wings of Pakistan. However, its base of support and organization in East Pakistan is very weak. During the Ayub decade, it remained a mostly West Pakistan–based party, although its ideology and program did not involve any secular or regional issues.[68] It is a fundamentalist religious party which advocates the revival of a truly Islamic society. According to the Jama'at, Islamic society rests on three fundamentals: (1) surrender to God as against secularism; (2) humanism as against nationalism; and (3) sovereignty of God and the

---

[66] For an elaboration of this point, see chap. VII.
[67] Personal interview with an East Pakistani intellectual.
[68] The Jama'at has recently focused more on regional and secular issues.

concept of the viceregency (Caliphate) of the people instead of their sovereignty.[69] The Jama'at holds that the Islamic polity is eternally perfect and hence incapable of evolution or change. In the early Islamic institution of tribal or intertribal consultation (*shura*) and in the principle of *ijma*, the Jama'at finds the nucleus of an ideal parliamentary system and consensus-building.[70] The Islamic polity is a "theodemocracy," since its sphere of activity is coextensive with the whole of human life.[71] *Sharia* is irrevocable, but *Fiquah* can be changed.[72] The non-Muslims living in an Islamic state have full economic and social rights, but are barred from political participation.[73]

The economic policy of the Jama'at is to revive the Islamic economy and thus avoid the disadvantages of both capitalism and communism. Since individual remains at the center of the Islamic economic system, the Jama'at has been against communism, socialism, and even land reform.[74] It recommends "Islamic" devices for socioeconomic justice— the abolition of interest and modern banking, the introduction of the Islamic law of inheritance, charity, etc. The Jama'at also rejects the notion of class struggle as un-Islamic and urges settlement of labor-management conflicts through constitutional means and reconciliation rather than through strikes.[75] In foreign policy, the Jama'at is generally regarded as pro-West because of its economic tenets, but it calls for friendly relations with all countries.

As I have stated, the Jama'at's organizational strength and base of support were confined to West Pakistan. According to a 1957 Jama'at publication, only one of the party's thirteen administrative divisions was allotted to the whole of East Pakistan.[76] The leadership also was largely West Pakistani. In the top party hierarchy, Professor Ghulam Azam was the only Bengali. In general, the party leadership was highly personal, with Maulana Maudoodi dominating the party. He was not only the leader but also the main ideologist and tactician.

[69] M. I. Faruqi, *Jama'at-e-Islami Pakistan*, p. 88.
[70] Maulana Maudoodi, *Islamic Law and Constitution*, 3d ed. pp. 85-95.
[71] *Ibid.*, pp. 147-52. Maudoodi argues that this theodemocracy will not be totalitarian, however, as Islam upholds the viceregency of every man in relation to God and hence rules out dictatorship.
[72] *Ibid.*, pp. 47-54.   [73] *Ibid.*, pp. 295-317.
[74] Ghulam Azam, *A Guide to the Islamic Movement*. The Jama'at has recently come out in favor of land reforms, however.
[75] Faruqi, pp. 80-81.   [76] *Ibid.*, p. 73.

134 / *The Basic Democracies and political parties*

One reason for the Jama'at's weakness in East Pakistan[77] was that there the social groups to which the Jama'at generally appealed were mobilized and recruited by other political parties. In West Pakistan, the Jama'at received its support from the orthodox religious people. But in East Pakistan, a large section of this group had already been recruited by the other religious party, the Nizam-i-Islam. Another important base of Jama'at support in West Pakistan was the refugees—partly because the Jama'at was the only organization doing social work among them, and partly because the idea of true Islamic community has been very real to the refugees, who sacrificed so much for it.[78] In East Pakistan, however, the refugees came mostly from Bihar and other non-Bengali-speaking areas. They have felt alienated from the indigenous people and have tended to look upon the nonvernacular central elite as their friends and allies. The refugees in East Pakistan have not joined an opposition political party like the Jama'at, for fear of changing the status quo, but have all along supported the central ruling group, who were generally Muslim Leaguers. In West Pakistan, the Jama'at has been successful in recruiting student support, but in East Pakistan the students have been mobilized by leftist and nationalist parties—namely, the National Awami Party and the Awami League.[79] Finally, in West Pakistan, the Jama'at received the support of some of the urban lumpen proletariat. (The rapid economic development and modernization in West Pakistan during Ayub's decade thus helped increase Jama'at's support. In East Pakistan, however, this group was recruited mainly by the Awami League and the NAP.

Though the Jama'at had a limited support base in East Pakistan,

---

[77] The relative weakness of the Jama'at in East Pakistan can be gauged by the Provincial Assembly election results of 1965 (though it must be admitted that such an indirect election can hardly be called representative); the Jama'at won only one seat out of a total of 23 won by the opposition.

[78] The refugees who underwent personal suffering and property loss for the cause of the Muslim state were shocked to find that the landlords in Pakistan were not ready to share their wealth with their "Muslim brothers." Poverty and governmental neglect led them to embrace the Jama'at's fundamentalist tenets.

[79] The two student parties which have the largest membership in East Pakistan are the East Pakistan Students Union and the East Pakistan Students League. According to the Pakistan Ministry of Education's *Report of the Commission on Student Problems and Welfare*, these two parties are closely affiliated with NAP and the AL, respectively. In West Pakistan, the only student party which has some affiliation with an outside political party is the Jama'at-e-Talaba, which is unofficially affiliated with the Jama'at.

it was a highly disciplined, cadre party, and was the only major party that avoided schism during the Ayub decade.

The Council Muslim League. The Council Muslim League was the section of the Muslim League which did not join the PML and remained in the opposition. It claimed to be the true heir to the old Muslim League, whose ideology and program it perpetuated. It advocated the establishment of an Islamic republic (in effect, a freely elected democratic polity with ideological commitments to Islam), a strong central government, direct election by universal adult franchise, a mixed economy, and a generally pro-Western foreign policy. In spite of its "national" program, the CML increasingly became a West Pakistan–based party during Ayub's decade. Its national leadership was mostly West Pakistani, particularly after Nazimuddin's death in 1964. Whatever organizational strength and base of support it had were generally confined to West Pakistan, especially the Punjab, though it remained organizationally weak in both wings during the decade. It did not launch any campaign to increase its mass support; rather it clung to its traditional support base. In West Pakistan, especially in the Punjab, it managed to retain the support of some old Muslim Leaguers and their constituencies. In East Pakistan, on the other hand, the Muslim League lost its main driving force, the rising Bengali middle class, to the Awami League in the early fifties. Before independence, this group had joined the Muslim League for the creation of Pakistan, which they thought would eliminate Hindu domination and competition. But following independence, Hindu domination was supplanted by West Pakistani domination, and the Bengali middle class joined the Awami League, which promised regional autonomy for East Pakistan and the elimination of West Pakistani control.

Since 1962, only two parties have managed to gain some degree of mass support—the National Awami Party and the Awami League. Both are secular parties, and both underwent schism on a roughly regional basis. The two parties exemplify the dilemma of a secular, programmatic party in Pakistan trying to be mass-based and national.

The National Awami Party (NAP). When the NAP was first founded in 1957, its program and leadership attempted to unite all the progressive forces in both wings by promising to make the party truly mass-based and national. The NAP's manifesto incorporated the popular demands of both East and West Pakistan. It called for full regional autonomy in both wings, with the center having control over defense, foreign affairs, and currency.[80] For West Pakistan, it demanded the reorganization of the old provinces on the basis of culture, language, and geography into a subfederation within the Pakistan federation.[81] It also advocated other democratic principles such as direct election by universal adult franchise, a joint electorate, and full fundamental rights.[82]

The NAP called for the substitution of peasant proprietorship for landlordism (without compensation); nationalization of the jute industry; guarantee of fair prices to primary producers; government initiative in establishing heavy industry; and establishment of economic parity between the two wings.[83] In foreign policy, the NAP advocated nonalignment, and withdrawal from all military pacts.[84]

The NAP leadership included nationally known figures from both wings who had some mass support. In East Pakistan, it had Maulana Bhasani. In West Pakistan, it had Abdul Gaffar Khan and the Pir of Manki Sharif from the North-West Frontier Province, Mian Iftikharuddin from the Punjab, and G. M. Syed and Mahmoodul Huq Usmani from Sind. The NAP was essentially an alliance of various groups with various popular demands. It had in its fold communists, socialists, and regional autonomists. Their points of agreement were a demand for full regional autonomy and an antiimperialist foreign policy. But this unity of purpose cracked after the revival of the party in 1964, when the split between the pro-Peking and pro-Moscow factions began.

The rift in the NAP was due to the division in the international Communist movement and to differences between the leftists and the regional autonomists within the party over the issues of foreign policy and autonomy. When the international Communist movement was divided between Moscow and Peking, the leftists in Pakistan were also divided. Foreign policy became a key factor to the pro-Peking group, who looked upon the United States as their number one enemy. The Ayub regime's initiative in establishing friendly relations with China was regarded as progressive by the pro-Peking group. This faction chose to avoid immediate confrontation with the regime, a policy which they argued would give the left time to build up its structural base. They were

[80] *National Awami Party Manifesto* (in Bengali) (Dacca, 1957), art. 3.
[81] *Ibid.*, art. 3.   [82] *Ibid.*, arts. 1-2, 6-8.   [83] *Ibid.*, arts. 21-36, 40-46.
[84] *Ibid.*, arts. 59-63.

opposed to joining other, "bourgeois" parties in a common movement. Thus, in 1964, when all the opposition parties, including the NAP, formed an electoral alliance against Ayub, the pro-Peking group reportedly worked in favor of Ayub. They were also opposed to joining the Six-Point Movement in 1966; and they criticized the Pakistan Democratic Movement (PDM) in 1967 on the grounds that it did not have an antiimperialist plank.[85]

The pro-Moscow faction, in contrast, did not regard the Ayub regime as progressive. They argued that in spite of Ayub's foreign policy, the regime's economic policies fostered capitalism and feudalism, the two main agents of international imperialism. Unlike the pro-Peking group, who wanted to keep the Ayub regime as a protective shield and work for an outright socialist revolution, the pro-Moscow faction advocated alliance with "bourgeois" opposition parties in a common movement against the Ayub regime. They argued that neither the objective nor the subjective conditions for a socialist revolution existed in Pakistan, and that the best strategy was to form an alliance with the opposition parties and work for an antiimperialist, anticapitalist, national democratic government, which would provide the left with more favorable conditions for a revolution.[86]

Though the factional disputes within the NAP had started in 1963, the party did not openly split until 1967. The internal feuds made the party's overall policies erratic and ambivalent, however. In 1962, for example, when Bhasani was first released from house arrest, he declared that he would launch a civil disobedience movement against the regime; but he soon led a government-sponsored delegation to China and quietly dropped the idea of the disobedience movement. And, as has been noted above, when the NAP joined the Combined Opposition Parties (COP) in an electoral alliance against Ayub in 1964, Bhasani and the pro-Peking left were accused of tacitly supporting the regime.

The rift between the two factions came to the surface in 1966, when Bhasani and the pro-Peking factions criticized the Awami League's Six-Point Movement, while the pro-Moscow faction tried to reach some settlement with the Awami League. Finally, in 1967, the party openly divided. The two factions held separate council meetings and elected

---

[85] Talukdar Maniruzzaman, "The Leftist Movement in East Pakistan."   [86] *Ibid.*

separate officers. What is significant from the viewpoint of national integration is that the split generally aligned with the division between the two wings of the country. The Pro-Peking NAP was mainly East Pakistan–based, and the Pro-Moscow NAP drew its strength primarily from West Pakistan.[87]

The two NAPs are themselves faction-ridden. The Pro-Moscow NAP has two centers of localized support dependent on the personal following of their leaders.[88] The pro-Peking group is fragmented into three factions.[89] The multiplicity of factions naturally limited the effectiveness of the NAP during the Ayub period, though the various factions did increase the party's mass support.

The Awami League. The Awami League also underwent a split during the Ayub decade. The party had always been predominantly East Pakistani in its program, leadership, and base of support; and attempts to make it an all-Pakistan party had in the past met with only limited success. After the party's revival, the task of integration became even more difficult. First, Suhrawardy's death created a vacuum in the League's leadership. There was no leader left who was nationally known and equally acceptable to both the wings. Sheikh Mujibur Rahman, the powerful secretary of the East Pakistan Awami League, was nationally known; but he was not yet "acceptable" in West Pakistan, because of his strong commitment to East Pakistan's autonomy. Second, since the party's reorganization in 1957, when it lost the West Pakistani "autonomists" to the NAP and recruited the support of the rightist landlords and bourgeoisie in West Pakistan, there had been inconsistency and conflict between the East Pakistan and West Pakistan branches of the League. The East Pakistan Awami League had always advocated full regional autonomy—a goal which the West Pakistan Awami League could hardly endorse wholeheartedly. The difficulty of creating a secular, liberal, democratic party with equal support in the two wings became

---

[87] This is due to the fact that the NAP in East Pakistan was composed mostly of leftists, whereas the West Pakistani NAP generally consisted of regional autonomists. The latter were naturally opposed to Ayub and his policy of centralization and were in favor of an alliance with the other opposition parties.

[88] The West Pakistan NAP's support base depends largely on the followers of Khan Abdul Gaffar Khan, or the former red shirts in the North-West Frontier Province and that of Achakzai in Baluchistan.

[89] See Maniruzzaman, "The Leftist Movement," for a detailed discussion of these factions.

all too evident through the seemingly diametrical opposition of the political and economic interests of the Awami League's bourgeois supporters in East and West Pakistan. This conflict made it difficult for the Awami League, after its revival, to adopt any coherent program of action. As a result, the East Pakistan Awami League lost ground to its rivals—the NAP and the National Democratic Front (NDF). The 1965 assembly elections were eye openers to the Awami League.[90] The East Pakistan Awami League realized that it must either become a "national party" on paper, like the PML and the CML, or reestablish its mass contact and risk forfeiting all claims to being a national party; it chose the latter course. The war with India and the subsequent frustration of the Bengalis gave the Awami League an excellent opportunity to win back its lost ground. In the spring of 1966, Sheikh Mujibur Rahman launched his now famous Six-Point Movement. The Six-Point demand—especially attractive to the Bengali nationalist bourgeoisie—was to date the most radical demand for East Pakistani autonomy.[91] The Six-Point Movement evoked widespread enthusiasm in East Pakistan. Mass meetings and rallies held throughout the province by the East Pakistan Awami League helped to rejuvenate the moribund party organization and the Awami-affiliated student party, the East Pakistan Students League.

Predictably, the Six-Point Movement broadened the Awami League's base of support in East Pakistan at the cost of West Pakistani support. While the Six-Point demand was overwhelmingly passed in the East Pakistan Awami League Council meeting,[92] and Sheikh Mujibur Rahman was made the party's east-wing president, the program drew criticism from the party's national president, Nasrullah Khan, and other West Pakistani leaders.[93] The rift between the east and west wings of the League became final with their disagreement on joining other parties to form the Pakistan Democratic Movement (PDM).[94] The Six-Point demand not only split the League but made it difficult for the East Pakistan

---

[90] In the National Assembly elections in 1965, the Awami League won six seats, the NDF five seats, and the NAP two seats. In the Provincial Assembly elections, the Awami League won eleven seats, and the NDF three seats.
[91] The Six-Point Movement is discussed in detail in chap. VII.
[92] *Ittefaq* (Dacca), February 22, 1966.
[93] *The Pakistan Observer* (Dacca), February 18, 1966.
[94] *Ibid.*, May 1, 2, 3, 5, 7, 1967.

wing to form an alliance with any other West Pakistan–based party. The CML decried the Six Points as a demand for confederation, not federation;[95] the Jama'at-i-Islami branded it as a separatist design;[96] the Nizam-i-Islam rejected it as a unilateral, dictatorial move on Mujib's part;[97] and the NAP dismissed it on the grounds that it was parochial and did not include any measures to free East Pakistan from imperialist agents.[98] The Awami League, thus, in increasing its mass base in the eastern wing, became isolated from other opposition parties in East and West Pakistan.

The Pakistan People's Party. The Pakistan People's Party was the last political party established during the Ayub decade. Founded in November 1967 by Zulfikar Ali Bhutto, Ayub's one-time protege and former foreign minister, its organizational structure is still in a rudimentary phase. It did draw up a manifesto which may be called national in the sense that it does not emphasize regional demands but rather focuses on militant nationalism.[99] While the party's stand on economic and foreign policy was clearly stated, its domestic political program was kept vague and evasive.

The party's slogan has been "Islam is our faith, democracy is our polity, socialism is our economy, all power to the people."[100] Its economic program included "transformation of Pakistan into a socialist economy,"[101] nationalization of key industries, and development of the infrastructures of the national economy.[102] In foreign policy, the party advocated an independent position, with special emphasis on friendship with Russia and China. It took a hard line on India, called for the "liberation" of Kashmir, and suggested the establishment of special relations with Assam.[103] The Party manifesto did not take a stand on most of the controversial political issues but rather left them for the people to decide.[104] It rejected the Six-Point demand, however, and by implication stands for a strong centralized state.[105]

The People's Party has been totally West Pakistani in its leadership

---

[95] *Ibid.*, February 15, 1966.
[96] *Ibid.*, February 17, 1966.
[97] *The Eastern Examiner* (Chittagong), March 6, 1966.
[98] *Ittefaq* (Dacca), April 8, 1966.
[99] Pakistan People's Party, *Foundation and Policy.*
[100] *Ibid.*, p. 89.   [101] *Ibid.*, p. 29.   [102] *Ibid.*, pp. 34–36.
[103] *Ibid.*, pp. 68–80.   [104] *Ibid.*, pp. 38–40.   [105] *Ibid.*, pp. 81–88.

and base of support. It recruited support from the students and youth in West Pakistan—who are attracted by the party's militant nationalism—and the leftists. But in East Pakistan both these groups were recruited by the Awami League and the NAP. To a large extent the party's original members were Bhutto's personal followers, who are confined to West Pakistan.

The Nizam-i-Islam. The Nizam-i-Islam was revived in early 1963, soon after the passage of the political parties act. In the parliamentary period, the Nizam had been an East Pakistan–based party. After 1963, when Chaudhri Muhammad Ali joined the Nizam, the party's leadership took on a national aspect. The strength of the party lay mostly in its leadership, however, since its organization remained nearly nonexistent in both wings of the country.

Failure of the political parties to develop nationally. During Ayub's rule, then, neither his own party, the PML, nor the other political parties developed as national institutions. The Jama'at, the CML, and the People's Party were largely West Pakistan–based; the Awami League was East Pakistan–based; and the two factions of the NAP, though they had interregional organizations, remained fragmented and weak. The regime did not pay enough attention to building a national party of its own, and its policy of repression prevented other parties from developing into broad-based national organizations. Imprisonment and harassment of party leaders and workers, censorship of the press and other media of communication, were hardly conducive to the development of constitutional parties. The prerequisites for national political organization— namely, a free political process fostering political negotiations, bargaining, and compromise, alignment and realignments of groups, and polarization on issues—were not permitted by the regime. While the regime's policies were partially responsible for the lack of growth of national parties, there were other more fundamental reasons. As discussed in Chapter II, political power is highly localized and fragmented in Pakistan. Political parties, instead of building up their organizations or mass support, generally coopt locally influential leaders with their own group of supporters. Since local leaders are coopted into the party, and do not join it because they espouse the party's program and ideology, they feel free to alter affiliation whenever they stand to gain by so doing. And, since parties are composed of local leaders with their own followers, factionalism is rife; political party differences are often based on factional rather than programmatic differences. Since the factions are the parties' major source of support and the factional bases are local, it is difficult to build national political parties. What is more significant, the party schisms are generally on an east-west basis. Political parties were fragmented even during the parliamentary period, but they always tried to form national parties or national coalitions. In the Ayub decade, however, the parties were less interested in organizing a national party. This growing inability and unwillingness to form a national party or a national coalition was an indicator of the process of national disintegration during the Ayub regime.

seven / The 1962 constitution and East Pakistani political movements

ON THE VERY DAY he took power, Ayub promised the return of constitutional government.[1] It was not a mere promise, for he already had in mind the broad framework of the future constitution,[2] which would provide for the strong, stable, and centralized government he felt was necessary to maintain national integrity.

The 1962 constitution

Like the Basic Democracies, the constitution of 1962 was in large measure Ayub's brainchild.[3] It was the second part of his grand plan

[1] Ayub Khan, *Speeches and Statements,* I, 3.
[2] See Mohammad Ahmed, *My Chief,* for a detailed discussion of the draft constitution Ayub prepared in 1954.
[3] Karl Von Vorys, *Political Development in Pakistan,* pp. 208–29, argues persuasively that the constitution of 1962 bore a close resemblance in all its essential features to Ayub's draft constitution of 1954.

of political institution-building. And like the regime's other institutions, the constitution was structurally centralized, with vertical power linkages. The structural distribution of power favored the center and the presidency.

Distribution of power. The constitution of 1962, which is said to have established a "constitutional autocracy,"[4] made the presidency, the cornerstone of the new system, even more powerful than the French presidency under the Fifth Republic. The president's veto powers were extensive. Even when the National Assembly passed a bill by a two-thirds majority, he could withhold his assent and send it to the electoral college for a referendum (article 27). The president's tenure was very secure, and his impeachment was a near impossibility (articles 13, 14, 15). Unlike the American president, he did not share his power of appointment with the national legislature. His emergency powers were overwhelming. He could issue a proclamation of emergency if he was satisfied that a grave emergency existed in which Pakistan or any part of Pakistan was threatened with war or external aggression or in which the security or economic life of Pakistan was threatened by internal disturbances beyond the power of the provincial governments to control. During the state of emergency, the president could legislate by ordinance, and the assembly had no power of veto.

The presidency was empowered mainly at the legislature's expense. Its power over national finances was severely limited (articles 41 and 42). It had no control over recurring expenditures and could vote only on new expenditures. Its power of legislation was greatly curtailed by the president's power of legislation through ordinances (article 29).

As for the structural distribution of power between the center and the provinces, the constitution favored the center. Though Pakistan was declared to be "a form of federation," and provisions were made for a governor, council of ministers, and assembly for the provinces (articles 66, 70, 82), the provincial executive did not have coordinate or equal status with the central executive organ; rather he was a mere agent of the central chief executive. The governor was not elected by the people or the National Assembly, he was appointed by the president and in the performance of his functions was "subject to the direction" of the

[4] Khalid B. Sayeed, *The Political System of Pakistan,* chap. 5.

president (article 80). Similarly, the provincial legislature was subordinate to the National Assembly. In case of a deadlock between the Provincial Assembly and the governor, the matter was referred to the National Assembly for resolution (article 74). And though more areas of legislative competence were delegated to the provinces than under the 1956 constitution, the essentially superior status of the center was maintained insofar as the provinces were denied exclusive jurisdiction over any subject. Article 131 granted the center overriding power to legislate, "for the whole or any part of Pakistan," whenever the national interest in relation to security (including economic and financial stability), planning or coordination, or the achievement of uniformity in any matter in different parts of Pakistan so required.

Such a highly centralized political structure was naturally an anathema to the Bengali counterelite, who had for a long time demanded a federal parliamentary government with full regional autonomy.

Participation: elections and assemblies. The first crack in the initial Bengali opposition to the constitution appeared with the decision to enter the election. The leaders of most of the political parties, who had been EBDO'd[5] or imprisoned, were in favor of boycotting the election and launching a mass movement to bring back democracy to the country. The non-EBDO'd, free politicians, who were generally second-echelon political leaders, were in favor of giving the constitution a try, of working through the constitution to change the system. As unrestricted political activity and political party organization remained banned, the non-EBDO'd politicians' position was strengthened; and there was no general boycott of the election. That the Bengali counterelite participated in the election — though they did so more on an individual than a party basis — meant in effect that they complied with the regime's system. Nevertheless, by failing to accommodate the "first string" of political leaders, the participation provided by the constitution proved to be inadequate and, indeed, counterproductive.[6]

[5] The term refers to the barring of politicians from electoral participation under the EBDO.

[6] Since most of the top leadership of the political parties were barred from entering the election, only members of the "second string" were elected. This had serious consequences later, when the regime felt compelled to come to some understanding with the politicians. It naturally looked to the assembly; but recruiting the support of the "second string" did not ensure the support of the whole party.

The election campaign of 1962 was low-keyed, and the candidates generally dealt with national questions. But the new National Assembly showed the same differences between East and West Pakistani members as had existed in the past (see Tables VII.1, VII.2, VII.3).[7] The new members were no more homogeneous a national elite than their predecessors. The East Pakistani members were older than their West Pakistani counterparts and had a higher educational level. They were mostly vernacular professionals, while landlords predominated in the western contingent.[8] Many of the young western members were the sons of former landlords or local religious figures, known as "Pirs," who had been EBDO'd by the Ayub regime; their sons inherited the safe constituencies of the fathers.[9] In addition, there were more political newcomers in the west wing than in the east.

The East and West Pakistani members of the National Assembly differed not only in age, literacy, and socioeconomic background but also in their attitudes toward the regime and the constitution. The groupings which gradually emerged in the assembly showed that the majority of opposition members came from East Pakistan, whereas the majority of supporters of the regime and the constitution came from the west wing. The division in the assembly thus reflected the general picture in the country: it was a "division between the political haves and

---

[7] In the Constituent Assemblies of 1947 and 1955, the eastern contingent was dominated by lawyers, and the western by landlords. The members of the Constituent Assembly of 1955 had the following occupations:

	East Pakistan	West Pakistan
Landlords	—	28
Lawyers	20	3
Retired officials	9	5
Industrialists and businessmen	3	4
Miscellaneous	8	—

(Mushtaq Ahmad, *Government and Politics in Pakistan*, p. 97.)

[8] Many of the landlord politicians of West Pakistan were, however, city-dwelling, educated, and modern in outlook.

[9] Noteworthy among sons of famous families in the assembly were Mir Ghulam Ali Talpur, 29, son of the former minister from Sind; Muzaffar Khan Malik, 28, of the Kalabagh family and son of the then governor of West Pakistan; Ghulam Mustafa Jatoi, 31, of the famous Jatoi family; Makhdum Zada Syed Hamid Raza Jilani, 26, of the Jilani family of Multan; Mian Gul Aurangzeb, 34, son of the Wali of Swat; and Noor Hayat Khan Noon, son of Feroz Khan Noon, the former prime minister of Pakistan.

Table VII.1 / Age distribution of members of the National Assembly, 1962 and 1965

	EAST PAKISTAN		WEST PAKISTAN	
	1962	1965	1962	1965
40 or below	25	17	35	31
41 to 49	12	30	22	21
50 or above	36	28	19	18

Sources: Mushtaq Ahmad, *Government and Politics in Pakistan*, 2d ed. (Karachi: Pakistan Publishing House, 1963), p. 272; Md. Nuruzzaman, *Who's Who* (Dacca: Eastern Publications, 1968); M. Rashiduzzaman, "The National Assembly of Pakistan under the 1962 Constitution," *Pacific Affairs*, XLII (1969–70), 488.
Note: Data on some members were not available.

Table VII.2 / Education of members of the National Assembly, 1962 and 1965

	EAST PAKISTAN		WEST PAKISTAN	
	1962	1965	1962	1965
Graduation and above	55	58	36	35
Matric and above	4	10	15	20
Below matric	10	5	14	14

Sources: Mushtaq Ahmad, *Government and Politics in Pakistan*, 2d ed. (Karachi: Pakistan Publishing House, 1963), p. 272; Md. Nuruzzaman, *Who's Who* (Dacca: Eastern Publications, 1968); M. Rashiduzzaman, "The National Assembly of Pakistan under the 1962 Constitution," *Pacific Affairs*, XLII (1969–70), 488.
Note: Data on some members were not available.

Table VII.3 / Occupations of members of the National Assembly, 1962 and 1965

	EAST PAKISTAN		WEST PAKISTAN	
	1962	1965	1962	1965
Lawyers	27	30	17	11
Businessmen and industrialists	9	20	4	10
Landlords	4	7	38	32
Others	23	19	8	18

Source: Md. Nuruzzaman, *Who's Who* (Dacca: Eastern Publications, 1968). (Mushtaq Ahmad's 1962 data in *Government and Politics in Pakistan* seem to be unreliable here, since his figures give a total of 83 East Pakistani members and 96 West Pakistani members, whereas there were 78 members from each wing. Rashiduzzaman, "The National Assembly of Pakistan under the 1962 Constitution," quotes Mushtaq Ahmad's figures.)

political have nots and not a division between differing economic and social programmes."[10]

Since the assembly was a national body, the East Pakistani opposition members initially tried, and to a large extent succeeded in, focusing their attention on national rather than regional issues. Because the regime's support in the assembly was at first shaky, the opposition was hopeful about amending the constitution through legislation. The first few bills and amendments proposed by Ayub's supporters were spiritedly fought by the opposition. But as the regime strengthened its hold in the assembly, through a judicious distribution of patronage and the revival of political parties, the opposition weakened. East Pakistani opposition members increasingly turned their attention to regional issues, and questions about economic disparity and East Pakistan's problems began to assume priority for them.

As the regional questions increased in number, the tone of the Bengali demands changed. In 1948-49, the Bengali complaint had been mainly one of neglect—accompanied by a demand that the central government do more for East Bengal. Thus one member of the Provincial Assembly, expressing the Bengali view, said on the house floor:

> I would respectfully submit that it is a disgrace that our Provincial Ministers could not impress upon the central government regarding our needs and demands. They could not push through their demands to the Centre and they could not make their grievances felt even by His Excellency the Governor-General to see that the members of the cabinet did not care to meet the legitimate demands to carry out the orders of this Government.[11]

By 1955, however, the complaint of neglect had become a complaint of exploitation:

> Sir I actually started yesterday and said that the attitude of the Muslim League coterie here was of contempt towards East Bengal, towards its culture, its language, its literature and everything concerning East Bengal . . . In fact, Sir, I tell you that far from considering East Bengal as an equal partner, the leaders of the Muslim League thought that we were a subject race and they belonged to the race of conquerors.[12]

---

[10] Mushtaq Ahmad, p. 280.

[11] East Bengal, Legislative Assembly, *Debates,* Vol. III, March 16, 1949, pp. 164-65, Shamsuddin Ahmad Khondkar.

[12] Pakistan, Constituent Assembly, *Debates,* Vol. I, September 7, 1955, p. 530, Ataur Rahman Khan.

And by 1963, the complaint against the central government and a political clique had turned into an alignment in a bitter, general, east-west controversy. Thus a member of the National Assembly from East Pakistan, speaking about the problems of the East Pakistani settlers in West Pakistan, commented:

> East Pakistan did contribute its mite to the settlement of refugees by paying refugee tax. East Pakistan contributed to the development of West Pakistan to the extent that during the last fifteen years East Pakistan has been drained out of Rs 1,000 crores of its solid assets by way of less imports and more exports. With that, sir, West Pakistan was developed and these million acres have been created. These big people now talk so loud leave East Pakistan out, we can maintain ourselves . . . Today in the 16th year, when we have been reduced as paupers to build West Pakistan, we are told get out boys, we have nothing for you, we do not require you.'[13]

But in spite of growing regionalism, the National Assembly of 1962 had been able to focus its attention on important national issues — political parties, fundamental rights, franchise, and foreign policy — and East Pakistani opposition members even focused interest in the regional problems of West Pakistan.[14] In fact, the 1962 assembly was a great educating device for the liberal democratic forces of the country, and it managed to mobilize nationally at least the literati opposition of the two wings. But the masses had not yet been reached. They were nationally mobilized by the elections of 1964-65.

The 1965 presidential election, unlike the assembly election of 1962, evoked tremendous enthusiasm in the country. It had a great unifying impact, which belied the regime's thesis that politics is a devisive and disintegrative influence in Pakistan; rather it showed how the exigencies of politics helped to develop a consensus among groups and leaders of diverse political opinion.

The regime at first thought that the election of 1965 would be as quiet as that of 1962; and that the opposition parties would not be able to offer a serious fight. It therefore called for the unanimous election of Ayub; and a "systematic campaign" on his behalf was launched through "speeches and statements which recounted in glowing terms his

---

[13] Pakistan, National Assembly, *Debates,* No. 2, May 29, 1963, p. 83, Mahbub ul Huq.
[14] For example, Mashihur Rahman of East Pakistan elicited information about the regime's oppression of Baluchi tribes and the bombing of Baluchistan.

services and achievements."[15] The opposition parties were hopelessly divided in their ideology and program, and no candidate could be found from among the party leaders who was acceptable to all parties and in both regions of the country. The right-wing, fundamentalist Jama'at-i-Islami stood for the revival of an Islamic polity and had some popular support in West Pakistan; the other rightist religious party, the Nizam-i-Islam, advocated an Islamic democracy and had limited support, only in East Pakistan; the center-left Awami League stood for the autonomy of East Pakistan and probably had the majority's support in East Pakistan; the far-left National Awami Party, which advocated autonomy in both wings of the country and a socialist economy, had moderate support in both wings; the center-right Council Muslim League wanted the return of the pre-1958 order and had some support in West Pakistan. The National Democratic Front was not a party at all and advocated abolition of all parties until democracy was restored. Its ideology and program were more or less the same as the Awami League's and it had limited support, only in East Pakistan.

Of the political leaders, Nazimuddin (Council Muslim League) was known in both wings but was old and none too energetic. Chaudhri Muhammad Ali (Nizam-i-Islam) was acceptable to the West Pakistani leaders but not to the East. Maulana Bhasani (National Awami Party) was known in both wings, but he was unacceptable to the west wing and to other parties, as was Sheikh Mujibur Rahman (Awami League). General Azam Khan had popular support, especially in the east, but he was too closely associated with the military.

But the opposition political parties realized that they stood no chance of challenging the regime unless they closed their ranks, despite all ideological differences and personality clashes.[16] Their rapprochement was finally brought about by the tireless efforts of Nazimuddin and Chaudhri Muhammad Ali.[17] On July 21, 1964, the five opposition

[15] Sharif al-Mujahid, "Pakistan's First Presidential Elections," *Asian Survey*, V (1965), 282.

[16] Personality clashes were probably a more important factor than ideological differences. The failure to incorporate the NDF in the COP was due more to personal rivalries between some of the NDF and Awami leaders, for instance, than to programmatic differences between the parties. The differences between the NAP and the Awami League were also often the result of personal rivalries.

[17] Sharif al-Mujahid, "Pakistan's First Presidential Elections," pp. 382–83, attributes the rapprochement to Nazimuddin; Von Vorys, *Political Development*, pp. 269–74, attributes it to Chaudhri Muhammad Ali.

political parties formed an electoral alliance, the Combined Opposition Parties (COP), and drew up a nine-point program as their election manifesto. The program was vague and general; among its demands were the restoration of democracy, a federal, parliamentary government, judicial review, political parties, direct elections, and fundamental rights, and the removal of interregional and intraregional economic disparity in ten years. While the program was at best a compromise,[18] and the COP had virtually no organization,[19] the fact that political parties with such divergent views as these five could agree on a common program was no mean achievement. To agree to the COP program, the Awami League and the National Awami Party had to moderate their stand on autonomy and foreign policy, and the Jama'at had to reverse its earlier stand on cooperation with parliamentary parties and the eligibility of a woman as head of state.

A consensus on the presidential candidate was reached with even greater difficulty. Finally, on September 19, Miss Fatima Jinnah, sister of the founder of the state, was announced as the COP's candidate. Since both candidates came from West Pakistan, one form of regional electioneering strategy was automatically ruled out.

The presidential campaign activated the masses in both wings of the country.[20] From the beginning, Miss Jinnah decided to take her campaign to the people. The COP's strategy was to build up sufficient popular support in both wings of Pakistan to pressure the Basic Democrats to vote for Miss Jinnah. Ayub was at first content with addressing the Basic Democrats and other select groups. But the mammoth public meetings of Miss Jinnah, and the popular enthusiasm they demonstrated, forced Ayub to go to the masses, too. Between September 1, 1964, and the end of the election campaign, Miss Jinnah addressed 43, and Ayub

---

[18] The Awami League was unhappy with the COP program, as it did not specify the scope of autonomy; the NAP was dissatisfied because it promised amendment of the Muslim Family Laws Ordinance, failed to support the subdivision of West Pakistan, and failed to demand Pakistan's withdrawal from all military and regional alliances.

[19] The COP organization was fragile at best. The coalition was not a true merger of political parties; each party retained its organizational integrity. It was decided that each candidate would be endorsed jointly by the COP but "for the record" would state his own party affiliation. This led to constant clashes among the component parties of the COP over the selection of candidates for the Basic Democracies.

[20] Miss Jinnah's campaign generated enthusiasm in both wings of Pakistan. Both Miss Jinnah and Ayub drew huge crowds in their public meetings. See K. P. Misra et al., *Pakistan's Search for Constitutional Consensus*, pp. 80–85.

28, public rallies.[21] Another strategy of Miss Jinnah's was to emphasize national political and constitutional problems and avoid regional issues. Also, she tried to polarize the issues; for example, she stressed that she stood for democracy and Ayub stood for dictatorship. Ayub at first wanted to base his campaign on his record in office and his socioeconomic policies, but he was soon forced to defend his system and to turn his attention to constitutional issues.[22] When his supporters in East Pakistan attempted to exploit regional sentiments,[23] the opposition did not follow suit. On the whole, the campaign issues remained highly ideological and, hence, national.[24]

But if the presidential campaign had some positive effect on national political integration, the outcome of the election did not. The campaign united the disparate groups of the two wings of the country by polarizing them on one issue, but the voting pattern in the two wings only underscored regional differences. While Ayub won an overwhelming majority in West Pakistan (73 percent), his victory in East Pakistan was narrow (53 percent). Additionally, the voting pattern within East Pakistan exhibited significant intraregional differences. As Table VII.4 shows, Miss Jinnah won a majority in four districts, all of which fall in the more "modern" center-east region. Ayub won a substantial majority in the less "modern" north-south. This difference might lead one to hypothesize that the more modern districts favored Miss Jinnah—because they were more politically conscious and imbued with liberal-democratic ideas,

---

[21] Von Vorys, *Political Development*, pp. 279, 285.

[22] *Ibid.*, pp. 280–86. According to Von Vory's calculations, Ayub and Miss Jinnah put 50.0 percent and 75.8 percent emphasis, respectively, on the political system in their major addresses and statements between September 1, 1964, and the end of the Basic Democracies election. From the conclusion of the Basic Democracies election until December 31, 1964, the emphasis was 62.9 percent and 57.3 percent for Ayub and 66.0 percent and 68.8 percent for Miss Jinnah in their major public addresses and statements and projection meeting speeches, respectively.

[23] Governor Monem Khan taunted the COP for failing to nominate an East Pakistani candidate; the commerce minister alleged that Miss Jinnah had not donated to East Pakistani cyclone sufferers from funds at her disposal; and, of course, Ayub and all his supporters claimed that he had done more for East Pakistan than any other politician (Sharif al-Mujahid, "Pakistan's First Presidential Elections," pp. 290–91).

[24] In Pakistan, interwing consensus has been possible only on general ideological issues— Islam vs. secularism; democracy vs. autocracy; left vs. right—and not on specific or local socioeconomic or political issues. On the latter issues, alignments have tended to be regional.

Table VII.4 / *Distribution of vote in East Pakistan districts in 1965 presidential election*

EASTERN AND CENTRAL REGIONS	AYUB	MISS JINNAH	% OF VOTE FOR MISS JINNAH
Dacca	1,764	2,193	54.9
Mymensingh	2,764	2,684	48.9
Sylhet	1,142	1,551	56.8
Comilla	1,536	1,874	54.5
Noakhali	682	1,174	62.8
Chittagong	1,284	1,042	44.5
Chittagong Hill Tracts	150	148	48.8
NORTHERN AND SOUTHERN REGIONS			
Faridpur	1,333	1,109	44.9
Barisal	1,920	1,389	41.7
Jessore	1,016	683	39.7
Khulna	1,240	662	34.4
Rangpur	1,727	1,229	41.3
Dinajpur	721	609	45.3
Rajshahi	1,445	730	33.2
Pabna	932	592	38.6
Bogra	841	379	30.7
Kushtia	515	386	42.1

Source: Pakistan, Election Commission, *Presidential Election Results, 1965.*

and because Miss Jinnah promised the return of democracy. One may test such a hypothesis by statistical correlation of socioeconomic indices of modernization in the seventeen East Pakistani districts with the vote percentages won by Miss Jinnah. The socioeconomic indices selected here were per capita income from agriculture and industry, rate of school enrollment, literacy, and urbanization, percentage of nonagricultural labor force, rate of industrialization, and electricity consumption.[25] Four separate multiple regressions were computed to correlate the different indices with voting. The first regression of three independent

[25] See Table II.5 for the exact values of these variables, and their source.

variables (per capita income from agriculture and industry, urbanization, and school enrollment) and the dependent variable (voting) resulted in a very low multiple correlation coefficient ($r^2 = 0.04$). The second regression substituted income from industry alone for income from agriculture and industry; this regression (of urbanization, school enrollment, and industrial income) and the dependent variable, voting, again resulted in an insignificant multiple correlation coefficient ($r^2 = 0.057$). A third regression involved the purely economic indices (income from agriculture and industry) and voting; it resulted in a correlation coefficient of $r^2 = 0.045$, again insignificant. Finally, the fourth multiple regression (of percentage of literacy, nonagricultural labor force, electricity consumption, and voting) resulted in $r^2 = 0.118$, also insignificant.[26]

Since the degree of modernization of the various districts does not explain the voting behavior in East Pakistan, one has to look for alternative factors—such as party organization, local factions, intra-regional conflicts, political culture—data on which is not readily available. A number of tentative hypotheses can be put forth, however. First, of the four districts where Miss Jinnah got the majority of the vote (Dacca, Comilla, Noakhali, and Sylhet), three were overcrowded districts which in the years between 1960 and 1965 had been food deficit areas. Though poor, these districts have a high rate of literacy and enrollment. Additionally, the people from all four districts are the most mobile in the whole province. The migration from these districts to other districts and abroad is high. These districts therefore can be expected to be characterized by a great sense of frustration. Second, the center-east, where Miss Jinnah got a relatively large vote, fall near the major lines of communication. The region, which is nearer the capital and more exposed to media communication than the north-south, was subjected to extensive campaigning by the COP leadership and workers. COP campaigning in the north-south was limited. In the north, which was presumed to be Bhasani's stronghold, the election campaign was left largely to the NAP, whose lukewarm campaign was blamed by the other members of the COP for Miss Jinnah's loss of the north. Third, since the north-south

---

[26] The scattered plot diagrams do not give a much better fit, since there are always three or four deviant cases ($N = 17$), and the deviants usually occur in the areas where Miss Jinnah got the majority of the vote.

was known to be Miss Jinnah's weak ground, the regime concentrated on winning this subregion with a large majority.

The presidential election returns came as a rude shock to the COP. The enthusiastic popular acclaim that Miss Jinnah had received during the campaign had made the COP think that they might win the election, especially in East Pakistan. Their defeat made them despair of working the Ayub-dominated system. The fragile preelection opposition coalition nearly broke up after the presidential election.[27] Controversy arose over whether or not to participate in the assembly elections. The West Pakistan–based parties, after their experience in the presidential election, leaned toward nonparticipation; while the East Pakistan–based parties, hoping to gain substantial representation, favored participation. After prolonged vacillation, the COP decided to participate. But the campaign lacked the verve of the presidential campaign. The COP candidates got little support from the national organization and national leaders, and were left to their own resources.[28]

From the viewpoint of the opposition's accommodation in the Ayub system, the assembly election results were disastrous. The PML, Ayub's party, won 120 seats in a house of 150. The opposition secured only 15 seats (COP, 10; NDF, 5) in East Pakistan and one in the west wing. The rest went to independents. Although the PML won 80 percent of the seats, it secured only 54.8 percent (in the east, 49.64 percent; in the west, 61.31 percent) of the votes cast; the opposition won a little more than 25 percent (34 percent in the east); the rest were gained by the independents.[29]

In the new National Assembly, even though the overwhelming majority of members from both wings belonged to the PML, the differences between the eastern and western members in age, literacy, and

[27] Tension within the COP developed even before the election campaign ended. First, the parties clashed over their nominees for the Basic Democracies. Later in the campaign, the NAP's halfhearted campaigning for Miss Jinnah drew suspicion and muffled criticism from the other parties. After the election, Awami League leader Mujibur Rahman publicly denounced the NAP for a breach of trust. For a detailed discussion, see K. P. Misra et al., pp. 203–8.

[28] Neither Miss Jinnah nor the top COP leaders did any campaigning for the assembly elections, and the COP candidates who did win in the National Assembly election did so because of their personal appeal, and not because of the party. There was no similarity in voting pattern between the presidential and assembly elections.

[29] Sharif al-Mujahid, "The Assembly Elections in Pakistan," *Asian Survey*, V (1965), 547.

socioeconomic background followed the same pattern as in previous years (see Tables VII.1, VII.2, VII.3), with one significant change: there was a sharp increase in the number of members with industrial or business background.[30]

Since the 1965 National Assembly was completely dominated by the ruling party, the opposition members had little hope of effectively challenging the regime. The opposition therefore spent most of its time in the assembly in eliciting information and venting grievances. They looked upon these functions as especially important because the press and other media of communication were more and more tightly controlled by the regime.[31] In addition, the West Pakistani component of the opposition was even smaller than before. This gave the opposition in the National Assembly a regional aspect.

Thus East Pakistani participation in the new political system established under Ayub's constitution was limited. First, since the representative institutions were themselves weak (as we have already noted, the assemblies and the councils of ministers had little real power), participation in these bodies failed to give the Bengali counterelite a sense of effective power-sharing. Second, as the leading political leaders of East Pakistan were either disqualified under EBDO or imprisoned, they could not participate in the system at all. In the later years of Ayub's rule, the Bengali political opposition's representation continued to dwindle as the regime adopted more repressive measures.[32] Ayub's constitution thus failed to give meaningful participation to the mobilized groups in East Pakistan.

Legitimacy: The regime initially wanted to involve the people in the constitution-making process, and thereby gain legitimacy for the new system. A commission was appointed to elicit public opinion on the future constitution and make recommendations to the president. But when the responses to the Constitution Commission's questionnaire revealed substantial opposition to some of the regime's cherished concepts, public debate on the constitution was discouraged.[33] The "Bengali view" of the constitution can be gauged by the responses of prominent

[30] See the discussion in chap. III, pp. 60–62.
[31] See the discussion on pp. 161–64.
[32] See the discussion on the East Pakistani governor's policy toward the opposition later in this chapter.
[33] *Dawn* (Karachi), July 4, 1961.

Bengali leaders and organizations to the Constitution Commission's questionnaire. Most of the published responses favored a federal parliamentary system of government, direct election by universal adult franchise, restoration of fundamental rights, and active political parties.[34] The Constitution Commission's report found that 65.5 percent of the respondents favored a strong federal government. The majority of replies from East Pakistan (765 respondents out of 1,357; or roughly 56 percent) advocated a weak center, however. The report warned the regime of the "strong feelings of East Pakistan in this matter," and it rejected the regime's plea for a unitary government, with the following caution:

> It is our considered opinion that if we impose a unitary form ignoring the state of feeling in East and West Pakistan, we would be driving the average Muslims of East Pakistan into the arms of extremists and disruptive elements which are active in that province.[35]

Of the respondents to the questionnaire, 50.6 percent favored parliamentary government, and 98.39 percent were in favor of incorporating fundamental rights into the constitution; an "overwhelming majority" were in favor of direct election by universal adult franchise.[36] As the framing of the constitution was protracted, the political demands of the East Pakistanis grew louder.[37] The regime came through with economic concessions to placate East Pakistan, but the constitution failed to incorporate most of the Bengali demands.

The regime failed to accommodate the "Bengali view" because, like its predecessors, it looked upon the demand for autonomy in East Pakistan as being essentially inspired by Communists, Hindus, and Indian agents and as posing a threat of disintegration to the country.[38] In a press conference before the introduction of the constitution, Ayub made these comments, which revealed his attitude toward the Bengali demands:

---

[34] Edgar A. and Kathryn R. Schuler, *Public Opinion and Constitution Making in Pakistan, 1958-62*, pp. 61-73.

[35] Pakistan, *Report of the Constitution Commission*, p. 37.

[36] The figures here are for Pakistan as a whole. But these demands were popular in both wings.

[37] Schuler and Schuler, pp. 83-151.

[38] Thus Ayub in a speech in Chittagong, East Pakistan, in July 1961, said that it was the Communists who were asking for federal parliamentary government in East Pakistan (*ibid.*, p. 86).

> I know in East Pakistan, some people think too much about direct franchise, parliamentary system and things like that. By God, one place which requires most stability is East Pakistan.

And then:

> Say for a moment that there is a demand in East Pakistan that we have a parliamentary form of government and we have this or that or the other, but that may not be the demand in West Pakistan. Then at once you tear the country into two factions straight way. If East Pakistan wants to have a Parliamentary form of Government and here somebody else wants to have something else, really you have got to have two countries then! I will appeal to your better sense in East Pakistan that for God's sake exposed to dangers and surrounded as you are look at things a little more realistically.[39]

Clearly the underlying principle here was to give the East Pakistanis not what they wanted but what the regime thought was good for them.

Since the constitution did not satisfy any of the Bengali counterelite's demands, its introduction was followed by widespread public protest in East Pakistan. As a precautionary measure, the regime arrested H. S. Suhrawardy before the constitution was introduced. Nevertheless, a nearly year-long strike by Dacca University students ensued, with almost daily burnings of copies of the constitution on the university campus. A statement was issued on June 24, 1962, signed by all the prominent East Pakistani politicians,[40] criticizing various aspects of the new constitution, and calling for a united movement to repeal the constitution and restore democracy. For a moment, the National Democratic Front, a loose alliance opposing Ayub's policies, looked like "a popular mass movement, spearheaded by a phalanx of national leaders and dedicated to the total destruction of the President's political system."[41]

However, the turbulence in East Pakistan quieted down somewhat after the elections of 1962. The Bengali counterelite did participate in the election of 1962 and 1964–65 — in the first one with skepticism, in the second one very seriously — and to the extent that they partici-

---

[39] G. W. Choudhury, *Documents and Speeches on the Constitution of Pakistan*, p. 806-7.

[40] This "Nine-leaders' Statement" was signed by, among others, Nurul Amin (Muslim League), Sheikh Mujibur Rahman and Ataur Rahman (Awami League), Mahmud Ali (National Awami Party), Pir Mohsenuddin (Nizam-i-Islam), Hamidul Huq Choudhury, A. H. Sarkar, and Yousuf Ali Choudhury (KSP). It was the first of a series of all-party alliances against the regime.

[41] Von Vorys, *Political Development*, p. 258.

pated the constitution did gain the appearance of legitimacy. But one of their objectives in participation was to change the constitution from within. Yet their pressure inside the system as well as outside had little impact in bringing about the major constitutional reforms they desired.[42] Ayub's system of election through the Basic Democracies and the built-in widespread patronage ensured the survival of the regime. The counterelite's failure either to induce the regime to amend the constitution or to change the regime itself led them to withdraw support for the constitutional order. That the constitution failed to gain legitimacy or even to govern the regime's authority was evidenced by the nearly three years of emergency rule imposed upon the country after the war of 1965. Laws were increasingly promulgated as presidential ordinances rather than legislative enactments.

The weak institutionalization of the constitution was best illustrated during Ayub's illness in the spring of 1967. Even though the constitution provided that the National Assembly speaker was to be acting president during the president's absence or incapacity (article 16), Abdul Jabbar Khan, a Bengali who was the assembly speaker at that time, was not allowed to act as president during Ayub's illness.[43] For the Bengalis, this situation underlined the discrepancy between the constitutional distribution of power and the actual power distribution in the country.

Political movements in East Pakistan

During the Ayub decade, political movements in East Pakistan changed from movements for competitive participation in the national system to radical provincial autonomy movements. The period saw not only a

---

[42] In spite of the opposition's persistent pressure, the regime refused to accept any of their demands for direct election, full freedom for political parties, independence of the legislature and the judiciary, or autonomy for East Pakistan.

[43] During Ayub's illness in the spring of 1967, all attention was focused on the working of the constitutional provision for succession. Not only was Abdul Jabbar Khan not allowed to become acting president, he was not even allowed to preside over the swearing-in of the chief justice or to take the salute in the ceremonial parade on March 23. Instead, it was the defense minister who took the salute. See *The Pakistan Observer* (Dacca), March 24, 1967.

radicalization of Bengali autonomy demands but also a growing polarization between the left and the right. From 1962 to 1965, political movements in East Pakistan aimed at the democratization of the constitution; their aim was to change the national system. But after 1965, all the political movements in the east wing took on a strongly regional aspect, largely because the regime's political institutions had failed to give the Bengali counterelite effective participation in the system. Two factors immediately contributed to the exacerbation of Bengali isolation and frustration and led to the Six-Point Movement. These were the actual workings of the center-province relationship under the 1962 constitution and the war with India in 1965.

The impact of Abdul Monem Khan's governorship. If the constitution made the governor the president's "agent," in practice Abdul Monem Khan, governor of East Pakistan from 1962 to 1968, was more like a vassal. Monem's appointment in October 1962 was the result of political necessity. Gulam Faruque, the previous governor, was an able administrator, but he felt the task of building political support for the regime, which the postconstitutional era demanded, to be beyond him. When he resigned, he suggested that a substitute with greater political aptitude be found.[44] The post fell to Abdul Monem Khan, a Bengali, a Muslim Leaguer, and a one-time protégé of Nurul Amin with a reputation for flair in organizing political support.[45] But Monem's greatest asset to Ayub was his complete loyalty. After the regime's experience with Gulam Faruque's predecessor, General Azam Khan (governor from 1960 to 1962), who had acted more as the province's spokesman to the center than as the center's spokesman to the province, the regime wanted a governor who would champion, explain, and support its policies in East Pakistan. Monem's complete subservience to Ayub more than qualified him for the job.[46] As governor of East Pakistan, Monem looked upon

---

[44] In his letter of resignation, Governor Faruque pointed out: "my experience is . . . confined wholly to matters connected with economic development and I am afraid I cannot lay a claim to any ability to organize or lead a party." *The Pakistan Observer* (Dacca), October 26, 1962.

[45] Abul Mansur Ahmad, *Āmār Dekha Rajnitir Panchāsa Bachara*, p. 249.

[46] Monem Khan was continued in his post even after he became extremely unpopular. He was reportedly favored over other contenders for the governorship (Sabur Khan, Fazlul Qader Chowdhury, and Kaji Kader), because of his complete loyalty and subordination to the will of the president.

building political support for the regime as his primary task. The regime's base of support in East Pakistan was shaky after the introduction of the constitution. Students were almost continually on strike; politicians were holding mammoth public meetings around the province calling for the restoration of democracy and the repeal of the constitution; the regime's supporters in the Provincial Assembly were having a hard time holding the line; and Ayub and his "ministerialist" supporters could hardly appear in public in East Pakistan without creating untoward incidents.[47]

To build political support for the regime, Monem adopted a dual policy. On the one hand, he took a tougher line with the opposition groups—i.e., students, intelligentsia, and opposition political leaders; on the other hand, through official support and patronage he tried to build a "government party"[48] in the university, the assembly, and the province at large.

He reversed Azam Khan's policy of reconciliation, moderation, and accommodation of the East Pakistani opposition. Azam Khan deliberately adopted a soft line to win over the Bengali opposition. By his friendly gestures and personal involvement he had endeared himself to the masses, especially the students. When student riots broke out in Dacca following Suhrawardy's arrest in 1962, for example, Azam reportedly counseled the regime against taking harsh steps. In contrast, Monem Khan's policy toward the opposition political parties and leaders was one of total suppression. Although the constitution legalized the free political process, Monem's administration frequently harassed and persecuted the leaders and workers of the opposition parties. During the election campaign of 1964-65, the COP in East Pakistan complained that more than five hundred of its political workers were arrested by the government.[49] During the Awami League's Six-Point Movement in

---

[47] Ayub's East Pakistan visit in March 1962 sparked public demonstrations. Similarly, two of his most vocal supporters—Fazlul Qader Chowdhury and Sabur Khan—faced hostile crowds in East Pakistan during their visits. *The Pakistan Observer* (Dacca), July 15, August 1, 1962.

[48] "Government party" is a literal translation of the Bengali term *Sarkari Dal*; it connotes a party which not only supports the government but whose sole strength is government support rather than popular support, a party which is engineered and maintained by the government and which collapses with the fall of the government.

[49] See *The Dacca Times,* January 8 and 15, 1965; and *The Pakistan Observer* (Dacca), January 5, 1965.

1966, most of its top leaders were imprisoned—and were kept in jail for more than two years. Awami League leader Sheikh Mujibur Rahman was imprisoned three times, on different charges, in one month. Section 144's ban on public meetings, rallies, and loudspeakers was indiscriminately invoked to limit free party activity.[50]

The press and other communications media were tightly controlled through various means. Lucrative government advertisements were withheld from recalcitrant newspapers (three East Pakistani opposition newspapers suffered from this form of discrimination). News was censored. Newspapers were often prohibited from publishing independent reports of antigovernment demonstrations. Publications and presses were seized outright, and newspaper editors were arrested. (The New Nation Press was seized on June 18, 1966, and remained under government seizure for over two years. The editor of *Ittefaq* was arrested.) Finally, by creating the Press Trust (which became the official source of news and had oversight of all elements of the press) in July 1966, the regime brought the press under stricter control.

An attempt was also made to "manage" elections to deny the opposition representation in the system.[51] Opposition parties and leaders were regularly accused of being "enemies of Pakistan" and "secessionists." Such a policy of suppression had a twofold effect: it led the opposition to adopt a more radical political position; and, by excluding the opposition from constitutional participation, it created a dangerous void in the political communication of the system.

Monem's attitude toward the intelligentsia was one of undisguised hostility and contempt. The intelligentsia, on their part, came to look upon Monem's arbitrary and high-handed policies with abhorrence.[52] Monem regarded the Bengali language and culture with the "old guard"

---

[50] The Awami League was repeatedly refused permission to hold public meetings in Dacca after its Six-Point demand. *The Pakistan Observer* (Dacca), August 16 and 28, 1966.

[51] The opposition charged the government with manipulating elections by using government machinery. One minister was later found guilty by the Election Tribunal of using his official power in pressuring circle officers to campaign for him. *The Pakistan Observer* (Dacca), March 19, May 1, 1965. See also K. P. Misra *et al.*, pp. 200-1.

[52] In my interviews with East Pakistani intellectuals, their mildest reference to the governor was that he was "uncouth." The intelligentsia were angry not only at his interference with university affairs and his "terrorist" tactic of "turning loose goonda elements" on the country but also at the arrogance and vanity he displayed in his private and public meetings with them.

Muslim League attitude, so much detested by the Bengali intelligentsia.[53] He revived the charge that Bengali is a non-Muslim language, and the bogy of cultural domination by Calcutta. Tagore songs were temporarily banned from Radio Pakistan; the importation of books and films from West Bengal was prohibited; and Monem underscored in public as well as in private the need for cultural independence from India.[54] The attack on the Bengali language and culture of the literate only led to a resurgence of linguistic nationalism, which for some time had been relegated to the background. The twenty-first of February was celebrated with more than usual fervor in 1966.[55] It was preceded by a weeklong campaign to popularize the Bengali language.[56] Almost overnight in Dacca, name plates, signboards, posters, and street signs, were written (or overwritten) in Bengali. Most newspapers published special editions on the Bengali language. In growing numbers citizen groups in public rallies and symposiums protested the government's negative attitude toward Bengali.[57] And even though the government-controlled Radio Pakistan neglected it, numerous private organizations celebrated Tagore's birthday, with more ardor than ever before.[58]

What distressed the intelligentsia most was Monem's policy toward students and the autonomy of the university. Monem realized that the students were the active support base of opposition to the regime. In order to tame the opposition, he had to tame the students. He first turned his attention to Dacca University, because it was the nerve center for province-wide student distrubances. Student strikers were severely dealt with, and police were frequently called in to put down demonstrations.[59] Monem soon realized that mere force would not be enough, however, and he began to build up a "government party" within the university that would "take care" of the student parties which for so

[53] According to the "old guard" Muslim League view, prevalent among the ruling elite in the early fifties, the Bengali language is very much under the influence of Sanskrit and hence is a Hindu language which should be Islamicized by the infusion of Arabic and Urdu words and by the changing of the script.

[54] *The Pakistan Observer* (Dacca), January 4, 1966, and September 8 and 16, 1967.

[55] *Ibid.*, February 22, 1966. *The Pakistan Observer* news report described the mass meeting as the biggest since 1954.

[56] *Ibid.*, February 15, 1966.   [57] *Ibid.*, June 25, July 2, and 3, 1967.

[58] *Ibid.*, May 10, 1966.

[59] Students and police clashed repeatedly during Monem's governorship. Police gradually took a tough line and even entered the university and dormitory premises to arrest students, thus violating university autonomy. *Ibid.*, June 8, 1966; April 6, June 8, August 1, 3, 1967.

long had dominated the academic political arena. The government party in the university, the National Students Federation (NSF), was soon built up through government support.[60] With the help of detailed university regulation promulgated in 1960, the governor, who was chancellor of the university, could influence the internal affairs of the university. It is charged that several methods were used to build up the NSF. Admission rules were allegedly relaxed in certain cases to admit NSF members to the university.[61] The grading and examination system was reportedly manipulated to keep them there. Finally, NSF students used strong-arm tactics, reputedly with impunity because of their government support. When they lost elections, they assaulted their opponents;[62] and after one assault on a university professor, for example, they were not arrested though they were definitely identified by him.[63] By terrorizing the general student body, they gained acquiescence from a great many persons who thought them to be inevitable. They also reportedly built strongholds in the two new student dormitories by controlling the admissions to these dormitories.[64] The university administration was subdued by sheer terror, pressure from "above," or by the forcing out of uncooperative members of the staff.[65]

Thus the autonomy of the university was seriously encroached upon both by ordinances and by informal means. Through force as well as patronage, Monem managed to plant a group of supporters in the university within the relatively short period of three years. While the student opposition had succeeded in breaking up the annual convocation in 1964, by 1968 they seemed cowed by NSF dominance.[66] Having

---

[60] According to the Ministry of Education's *Report of the Commission on Student Problems and Welfare,* the NSF was the student counterpart of the Pakistan Muslim League. Additional information on the NSF was gathered by me in interviews with Dacca University teachers and students in 1968.

[61] *The Pakistan Observer,* February 13, 1969.

[62] *The Pakistan Observer,* May 3, 1965; February 15, 1966; January 30 and May 17, 1967.

[63] *Ittefaq* (Dacca), February 16, 1966.

[64] *The Pakistan Observer* (Dacca), February 13, 1969.   [65] *Ibid.*

[66] The Dacca University students and teachers I interviewed in the summer of 1968, gave me the impression that the general body of students and teachers were greatly cowed by the NSF's tactics. According to an article in *The Pakistan Observer,* on February 13, 1969, "students who sought residence in some halls were to produce certificates from a particular party of students"; further, that the vice chancellor had to withdraw an order of resignation to a provost when student "leaders of a particular party wanted it."

gained a stronghold in Dacca University, Monem was encouraged to take a hard line at other educational institutions. When Jagannath College students went on strike in 1968, the college was closed sine die, and its structure was completely changed. Finally, in a move to bring all the higher educational institutions under closer control, the government provincialized (i.e., took over) all the private colleges.[67]

A dual policy was followed toward established members of the intelligentsia as well. Government-sponsored research, awards, honorary titles, jobs in autonomous agencies, etc., were used as bait to win over or at least to silence scholars and other members of the intelligentsia. And those who could not be won over or neutralized were often victimized. In the words of one Dacca intellectual, Monem created "the atmosphere of a fascist state."[68]

In organizing political support for the regime, in the assembly or in the elections, Monem used the same kind of tactic. A correspondent for the *Observer* of London reported during the uprising of 1969:

> ... young officials ... told me how they had been harassed into unlawful acts. Everything began happening by telephone, one of them said. Ministers of the Regime would call a remote district magistrate directly and order him to imprison a man ... to harass and disperse his family. No clerk, however incompetent, could be dismissed if he had a local friend of the Regime. No criminal, however ruthless, could be brought to justice if his zeal for the Regime absolved him.[69]

Such interference with day-to-day administration was naturally resented by the civil servants. But Monem's perfect rapport with the regime meant that in a conflict between him and a civil servant, it was the latter who had to give in or quit.[70]

Thus Monem's administration, like that of his chief, was a personal one. Through him, the center could control and manipulate even the minutest detail of East Pakistani administration and politics. Though his

---

[67] *Ibid.*, April 23, 1968.
[68] Personal interview, 1968.
[69] Cyril Dunn, *The Observer* (London), March 23, 1969.
[70] The East Pakistani civil servants interviewed by me testified to the governor's power and their own vulnerability. They cited several instances where a senior civil servant had to quit his post because of policy or personal differences with the governor. As in the center, so in the provinces, a civil servant's effectiveness depended on his personal relationship with the chief executive.

policies made him thoroughly unpopular in East Pakistan, Monem could not be removed, except by the will of Ayub.

Effect of the War with India on East Pakistan. While Monem Khan's administration revealed the political impotency of East Pakistan, the province's physical vulnerability was made manifest by the 1965 war with India. The war may truly be called a watershed in East Pakistan's relationship with the center. During the weeks the war was actually fought, national sentiment in East Pakistan was high, and emotional bonds between the two wings were strengthened. But the break in communication between the two wings, and East Pakistan's actual physical isolation, left a deep sense of insecurity in East Pakistan. The war exposed more than ever some of the practical disadvantages of the centralization policy the regime was following, and underscored the east wing's need for autonomy.

With only one army division, and limited military supplies, the Bengalis realized that East Pakistan could hardly defend itself in the event of foreign aggression. The fact that India did not attack the east wing, for a variety of reasons, was no satisfaction to the Bengalis, who for so long had demanded their right to defense capability.[71] Moreover, the Bengalis resented the fact that they were exposed to the danger of Indian occupation for the sake of Kashmir.

The Bengalis' feelings of insecurity were coupled with a renewed sense of pride in East Pakistan. During the war, the courage of Bengali soldiers fighting in West Pakistan was given wide publicity by the government, with an eye to national integration and the boosting of morale in East Pakistan. But at a time when the Bengalis were disillusioned with the army's handling of the war and had lost faith in the old myth of the "invincibility" of the West Pakistan-based army, the stories of Bengali fighting prowess only emboldened them to take a more radical stand on autonomy.

During the period when the two wings were virtually cut off from each other, East Pakistan realized more than ever the economic difficulties involved in depending too much on the center. While East Pakistan was totally isolated and left to fend for itself, it did not have enough

---

[71] The 1950 All Parties Resolution, as well as the 1954 21-Point Manifesto, demanded the establishment of a regional defense force for East Pakistan and the transfer of Naval Headquarters to this province.

resources within the province to work with. The prices of most of the essential commodities, which were usually imported from West Pakistan, went up.[72] The war meant general economic depression. As the United States cut off all arms aid and economic supplies, Pakistan was forced to rebuild her military strength from her own resources, and had to divert development funds to the military. Administrative delays due to isolation from the center also held up much development work. The 1966-67 budget saw a severe cutback in development programs, especially in the social sector.

Sheikh Mujibur Rahman's Six-Point demand in February 1966, came at a time, therefore, when the Bengalis were looking for a new formula to express their recently intensified national pride and desire for a substantial measure of independence from the centralized political structure.

From Six Points to eleven points: the radicalization of Bengali politics. The Six-Point Movement started by the Awami League in 1966, though short-lived, marked a significant radicalization of Bengali politics and played a crucial role in shaping later political movements. The movement was a departure from past East Pakistani political movements in both its program and its tactics.

The Six-Point demand was a remarkable document. Unlike previous Bengali demands, it did not call upon the central government to do more for East Pakistan, but asked the central government to let East Pakistan do more for itself. The first point called for the establishment of federation "on the basis of the Lahore Resolution and a parliamentary form of government, with supremacy of legislature to be directly elected on the basis of adult franchise."[73] The second point demanded that the federal government deal with only two subjects—defense and foreign affairs—and that all other subjects "rest in the federating states."[74] The third point suggested that there be either two separate but freely convertible currencies for the two wings or one currency for the whole country, provided that effective constitutional provisions were made to stop the flight of capital from East to West Pakistan. There should be a separate banking reserve and a separate fiscal and monetary policy for East Paki-

---

[72] See Figure 2 on p. 79.
[73] Sheikh Mujibur Rahman, *Six Points—Our Demand for Survival*, p. 2.
[74] *Ibid.*, p. 3.

stan.⁷⁵ Point four denied the center the right of taxation, which was to be vested in the hands of the federating states with the center receiving a fixed share.⁷⁶ The fifth point made these recommendations for foreign trade: there shall be two separate accounts for the foreign exchange earnings of the two wings; the earnings of East Pakistan shall be under the control of the East Pakistan government, and those of West Pakistan under the control of the West Pakistan government; the foreign exchange requirements of the federal government shall be met by the two wings either equally or in a ratio to be fixed; indigenous products shall move free of duty between the two wings; the constitution shall empower the unit governments to establish trade and commercial relations with, set up trade missions in, and enter into agreements with, foreign countries.⁷⁷ And the sixth point demanded the setting up of a militia or a paramilitary force for East Pakistan.⁷⁸

The Six Points differed from the Bengali autonomy demands of 1950 and 1954 in that it specifically denied the center the right of taxation, and advocated that the units have the right to establish separate trade and commerical relations with foreign countries and keep separate accounts of their foreign exchange earnings. In fact, for all practical purposes, the Six Points envisioned a confederate, rather than federal, structure. The movement was also significant in its militant emphasis on linguistic nationalism. A drive for the expansion of Bengali was carried on by the East Pakistan Students League—the student party unofficially affiliated with the Awami League—side by side with the Six-Point Movement. Street-corner meetings and widespread picketing resulted in an almost overnight shift to Bengali, at least on all public signboards and name plates.⁷⁹ This appeal to Bengali nationalism was again revived in the 1969 popular movement in East Pakistan.

The movement which launched the Six-Point demand adopted more radical tactics than had been used before in East Pakistan. In the past, the student-literati alliance had played the leading role in political movements. Now workers and "street mobs"⁸⁰ for the first time had a

---

⁷⁵ *Ibid.*   ⁷⁶ *Ibid.*, p. 8.   ⁷⁷ *Ibid.*, p. 9–10.   ⁷⁸ *Ibid.*, p. 11.

⁷⁹ After 1966 there were hardly any English or Urdu signboards left in any public place in Dacca.

⁸⁰ The term "street mob" as used here includes such heterogeneous participants as rickshaw pullers, small shopkeepers, bus and taxi drivers, and day laborers.

significant part, and the brunt was borne not by the students, though they also participated, but by the workers. Worker and mob participation naturally meant a more "violent" movement.[81] In the previous, student-dominated movements, the strategy had included the staging of mass meetings and peaceful processions, both of which often resulted in mild clashes with the police. But the Six-Point Movement for the first time involved raids on police stations, looting of arms, and violent confrontations with the police. While the students' wrath was directed against one or two progovernment newspaper offices, the workers' and mobs' wrath was directed at local symbols of authority—police stations, banks, and government administration buildings.[82] The workers' radical methods soon led to the radicalization of the students. While disagreements among student parties prior to 1966 had been settled by meetings and at worst by fist fights, after 1966 they were increasingly settled by terrorist methods.[83]

The regime's policy toward the Six-Point Movement revealed, once again, its inability to respond politically to political demands. When Sheikh Mujibur Rahman first launched the movement, he hinted that the demands were negotiable;[84] but the regime, instead of trying to reach some settlement with him, embarked on a course of head-on confrontation. While Mujib was touring East Pakistan trying to galvanize mass support for the movement, Ayub made a similar east-wing tour, during which he engaged in a running verbal battle with Mujib, branding the latter's demands as "secessionist," "disruptionist," "a demand for greater Bengal," etc.[85] But such accusations were hardly heeded in East Pakistan, where for the past nineteen years any demand for autonomy or

---

[81] The demonstration and rioting were more violent in the industrial city of Narayanganj than in Dacca because of the workers' predominance in the former. Worker participation was obtained because trade unions in the Narayanganj area were affiliated with the Awami League.

[82] *The Pakistan Observer* (Dacca), June 8, 1966.

[83] Students and teachers of Dacca University readily admitted during my interviews with them in 1968 that many student leaders carry knives and guns and use them frequently to settle political disputes.

[84] In a speech in the town of Pabna, Mujib said that he was willing to drop the Six-Point demand if the capital were moved to East Pakistan. *The Eastern Examiner* (Chittagong), April 9, 1966. Also, throughout the movement, he repeatedly said that he was willing to cooperate with any party on the basis of the Six Points. *Ibid.*, February 18, 1966; and *Ittefaq* (Dacca), February 11, 12, 27, 1966.

[85] *The Pakistan Observer* (Dacca), March 15, 19, 20, 1966.

political freedom had been branded as secessionist. Ayub's threats of force and "civil war"[86] only enraged the Bengalis more and evoked further support for the Six Points.

The regime adopted a policy of total suppression toward the movement. Nearly all the top Awami Leaguers were imprisoned. *Ittefaq*, the movement's mouthpiece, was closed down, its bond of good behavior forfeited, and its editor thrown in jail. The Awami League leadership was kept behind bars for over two years, until February 1969. This policy of supression gave the movement a kind of martyrdom. The memory of the movement lingered on, and its deep imprint on East Pakistani politics was made evident during the 1968-69 "popular revolution," when the same demands and tactics were again adopted by the Bengalis.

One weakness of the regime's political response was its failure to rally the other East Pakistani opposition parties, all but one of which viewed the Six-Point Movement unfavorably. Some of these parties— especially the Council Muslim League and the Nizam-i-Islam, which advocated a strong center—looked upon the Six-Point Program as an end to one Pakistan.[87] Others rejected it because they saw it as an attempt by Sheikh Mujibur Rahman to increase his personal following. And others looked upon it as a threat to their base of support. All the East Pakistani opposition leaders publicly rejected and criticized the program.[88] But Ayub did not try to enlist their support, even though they indicated that they were willing to negotiate with the regime.[89] Instead of winning the moderate autonomists to his side, Ayub rejected their demands in toto and drove them to take a more radical stand on autonomy. The Pakistan Democratic Movement (PDM), which was formed in May 1967 of moderate autonomists and centrists from both wings (i.e., the NDF, the CML, the Nizam-i-Islam, and the Jama'at-i-Islami), adopted an eight-point formula which proposed greater autonomy than that provided

---

[86] *Ibid.*, March 21, 1966.

[87] Farid Ahmad (Nizam-i-Islam) in my interview with him said that if the Six Points were accepted, Pakistan would not remain one country (July 28, 1968). Nural Amin, former Muslim Leaguer and at present in the PDP, expressed similar views (July 15, 1968).

[88] The only opposition party which sympathized with the Six Points was the pro-Moscow NAP.

[89] Nurul Amin repeatedly asked the regime for a round-table conference of opposition parties to settle all disputed constitutional issues.

for by the 1956 constitution but less than that demanded in the Awami League's Six Points.

The PDM's formula was more radical than the 1956 constitution insofar as it set a ten-year limit for the removal of economic disparity between the two wings (point 4); recommended establishment of a special board consisting of equal members from the east and west wings to deal with currency, foreign exchange, central banking, interwing trade, communications, and foreign trade (point 5); and suggested bringing to par "the fighting and fire power of the two wings" (point 7). It fell short of the Six Points, however, in that it assigned control of currency, federal finance, and interwing trade and communications to the center (point 2). In general, the Six-Point Program attempted to take power away from the center, while the PDM's eight-point formula concentrated on devising means for equal participation at the center.[90]

The cause of the radical autonomists was further strengthened in December 1967, when the regime brought the Agartala conspiracy case to trial.[91] While the regime thought that a public trial would terrorize the radical autonomists into silence and would win over the mass of the people, in actuality almost the exact opposite happened. The open trial broke the taboo on open discussion of secession; the radical autonomists were made heroes; and the defense of the case was used as an excellent platform for propagating the cause of autonomy.

The decade also saw the growing polarization of left and right in East Pakistan. With Ayub's policy shift toward China, the leftists in East Pakistan, especially the National Awami Party, looked upon the regime more favorably and were pitted mostly against the right nationalists of Mujib's Awami League. After the elections of 1965, the rift between Mujib's Awami League and Bhasani's NAP widened. The

[90] *Pakistan Democratic Movement* (Dacca: PDM series 1, 1968).
[91] The Agartala conspiracy case, in brief, charged thirty-three East Pakistani politicians, civil servants, and army men with conspiring to bring about East Pakistan's secession from the center in collusion with India. The list of alleged conspirators included three high-ranking East Pakistani civil servants and Sheikh Mujibur Rahman. The open trial evoked unprecedented nationalist feeling in East Pakistan. The defendants' allegation of police torture, and the fumbling of some of the prosecution's witnesses, left most Bengalis with grave doubts about the credibility of the case. Instead of believing the regime's allegation of a secessionist plot, they looked upon the case itself as a plot against Bengali autonomists. The defense was excellently handled by Abdus Salam Khan, himself an Awami Leaguer, so as to champion the cause of autonomy.

schism in the NAP between the pro-Peking and pro-Moscow factions further polarized the leftists and the nationalists in East Pakistan.

The people's uprisings of 1968–69, which toppled the Ayub regime, clearly illustrated this radicalization and polarization of Bengali politics. The mass movements in East and West Pakistan differed in emphasis. In West Pakistan the movement was simply against Ayub and his system; in East Pakistan it was against Ayub and his system "as the vehicle of West Pakistan's domination."[92] The radical autonomy demands put forth in 1966 were reiterated with greater vigor, and a very direct appeal was made to Bengali nationalism.

The movement in East Pakistan, which started nearly a month after that in West Pakistan, was initially led by the students. In early December 1968, the various student parties forged a united front known as the All Parties Students Action Committee (SAC), and adopted an eleven-point program which incorporated, in addition to the Six Points, certain popular demands, such as nationalization of banking, insurance, and big industries; reduction of taxes on the farmers; and better wages for the workers. Thus, while the Six Points had been devoted solely to autonomy demands, the eleven-point program was broadened to appeal to the left, the workers, and the peasants; and it became *the* program of the popular movement in East Pakistan.[93]

Spurred on by the success of the students, the moderate opposition political parties, which for so long had been in disarray,[94] formed an alliance known as the Democratic Action Committee (DAC) to provide a united leadership to the mass movement. The DAC brought together the PDM, the Awami League, and the pro-Moscow NAP on a platform whose main thrust was the restoration of democracy. Only the Bhasani group and Bhutto's People's Party were left out of this front. It was thus essentially an alliance of all the non-left political parties. There were, however, some differences within the DAC which later proved to be disastrous. While the Awami League and the pro-Moscow NAP were

[92] *The Times* (London), March 26, 1969.

[93] Thus all the political parties and leaders supported the eleven-points demand, and the students insisted that any future constitutional settlement would have to accede to the eleven points in toto.

[94] After the election of 1965, the moderate political parties were completely disorganized. They were seriously thinking of not entering the forthcoming election. It was only the autonomists and the leftists who carried on mass movements between 1965 and 1968.

in favor of full regional autonomy, the PDM preferred a relatively strong center.

Though the 1968–69 movement in its early stage was mostly student-dominated and centered in Dacca, as it progressed it involved other groups and spread to small towns and rural areas. The student-worker-mob alliance, used successfully in 1966, was again in the forefront, and in the later, more violent stages of the movement, the workers and the street mobs predominated. While the students had provided the first few known martyrs, the workers ultimately led in the attacks on factories and administration buildings and in other disruptive activities.[95]

The Ayub regime's response was to give too little too late. Initially, it tried to brush off the movement as a mere disturbance started by "riff raff elements."[96] But when the street rioting continued for over four months in both wings of the country, Ayub offered to talk to the "responsible leaders" in a round-table conference to amend the constitution — an idea which had been put forth by some of the "responsible leaders" since 1966.[97] While Bhutto and Bhasani refused to participate in the proposed conference, the DAC was willing to talk provided emergency rule was revoked and all political prisoners, including Sheikh Mujib and Bhutto, were released. Ayub was willing to revoke emergency rule and release some of the political prisoners, but he was reluctant to free those against whom there was a "genuine case," presumably referring to Mujib. Mujib refused to participate in the conference unless the whole Agartala conspiracy case was dropped and he was allowed to join the talks as a free man. Ayub demurred, and the round-table conference was postponed.

The popular movement continued and took a more violent turn in East Pakistan in mid-February, when a university professor and an

---

[95] Troops had to be called out to fight back the workers and mob who tried to storm the East Pakistan Secretariat, the seat of the provincial government, and the Adamjee jute mills, for long regarded as the symbol of "West Pakistani capitalism" in the eastern wing. See *Dawn* (Karachi), January 25, 28, 1969.

[96] The deputy commissioner of Rawalpindi quoted in *ibid.*, November 8, 1968.

[97] Nurul Amin, other PDM leaders who did not agree with the Awami League on the autonomy question, and the leftists of the Bhasani NAP wanted to come to some understanding with the regime by settling constitutional disputes such as the restoration of democracy. But the regime ignored their overtures.

accused in the Agartala conspiracy case were killed by the police.[98] Curfew was repeatedly broken, and antimilitary, anti–West Pakistani feelings ran high. It was this surge of separatism in East Pakistan that led to Ayub's decision to resign.[99] On February 21, Ayub announced his "final and irrevocable" decision not to run again after the expiration of his term. He urged the opposition leaders to join him in working out a formula for a new political system according to popular wishes. The next day, Sheikh Mujibur Rahman was released, and the Agartala conspiracy case was dropped.

With Ayub's decision to resign, his erstwhile powerful system crumbled completely. The East Pakistani governor fled the province secretly. The police and the army were withdrawn from the streets. The whole administrative process appeared to come to a halt. There was continual unrest in both wings among the laborers, who successfully used the "gherao" tactic to force a pay raise.[100] In East Pakistan, the head of the Dacca University Central Student Union was reportedly the de facto governor, and student peace parties were formed to maintain law and order and arbitrate industrial disputes. The students reiterated their eleven-point demand and warned the politicians participating in the round-table conference that nothing short of the eleven points would satisfy them.

The difference between the popular movements in the two wings became more obvious after Ayub's decision to resign. The West Pakistani movement, directed against Ayub's system, subsided after his decision to resign. But in East Pakistan, Ayub's resignation was looked upon as only the first step toward the achievement of Bengali objectives. Thus Mujibur Rahman, one day after his release, demanded proportional representation for the east wing. Mujib now wanted for East Pakistan not just more autonomy but a dominant position at the center. Dismissing the idea of secession on the ground that the East Pakistanis, being the majority, could not and would not secede, he not only reiterated his Six Points and the students' eleven points but demanded removal of the central capital from West to East Pakistan.[101] He also urged the divi-

---

[98] *The Pakistan Observer* (Dacca), February, 17–21, 1969.
[99] *The New York Times*, February 22, 1969.
[100] The "gherao" tactic—of holding employers captive until they accede to demands—was successfully used before by West Bengali industrial laborers.
[101] *Dawn* (Karachi), February 23, 1967.

sion of West Pakistan into the former provinces of Sind, the Punjab, the North-West Frontier Province, and Baluchistan. The regime was willing to concede parliamentary government, direct election by adult franchise, and federalism based on the 1956 constitution, but rejected the regional autonomy demands, which were the crux of the movement in East Pakistan. The PDM members of the DAC tended to support the regime on this, but the Awami League and the Pro-Moscow NAP insisted on full regional autonomy. The round-table conference was deadlocked, and Sheikh Mujibur Rahman submitted detailed amendments to the constitution which envisaged a federal parliamentary government with full regional autonomy. The amendments were rejected by the regime. Imposing martial law on the country on March 25, 1969, Ayub referred to Mujib's demands as spelling the liquidation of Pakistan, and made it quite clear that any attempt to bring about a fundamental restructuring of the political system would not be tolerated by the regime. To quote from his final address:

> I have always told you the secret of the continued existence of Pakistan is in a strong center. I accepted the federal parliamentary system because even in this system, there are possibilities of keeping a strong center. But now it is being proposed that the country be divided into two parts, the center be made weak and helpless, the defense forces be paralyzed completely and West Pakistan's political position be ended. I cannot preside over the destruction of my country.[102]

Once again, then, as the Bengali counterelite threatened to play a dominant role in national decision-making, they were thwarted by the ruling elite.

The five-month-long turbulence that resulted in Ayub's ouster and the reimposition of martial law had highlighted the limitation of the regime's political institution-building efforts, as well as the changing nature of Bengali politics. The movement had not only revived earlier autonomy demands, it had evoked a strident appeal to Bengali nationalism.[103] Finally, as the movement progressed, it had gradually polarized the left and the right. In the beginning an essentially bourgeois nationalist movement for regional autonomy, it was soon taken over by industrial labor and the lumpen proletariat in the urban areas, and later by the

---

[102] *The New York Times,* March 26, 1969.
[103] The term "Bengali" (instead of "East Pakistani") was frequently used. Mujib was given the epithet "friend of Bengal."

poor peasants in the rural areas.[104] When the demands of labor were put forth side by side with the demands for autonomy, some of the Bengali bourgeoisie felt threatened, for the enemy then was no longer the outside, "colonial" power, but someone within.[105] The division between the left and the right was clearly illustrated after Ayub's resignation, when Mujib went to the round-table conference, still deadlocked, and advised peace, while Bhasani boycotted the conference and claimed that the problem would be settled not through ballots but on the streets.

The people's uprising also revealed the inadequate development of political institutions in the decade. In both wings, the uprising was a "spontaneous" popular movement, with little organization or leadership from the political parties. The parties and leaders joined the movement after it was already a success, and hence were in no position to control or guide the "people's revolution." Instead of leading the movement, "they were following the people who were supposedly following them."[106] Even the hurriedly formed DAC, which did not include the leftists, was deeply divided between moderates and radicals, autonomists and centrists, secularists and Islamicists. Thus, when Ayub resigned and conceded to hold talks with political leaders to bring about a smooth transition of power, there was no "national" party or "national" leader with mass support who could make such a transition possible.

In sum, political movements in East Pakistan in the early years of Ayub's rule were directed at gaining participation in the national system. But after the election of 1965, when the Bengali counterelite found it difficult to participate in Ayub's system, demands for autonomy were revived with greater force in East Pakistan. The Six-Point Movement of 1966 marked a significant radicalization of Bengali demands for autonomy. The regime's response to the Six Points was one of total suppression. But this policy led to intensified frustration that partially explains the spontaneous mass movements of 1968–69. The people's

---

[104] Peter Hazelhurst, "Mob Slayings Sweep Rural East Pakistan," *The New York Times*, March 20, 1969.

[105] The Bengali bourgeoisie, many of whom supported the autonomy movement, naturally felt threatened when the "gherao" tactic was used against Bengali entrepreneurs, managers, and administrators and when reports of rural unrest came in. The students and the DAC pleaded for peace and the restoration of law and order.

[106] Joseph Lelyveld, "Ayub's Hopes Dissolve into Martial Law," *The New York Times*, March 30, 1969.

uprising of 1968–69 illustrated the radicalization and polarization, as well as the structural social changes, that Bengali politics underwent in Ayub's decade. It saw not only widespread support for radical demands for full autonomy but also a division between the left and the right which made consensus-building a difficult process. Finally, the uprising showed that after ten years of Ayub's centralized, personal rule the country was left with no national institution that could usher in a smooth transition for a successor regime or hold the two wings together.

eight / Dilemmas of political development in Pakistan

THE GRANTING of a nation-state to the Indian Muslims, and their troubled twenty-five-year attempt to fashion both a state and a nation from diverse provinces and personalities, illuminate most of the key problems of the new states. The spatial separation of the two wings of the country and its extreme poverty are perhaps exceptional factors, but their political effects are not unlike those found in other developing countries. Pakistan's path, in emphasizing state-building and deemphasizing nation-building, follows the guidance given many new states by both theorists and policy-makers; its effect, under Pakistan's conditions, was the disintegration of the country.

The Ayub Khan government consistently acted as though it believed that East Pakistan's grievances, expressed politically, were the product of insufficient policy "outputs." This view was thought to be understandable because of the poverty of the country and the assumption that the distribution of benefits of economic growth would soon follow investment-oriented, rather than distributive, allocation patterns. The real problem of east-west integration in Pakistan, however, was political. The main factor in Bengali alienation during this period was the lack of substantial participation in the national decision-making process.

The major mistake of the Ayub regime's nation-building strategy was its failure to integrate East Pakistan politically. None of the political institutions introduced by the regime succeeded in giving the Bengali counterelite effective participation in the national system.

While Ayub's political institutions limited the Bengali counterelite's participation in the system, his economic policies helped swell their number. The regime's economic policies did succeed in increasing the tempo of economic development and modernization in East Pakistan. But by increasing social mobilization, they increased social frustration.[1] Expectations rose, and the Bengalis, dissatisfied with the rate at which their economy was developing, demanded the adoption of a two-economy system. The regime's emphasis on economic growth, without the simultaneous development of political institutions, created a crisis in political management. The regime depended on the civil administration to manage these increasingly articulate socioeconomic groups; but in the absence of an ideology and effective political institutions, the civil bureaucracy proved of limited value as an integrative force.

From the viewpoint of east-west integration, the crucial development in the Ayub period was the growth of an intensified Bengali nationalism and mass Bengali support for the cause of autonomy in East Pakistan. As the decade progressed, the radical autonomists succeeded in picking up the support of most sectors of the East Pakistani population.

The urban intelligentsia, who might have supported the regime because of the regime's commitment to modernization and economic development, instead became the main support base of the autonomists as the regime denied civil liberties. Urban industrial labor's support was won over, since the real wages of labor had remained static, if they had not declined during the decade, and the right to strike had been curtailed, while the GNP and the wealth of industrial entrepreneurs increased significantly—and visibly. Urban salaried employees suffered from the rising inflation. And the ulema were unhappy with the regime's policies of modernization—such as its drive for family planning and the

---

[1] Samuel P. Huntington, *Political Order in Changing Societies*, pp. 55–56.

181 / Dilemmas of political development in Pakistan

Muslim Family Laws Ordinance. The autonomy demands also helped to win over a section of the civil bureaucracy and the rising business group, who wanted to be free of West Pakistani competition. And the rural poor were at least neutralized politically during the decade by the growing economic inequalities in the rural areas as a result of the regime's works program.

The mobilization of the various strata of East Pakistani society behind the banner of radical autonomy compounded the problem of east-west integration. It is likely that new factors in the seventies will serve to make integration more difficult than ever.

In East Pakistan human ecology will create a host of problems for any future government. East Pakistan is already overcrowded. Its population, estimated to be 75 million in 1970, is projected to go up to 125 million by 1985.[2] According to one estimate, food supplies will have to be doubled by 1985.[3] This will require a shift from relatively unproductive agriculture to sharply improved agricultural output, which, in turn, will depend on overall industrial and economic development.

Increasing population pressure will result in greater internal tensions and a higher rate of internal migration. There is even now a pattern of migration from the rural areas to the urban areas and from the overcrowded districts in the center-east to the less crowded districts in the north-south and the big cities.[4] Such interdistrict migration creates interdistrict conflict. The riots against predominantly Noakhali-born labor in the industrial city of Khulna in 1964 were an example of this kind of conflict. Any increase in internal migration can be expected to lead to heightened subregionalism in East Pakistan.

The increase in population will of course mean an increase in the labor force, which will probably create a greater problem than food production or internal migration in the seventies. There is already a high rate of unemployment and underemployment in East Pakistan. According to one estimate, in 1970 East Pakistan had a labor force of 25.7 million, of which 3.5 million, or 18 percent of the rural labor force, were "either seeking employment or working outside agriculture."[5]

[2] Roger Revelle and Harold Thomas, "Population and Food in East Pakistan."
[3] *Ibid.*, pp. 17–18.
[4] See Haroun er-Rashid, *East Pakistan*, pp. 364–65.
[5] Revelle and Thomas, p. 22.

Assuming that agriculture will be modernized, and that the rate of urbanization and industrialization will increase at a moderate pace, the seventies will see a rapid rise in agricultural unemployment. One estimate is that 11.5 million people in the countryside will need employment outside agriculture, whereas only 4 million will be provided with jobs.[6] In the urban areas, there will be unemployment and underemployment for the new migrants. The number of industrial laborers will also multiply. By 1985, 3.8 million workers are expected to be engaged in mining, manufacturing, and public utilities, as compared to 1 million in 1965.[7]

The increasing population will also require increased social services—more schools, teachers, doctors, hospitals, and transport and communication facilities—which will be difficult to provide, given the low resource base of the province. The lag between the need and the supply will be critical, especially for the multitude of students who will be enrolled in schools in the next decade.[8] According to one estimate, by 1985, 73 percent of the children aged five to twelve will be enrolled in primary schools, as compared to the present 39 percent.[9]

Of the major social groups, in the future, the students, who are already a powerful lobby and have been the main driving force of all popular movements in the past, can be expected to support the radical autonomists. Though the vast majority of Bengali students come from the rural areas, they are mostly modern in their outlook and show a marked difference from the "traditional" cultivators and even factory workers in their attitude.[10] Additionally, the students in the next decade will

---

[6] *Ibid.*

[7] Pakistan, Planning Division, *Growth Rates of Labor Productivity and Related Coefficients Needed for Projecting Sectoral Employment Composition of the Fourth Plan.*

[8] Alex Inkeles's survey shows that students feel a higher sense of deprivation than other groups. In reply to the question of whether the opportunity for the poor to improve their lot is increasing, 40 percent of the students surveyed answered that it was decreasing greatly. The corresponding percentage for cultivators and factory workers was 17 percent. (Mimeograph, Center for International Affairs, Harvard University, Cambridge, Mass.)

[9] Pakistan, Planning Division, Manpower Section, *Selected Tables on Projections of Education and Labor Force for Pakistan and Provinces, 1960–1990.*

[10] In Alex Inkeles's survey, while 89 percent of the students consider birth control necessary, for example, only 37 percent of the cultivators and factory workers think so. Similarly, 82 percent of the students prefer jobs that please them as against what pleases their parents, whereas in the case of the cultivators and the factory workers, the percentage is 29.7 and 70.3, respectively.

have been born after independence and partition, and will not share the memories of the independence movement. The students in East Pakistan attach little value to Islam as a uniting bond between East and West Pakistan, and few of them have any respect for the current political system.[11] Though the students are probably the best-organized social group, they act less as a functional group attempting to influence specific policies pertaining to their interests than as a political group aiming at systemic change. Similar is the case with the other rising social group — labor. It is also highly politicized and played a dominant role in the popular movements of the sixties. In the next decade labor can be expected to continue its support of the radical autonomists. But neither the students nor labor act as unified pressure groups. They are closely aligned with the political parties of the country and are as faction ridden.

In sum, the seventies will see a great increase in social and political conflict in East Pakistan. It is not at all clear whether the various social groups that are becoming increasingly active will organize themselves for political action within a viable political system. The fragmentation and the diffuse nature of political organizations are likely to continue in the next decade unless a prolonged war and/or revolution forces the birth of a dominant, coherent political organization.

[11] Talukdar Maniruzzaman, "Political Activism of University Students."

*epilog/ The disintegration of Pakistan
and the birth of Bangladesh*

THE DISINTEGRATION of Pakistan was not an unexpected phenomenon. As the previous analysis in this study has illustrated, the alienation of the Bengalis from the Pakistani political system started almost immediately after independence and was exacerbated during the Ayub period. However, the timing of the breakdown of Pakistan, so soon after Ayub's fall, caught most political observers by surprise. Even the actors themselves were unprepared and appear to have been swept up in a tide of events over which they had little control. The immediate background leading to the emergence of Bangladesh is significant because it sheds light on the configuration of forces that resulted in the final disintegration of Pakistan. Here an attempt will be made to discuss briefly the policies of the post-Ayub period and their impact on the eventual disintegration of the country. I shall analyze policies of the Yahya regime which precipitated the East-West confrontation and the national liberation movement that led ultimately to the birth of Bangladesh as a sovereign nation state.

The Yahya Regime (1969-71): from Conciliation to Confrontation

After the collapse of the Ayub regime, Yahya Khan, then commander-in-chief of the Pakistani army, was brought to power by the ruling elite of the civil-military bureaucracy. The second marital law of March 1969 was very much a defensive maneuver on the part of the ruling elite to maintain its position, which had been threatened by the mass movements of 1968-69. The round-table conference (RTC) of leaders convened in February and March 1969 to resolve the country's political impasse failed because the ruling elite was not willing to accede to any fundamental restructuring of power. In his farewell address Ayub stated explicitly that Sheikh Mujibur Rahman's alternative proposals, i.e., dissolution of one unit in West Pakistan and full regional autonomy for East Pakistan, were not acceptable since they threatened the position of the military and the Punjabi-dominated West Pakistan.[1] The task of the Yahya regime, therefore, was to seek a new political order which could maintain the status quo, although granting concessions to the counter-elite.

The policies pursued by the Yahya regime differed from those of Ayub. After the mass movements of 1968-69 it became obvious to the ruling elite that some of the demands of the more vocal groups in the mass movement would have to be met. Yahya therefore adopted a number of conciliatory policies specifically designed to placate the groups that spearheaded the mass movement. New education and wage policies were announced to meet the demands of students and labor, and the pay scale of salaried professionals was improved. It is in his attitude toward politics and politicians, however, that Yahya showed his most marked difference from the previous regime. Unlike Ayub, who disdained politicians and wanted to stay above politics, Yahya recognized the necessity of both politics and politicians, and decided to play the role of arbitrator among the conflicting political groups. He could not remain neutral, however; the regime's policy was to maintain the fundamental interests of the ruling elite through roles of mediator and power broker.

Upon assuming power, Yahya, unlike Ayub, did not ban political

---

[1] See Ayub's speech quoted in the *New York Times,* March 26, 1969.

parties, nor did he adopt restrictive political measures like EBDO or the arrest of opposition leaders. In his first broadcast to the nation Yahya clearly spelled out the transitional nature of his regime and stated that the sole ambition of his regime was the "creation of conditions conducive to the establishment of constitutional government . . . . and smooth transfer of power to the representatives of people elected freely and impartially on the basis of adult franchise."[2] Yahya revealed his scheme for this transfer of power on November 28, 1969. He announced that in October 1970 elections would be held to elect members of the National and Provincial Assemblies;[3] and that to facilitate electioneering, free political activity would be permitted after January 1, 1970. In the same speech Yahya announced two major concessions to the Bengali counter-elite which had previously been denied by Ayub at the RTC, that is, dissolution of one unit in West Pakistan and representation in the National Assembly apportioned on the basis of population rather than parity, thus giving the Bengalis a majority in the assembly. No concession was granted, however, on the third and major Bengali political demand, i.e., autonomy for East Pakistan on the basis of the Six-Point Program. This question was left for the people's representatives to decide.

That the regime had strong views about the future constitutional arrangement was also indicated by the Legal Framework Order (LFO) that Yahya proclaimed in March 1970. The LFO spelled out directive principles envisioning a democratic and federal government for Pakistan. The LFO did not specify the details of the constitution, but it set the parameters of the future order. On the question of autonomy for the federating units, the only remaining controversial political issue before the country, the LFO stated pointedly that while "provinces shall have maximum legislative, administrative and financial powers," the federal government also "shall have adequate powers including legislative, administrative and financial powers to discharge its responsibilities in relation to external affairs and to preserve the independence and territorial integrity of the country."[4] In addition, the LFO gave the president

[2] *Bangladesh: Contemporary Events and Documents* (Peoples' Republic of Bangladesh, n.d.), p. 52.
[3] The election date was later postponed to December 7 because of the severe floods in late summer, which hampered the election campaign.
[4] *Bangladesh: Contempory Events and Documents,* p. 54.

the power to validate the constitution. Thus the regime maintained two mechanisms through which it could have a decisive say in the future constitutional order in Pakistan. First, since the elections were expected to return a multiparty system to the assemblies, and since the National Assembly was given only 120 days to frame the constitution, the regime hoped to play a key role in balancing the different parties. Second, even if one party were to obtain an absolute majority in the National Assembly, Yahya still retained the power to refuse validation of the constitutional bill if it upset the basic interests of the ruling elite.

In spite of these restrictions in the LFO, the policies adopted by Yahya included major concessions to the political opposition; and the Bengali autonomists decided once again to work through Yahya's system. LFO was accepted with little opposition by the political parties, and on January 1, 1970 electioneering started in Pakistan.

The elections of 1970, the first general elections held in Pakistan on the basis of universal adult franchise, worked as a catalyst to sharpen the east-west confrontation. Nine political parties participated in the elections. They included religiopolitical parties, i.e., Jama'at-i-Islami, Jamiat-ul-Ulema-i-Islam and the Markazi Jamiat-ul-Ulema-i-Pakistan; and democratic, social-democratic, and leftist parties such as the Pakistan Democratic Party, the three factions—Council, Qayyum, and Pakistan—of the Muslim League, the Awami League, the National Awami Party, and the Pakistan People's Party. During the election campaign it became obvious that the "national" parties had little grass-roots support, while parties with mass support tended to be regional—a trend noticeable in the last stages of the Ayub decade (see the discussions in chapter 7, pp. 150–51). Thus, the Jama'at, the PDP, and the three factions of the Muslim League, the "national" parties, had little support either in East or West Pakistan; and the Awami League and the People's Party had strong mass support but were mainly regional.

Election campaigning varied widely in the two wings of Pakistan, since the brunt of the electioneering was carried out by a different party in each wing, with separate strategies based on different issues. In East Pakistan the Awami League was the major contestant. It faced opposition from both the left, i.e., the two factions of the National Awami Party,[5]

---

[5] Of the two factions of the National Awami Party, only the pro-Moscow faction actually

and the right, i.e., Jama'at, PDP, and the Muslim League factions. The Awami League's aim was to win a commanding majority in the National Assembly by maximizing support in East Pakistan—a feasible strategy, since the east was allotted a majority of seats in the assembly. The League's major campaign theme was a pledge to frame the constitution on the basis of the Six-Point and Eleven-Point Programs.[6] Sheikh Mujibur Rahman emphasized his image as a Bengali nationalist to undercut support for both the left and the right. The right was easier to deal with. Since the Six Points were portrayed as a Magna Carta for the Bengalis, parties to the right of the Awami League, who wanted a strong center, were easily discredited. The left, however, was a different story. Like the Awami League, the left also championed the Bengali cause, but in fact went a little further. They maintained that Bengali rights could not be achieved through the electoral and constitutional processes and demanded an immediate armed confrontation. Indeed, after the cyclones of November 1970, Maulana Bhasani in a public meeting voiced a demand for an independent East Pakistan, and his party decided to boycott the election. Challenged by leftist propaganda concerning the futility of the electoral process, the Awami League had to show that it could win people's rights without a revolution by participating in the election. It concentrated on its East Pakistani constituency in order to roll up an overwhelming majority, which, it thought, would insure its getting into power. In West Pakistan the League's strategy was to depend on the regional autonomists, the same strategy that the Bengali leaders had followed in the 1950s.

In West Pakistan there were more contestants, and no one party was in a commanding position similar to that of the Awami League. There was also no single issue comparable to autonomy. The major schism in

---

participated in the election. The pro-Peking faction, led by Bhasani, debated for a long time over the issue of participation in the election. The Marxist-Leninist faction of Bhasani's party was against participation in elections and other constitutional methods. Later they formally broke with Bhasani and declared their opposition to the concept of elections. Bhasani decided to contest the election; but at the last moment, after the cyclone, he demanded a postponement of election date, which was not forthcoming. He asked his candidates to withdraw from the election. Bhasani's decision to boycott the election could also have been due to early indications of the Awami League's landslide victory.

[6] See the Awami League election manifesto and Sheikh Mujibur Rahman's election broadcast in *Bangladesh: Contemporary Events and Documents*, pp. 56–69. For an elaboration of the Six and Eleven Points see discussion in chapter 7, pp. 167–72.

West Pakistan was between the "old guard" leadership and youth, between the established parties and the new social groups that had participated in the mass movement against Ayub. Naturally, the People's Party, itself new and led by a youthful leader, attracted these newly mobilized groups. Bhutto's electoral strategy was to coalesce all the antiregime forces, and especially to exploit the new social groups and the demands brought to the surface during the mass movement of 1968–69.[7] Because his party was an amalgam of different forces, Bhutto appealed to different groups in different languages and kept his party's platform relatively vague. The People's Party promised Islamic socialism, but the precise nature of that socialism was not spelled out. The party's major campaign theme was the promise of change, change from the "old guard" leadership. The party did not contest seats in East Pakistan; its alliance strategy was to keep maximum options open. During electioneering the party did not publicly reject the Six-Point Program, though in a pamphlet written in 1967 Bhutto criticized the Six Points and by implication called for a strong center.[8]

The election results saw the Awami League and the People's Party sweeping polls in East and West Pakistan respectively. The Awami League won an absolute majority in the National Assembly (160 out of 300 seats).[9] It won a landslide victory in East Pakistan, receiving all but two of the 162 seats. The People's Party was the second largest party in the National Assembly, with 81 seats. All the "national" parties fared badly. The Qayyum Muslim League won 9 seats, the Council Muslim League 7, Jamiat-ul-Ulema-i-Islam 7, Markazi Jamiat-ul-Ulema-i-Islam 7, the National Awami Party (Wali group) 6, Jama'at-i-Islami 4, the Pakistan Muslim League 2, PDP 1, and independents 16 seats.[10] In the provincial assembly elections the pattern of the National Assembly was repeated. In the East Pakistan provincial assembly, the Awami League was another resounding victory (288 out of 300 seats). The People's Party won a majority in the Punjab (113 out of 180 seats) and Sind (28 out of 60) assemblies. In the Baluchistan and North-West Frontier Province assem-

---

[7] See Shahid J. Burki, *Social Groups and Development: A Case Study of Pakistan* (forthcoming) for a detailed discussion of these groups.

[8] *Foundation and Policy* (Lahore: Pakistan People's Party, n.d.), pp. 81–88.

[9] The figures here include only the general seats. There were 13 more seats reserved for women, of which the Awami League won 7.

[10] See Craig Baxter, "Pakistan Votes—1970," *Asian Survey*, XI (1971), p. 211.

blies there was a plurality of parties, with the National Awami Party (Wali group) being the dominant one.[11] The elections thus crystallized the polarization between East and West Pakistan. The Awami League, which won a national majority and a majority of seats from East Pakistan, did not win any seat from any one of the provinces of West Pakistan. The People's Party, which won the majority of seats from the Punjab and Sind, did not win any from East Pakistan or Baluchistan.

The election results caught everybody by surprise. The Awami League was expected to win in East Pakistan, but not by such a large margin (experts gave the Awami League at best 60 percent of the seats). The November cyclone in the coastal region of East Pakistan and the administration's inadequate response to the cyclone victims had served to vindicate the Awami League's stand on autonomy, and in the elections that soon followed, the Awami League won a clear mandate from the people.[12] The People's Party's victory, however, was even more surprising. In West Pakistan the "old guard" leadership, especially the Council Muslim League and the Jama'at, had been expected to win in the Punjab and Sind. The People's Party's victory marked the successful assertion of the new groups in West Pakistani politics.

The emergence of the Awami League and the People's Party as clear winners upset the Yahya regime's plan concerning postelectoral alignments. The regime had expected that the election would either bring parties to power, for example, the PDP or the *Islam Pasand* parties,[13] who would not fundamentally threaten the ruling elite's position, or that it would result in such a plurality of parties that no party would have absolute command, and the military would be able to consolidate its position by working as a mediator among parties. The general expectation of the regime was that the Awami League would at best win a bare majority in East Pakistan, which would make it possible for the ruling elite to keep the Awami League out of power, or that if it should come

[11] *Ibid*, p. 211.
[12] The national election on December 7 came barely three weeks after the cyclone in which reportedly over half a million people died in the coastal regions of East Pakistan. The regime showed extreme apathy toward the cyclone victims, and this helped the Awami League to focus attention on the need for self-rule in East Pakistan. Most observers agree that the Awami League landslide was made possible by the party's exploitation of the cyclone issue.
[13] The right-wing parties with Islamic ideologies were called *Islam Pasand* in the Pakistani press.

to power with West Pakistani alliances, it would be forced to water down its Six Points and would not be a threat to the military. The Awami League's dominance of the National Assembly nullified the regime's first strategy of having a PDP–*Islam Pasand* alliance in power. The second strategy, however, was still possible, especially since the Awami League and the People's party appeared to represent conflicting constituency interests.

The landslide victories of the Awami League and the People's Party compounded the problem of east-west confrontation. The Awami League owed its victory to its image as a champion of Bengali rights. The Awami League's major constituencies were the students, literati professionals, and the rising business groups—in other words, the nationalist bourgeoisie, who wanted a share in the national pie and who looked upon the West Pakistani bourgeoisie as their natural adversaries. The constituencies of the People's Party were the students, labor, literati professionals and the lumpen proletariat of West Pakistan. The party owed its victory to its image as a socialist and nationalist—or rather statist—party. Thus like the Awami League in the east, the People's Party found its greatest support in the west among the students and petty bourgeoisie groups, who were outside the system and demanded an immediate share in power. Conflict between the two parties was thus innate in their respective constituency support.[14] The People's Party, however, had one advantage over the Awami League in that it never took any firm stand on any particular issue, as the Awami League had done on the Six Points, and was thus in a relatively better bargaining position.

The postelection period in Pakistan thus left three political actors on the scene, the Yahya regime, the Awami League, and the People's Party. All three had divergent, conflicting, and uncertain bases of power, which made accommodation among them difficult. The Yahya regime represented the old ruling elite, but the elite was no longer a united force. It had been shaken up by Ayub's fall and the mass movement; and some of its members had joined the counterelite (the People's Party in the west

---

[14] For a detailed discussion of how the divergent constituency support of the three political actors, Mujib, Yahya, and Bhutto, limited their capabilities for negotiations see Rounaq Jahan, "Elite in Crisis: An analysis of the Failure of Mujib-Yahya-Bhutto Negotiations" (unpublished paper presented at the National Seminar on Pakistan, Columbia University, February 1972).

and the Awami League in the east). Yahya's control over the ruling elite was shaky, and he survived by balancing the feuding factions among them. In the postelection period his conciliatory policies came under fire from the hawks among the military generals, and his bargaining position with the counterelite was greatly undercut. The counterelite, i.e., the Awami League and the People's Party, also had divergent and weakly organized power bases. Both were organized for electoral purposes and both had radical/moderate, left/right factions within them. The leaders of both parties—Sheikh Mujibur Rahman and Zulfikar Ali Bhutto— depended strongly on personal charisma and manipulation of symbols.

The crisis of 1971 that led to the final disintegration of Pakistan was precipitated by Bhutto and his People's Party. After the Awami League's overwhelming electoral victory, the mood in East Pakistan was one of confidence, and there was no talk of secession. With an absolute majority in the National Assembly, the Awami League expected to come to power, and it was busy working out the details of the draft constitution and other national and international problems. Mujib himself played up his image as the leader of the majority party in the National Assembly. He interpreted the election returns as a de facto transfer of power to his party, as is the custom in a parliamentary democracy, and chided Yahya for not briefing him on foreign policy issues.[15] But for Bhutto, and indeed for the West Pakistani leadership in general, it was psychologically difficult to accept Mujibur Rahman's domination of the center. That Mujib was no Nazimuddin, Mohammad Ali, or Nurul Amin (all of whom believed in token Bengali participation) was obvious; hence Bhutto came out with a demand for a power-sharing arrangement with Mujib.

In January, Bhutto and other People's Party leaders visited Dacca for talks with Mujib and other Awami League leaders. The full details of the Mujib-Bhutto talks have not yet been made public, but from all accounts it appears that Bhutto's demand for power-sharing was rejected by Mujib. Having failed to get a share of power, Bhutto used his anti–Six Points stand as a bargaining point. After returning from Dacca, Bhutto advised Yahya to delay the calling of the National Assembly session, which, he argued, would give him more time to bargain with Mujib.

---

[15] Mujib criticised Yahya for not briefing him on foreign policy issues in the wake of the hijacking and destruction of an Indian plane in Lahore which led to a worsening of Indo-Pakistani relations.

Bhutto hoped that by mobilizing the anti–Six Points sentiment in West Pakistan, he could put pressure on Mujib to share power with his party. Mujib felt the pressure but decided to pick up the all-too-willing support of the anti-Bhutto minority parties in West Pakistan. Outmaneuvered, Bhutto announced on February 15 that he had decided to boycott the proposed National Assembly session on March 3, 1971. But his decision did not have any impact on the other minority parties of West Pakistan, except for the Qayyum Muslim League. As the date of session drew near, even some members of the Qayyum League and the People's Party grew restive. To increase the pressure on both the regime and Mujib, in a public speech on February 28 Bhutto threatened West Pakistani members participating in the National Assembly with "liquidation" and revenge, and asked Yahya either to postpone the National Assembly session or to withdraw the 120-day time limit imposed on the Assembly in order to facilitate continuation of his dialogue with his "elder brother Mujib."

On March 1, Yahya announced his fateful decision to postpone the National Assembly session, citing Bhutto's unwillingness to participate in the National Assembly as the primary cause for his action and urging the political leaders of East and West Pakistan to come to a reasonable understanding on constitution-making.[16] The postponement sparked off spontaneous, rebellious demonstrations in East Pakistan, and in the next few weeks Mujib came under tremendous pressure both from other parties and from the radicals of his own party to declare independence.[17] Pressure from the military was also visible as troops were flown in, the moderate governor in East Pakistan was replaced, and Yahya delivered some tough speeches.[18] Under cross-pressures from the military and the political radicals, Mujib decided to chart a middle course. He rejected the options of unilateral declaration of independence or bowing down

---

[16] *Dawn* (Karachi), March 2, 1971.

[17] After Yahya's announcement of the postponement of National Assembly session, the pro-Moscow faction of the National Awami Party was the first group to call for a declaration of independence. The Bhasani faction also did the same, as did other parties. Mujib at first urged a constitutional movement, but the radicals of his party and the Student League did not want to fall behind the popular mood, which enthusiastically supported the other parties' call for independence. After a period of initial hesitation, the radicals of the Student League supported and, in fact, overshadowed the other groups demanding independence.

[18] See Yahya's broadcasts of March 1 and 6 in *Bangladesh: Contemporary Events and Documents*, pp. 84–86, 90–93.

under military threat. Instead, he chose to launch a nonviolent noncooperation movement, which gave him the opportunity to combat the military on his own strong ground. His strategy was to build up such unprecedented popular pressure as to deter military action and to force the regime to negotiate with him. Between March 1 and 7, the regime offered Mujib a round-table conference and a recalling of the National Assembly session. But while the regime was offering negotiating terms, violent clashes between the army and the people continued to occur on the streets of Dacca and other cities, making acceptance of these terms difficult. On March 7 Mujib laid down his four preconditions for joining the National Assembly session, the crucial precondition being immediate transfer of power to the elected representatives of the people. Simultaneously, the Awami League launched a noncooperation movement which placed Mujib in complete control of East Pakistan. The whole of the East Pakistani administration, even the Bengalis serving in central government agencies and in the civilian branch of the armed forces, complied with Mujib's call for noncooperation. Faced with Mujib's de facto assumption of power, Yahya came to Dacca on March 15 to work out a political settlement of the crisis. The minority party leaders of West Pakistan also came and demanded an interim arrangement under which power could be transferred to the Awami League.

Detailed information about the Mujib-Yahya talks in Dacca is not yet available. From published accounts of talks,[19] it appears that after an initial period of difficulties, Yahya agreed in principle to Mujib's four preconditions; and on March 20, the combined advisers of Yahya and the Awami League agreed on a draft proclamation to be issued by Yahya which contained the outlines of an interim arrangement for power transfer. The proposed proclamation provided for immediate cessation of martial law and transfer of power to the five provinces, without such a transfer of power in the center. It also provided for the division of the National Assembly into two committees to draft separate reports, on the basis of which the constitution would be framed. Automony was granted

---

[19] The published accounts include *White Paper on the Crisis of East Pakistan* (Islamabad: Government of Pakistan Press, August 1971), which gives the regime's side of the story; Zulfikar Ali Bhutto, *The Great Tragedy* (Karachi, 1971), which gives Bhutto's version of the negotiations; and the press reports. The Awami League's side of the story still remains untold.

to East Pakistan on the basis of the Six Points, while the amount of autonomy for the four other provinces was left to mutual arrangement.[20] This agreement, however, was not acceptable to Bhutto and the People's Party, who termed the arrangement a "massive betrayal of West Pakistan."[21] Bhutto objected to the provisions concerning the two committees and the differential amounts of autonomy for the two wings. Bhutto's alternative proposals were to call the National Assembly session first, or to allow him more time to negotiate directly with Mujib.

Bhutto's plea for protracted negotiations was not sympathetically received by the Awami League. By that time, the pressure on Mujib either to get a quick settlement or to declare independence had nearly reached the breaking point.[22] The Awami League had been continuing its noncooperation movement for nearly a month, and it was becoming increasingly difficult to sustain such a prolonged mass movement while at the same time keeping it nonviolent. Confrontations between the military and the people became more frequent. Animosity toward the non-Bengali population rose also, resulting in the migration of some panic-stricken non-Bengalis to West Pakistan. The plight of these groups was used as a counterpressure on the Yahya regime, and it hardened its bargaining stand. On March 23 the Awami League advisers presented a draft proclamation which, in effect, granted East Pakistan autonomy on the basis of the Six Points.[23] The Awami League pressed for quick acceptance of the draft proposal, and the general secretary of the party warned that unless it were issued within 48 hours, even that proclamation would be too late.[24] On March 25, while the Awami League leaders were still hoping to hear the draft proclamation, Yahya, without formally breaking the talks, launched a policy of military solution to the crisis. On that night units of the Pakistani army attacked the Dacca University cam-

---

[20] *White Paper on the Crisis of East Pakistan* (Islamabad: Government of Pakistan Press, August 1971), pp. 18–20.

[21] *Dawn* (Karachi), March 20, 1971.

[22] As the negotiations became protracted, Mujib came under increasing pressure from the radicals of his own party. In mid-March four leaders of the Awami League–affiliated Student League formed a *Shadhin Bangla Kendriya Sangram Parisad* (independent Bangladesh central students' union) and started a program of paramilitary training on the campus of the university and at other educational institutions. Some of the Bengali members of the EBR and EPR also warned Mujib about the Pakistan army's plan of military action and advised him to preempt the army's move by declaring independence.

[23] *White Paper on the Crisis of East Pakistan*, pp. 22–27.   [24] *Ibid.*, p. 26.

pus, the headquarters of the East Pakistan Rifles and police, and offices of Awami League newspapers, and killed innumerable unarmed civilians. Skeikh Mujibur Rahman was arrested. The military action destroyed the last hope of saving the unity of Pakistan, and on March 26, the independence of Bangladesh was formally declared in the name of Awami League and its leader, Skeikh Mujibur Rahman.

Thus, in the post-Ayub period a number of factors converged to accelerate the process of disintegration. Ayub's successor Yahya at first followed a different policy and it appeared for a time that the policy might hold the two wings of Pakistan together. Yahya adopted a conciliatory attitude toward the Bengali autonomists, and by granting representation on the basis of population, he increased the Bengali's stake in the union. Indeed, the Awami League contested the election and worked within Yahya's system, in spite of its restrictions. In the postelection period, the Awami League and Mujib wanted and worked to save the union right up to the last moment, until the regime took military action against East Pakistan. Though under tremendous pressure from both his supporters and his opponents in East Pakistan to declare independence, Mujib rejected the option; the declaration of independence was made after the military crackdown. In the final analysis, the union could not be saved because the ruling elite was not willing to renounce its fundamental interests, even though the election results clearly signaled the victory of the counterelite; and the counterelite in the east and west, with divergent power bases, could not accommodate each other. The counterelite in East Pakistan was no longer interested in saving the unity of Pakistan, if this were to be done again at the expense of the Bengalis; and the counterelite in West Pakistan did not care to save a union that was no longer profitable to them.

While the adoption of a policy of brutal military action destroyed the concept of Pakistani "nationhood," final disintegration of the state did not come about until nine months later after a successful national liberation movement. It is worthwhile to discuss briefly the nine-month-long period of Pakistani occupation and the liberation movement, since only during this period did Bengali nationalism change from an elite phenomenon to a mass one,[25] making possible the breakup of Pakistan

[25] Howard Schuman, "A Note on the Rapid Rise of Mass Nationalism in East Pakistan," (unpublished paper presented at the National Seminar on Pakistan, Columbia University,

and the emergence of Bangladesh. An analysis of the national liberation movement can also help in understanding why the Bangladesh movement succeeded while similar movements failed elsewhere, and what the problems the policy-makers in Bangladesh are likely to face in their task of nation-building.

The National Liberation Movement

Historically, the national liberation movement in Bangladesh can be divided into three phases. The first phase ran from March 25 to the middle of May, when the Pakistani army occupied all the major cities of East Pakistan; the second phase was between mid-May and September, when the status quo was maintained; and the third phase was from October to the middle of December, when Dacca and the whole of East Pakistan was liberated. My analysis here will focus mainly on the changing leadership and strategies of the movement in the three phases.

The first phase was one of spontaneous resistance and revolt, often uncoordinated and amateurish in nature. When the Pakistani army began its campaign of murder and oppression, the Bengali reaction was one of immediate revolt. Even on the night of March 25, when the Pakistani army, without warning, attacked the headquarters of East Pakistan Rifles (EPR) and the police, Bengali members of the EPR and police fought back. This skirmish, however, was mainly a defensive action to facilitate the escape of fellow members, who at that point were unarmed and did escape to regroup later. As news of the Dacca massacres reached the districts, they rose in immediate revolt and prepared a resistance to the Pakistani army. On March 26 the independence of Bangladesh was declared over Chittagong radio. The next day a more formal declaration of independence was made by a military officer of the East Bengal Regiment (EBR). On April 10, a provisional government composed of Awami Leaguers was sworn in at Mujibnagar.

The leadership of the movement in the first phase rested mainly

---

February, 1972). Schuman's data reveal that as late as 1964 there was a low level of identity with Bengali nationalism in East Pakistan. He argues that the spread of mass nationalism was a relatively recent phenomenon, mostly done by the Pakistani army through its policy of mass killings.

with the Awami League and in some places Bengali members of the EBR, EPR and the civil service; in other words, the established authority in the districts. The Awami League members came mostly from the middle class, as did the members of EBR, EPR, and the civil service.[26] In the first phase there was hardly any well thought out military strategy. The war of resistance in the districts was spontaneous and involved mass participation. In small garrison cities, literally human waves overran the garrison and distributed arms among the people. The arms supply and the number of trained people, however, both remained pitifully low. While short of arms, the freedom fighters were successful in destroying lines of communication, i.e., roads, bridges, railroads, etc., a defensive measure to deter the Pakistani army's advance. This, too, involved mass participation.

The Pakistan army's strategy was to conserve its strength as much as possible and slowly occupy one city after another. Though its numerical strength was not all that great, the Pakistan army had vast superiority in fire and air power. In a conventional war against the Bengalis, the Pakistan army naturally had an advantage. By the middle of May, the army had occupied all the major cities of Bangladesh, though that did not give them control over more than one-third of the population or land area. Initial campaigns against the cities were quite brutal. Heavy firepower was used, which meant massive civilian casualties. There were also wanton killings, looting, and destruction. These policies had a twofold impact on the liberation movement. First, they resulted in large-scale migration of the population to India, which put pressure on India to intervene on the side of the liberation movement. (According to Indian sources, roughly ten million people migrated to India from Bangladesh during the nine-month-long occupation.) Second, large-scale destruction of life and property effectively spread a sense of Bengali nationalism at the mass level.

The second phase of the liberation movement was a period of long-term planning. Leadership of the movement during this phase either went underground or into exile in India. Two sets of leaders emerged. One belonged to the government-in-exile in Calcutta, the other to the

[26] M. Rashiduzzaman, "Leadership, Organization, Strategies and Tactics of the Bangladesh Movement," *Asian Survey* XII (1972). Rashiduzzaman's data reveal the essentially middle-class nature of the leadership of the Bangladesh movement.

Mukti Bahini (liberation army). The former was comprised mainly of top Awami Leaguers and government officials; the latter included the members of EBR and EPR, as well as other student guerrilla leaders. The government-in-exile handled external relations, for the most part, while the Mukti Bahini was mainly concerned with the actual fighting. There was little coordination between the two sets of leaders, and in the later stages of the revolt one heard rumours of conflict between the two. The leadership of the movement still came from the middle class, though some student and guerrilla leaders reportedly believed in revolutionary ideology.

During the second phase, the tactic of guerrilla warfare was adopted and both short- and long-term military strategies were worked out. The recruitment drive for the Mukti Bahini was intensified, and reportedly more than a hundred thousand young men joined the liberation army. Military training camps were established both in Bangladesh and in India, and a program of rigorous military training was instituted. There was, however, a lull in the actual fighting because of the heavy monsoons. Both the Pakistan army and the Mukti Bahini essentially dug into their own respective holds and prepared for the inevitable confrontation in the winter. While frontal confrontations were rare, the guerrilla ambushes of the Pakistani army continued and increased in frequency during the later stages of the fighting. Destruction of communication lines also went on unabated, though during the second phase the goal was to disrupt the Pakistan army's supply lines and its efforts to bring life back to normality in the occupied areas. Railroads were for the most part unusable, and river and road transportation at night was hazardous. Successful attempts were also made to disrupt the economy, and especially to sabotage the jute and tea export, thereby denying the Pakistan army its major medium of foreign exchange.

During the second phase, external publicity to mobilize support for Bangladesh was undertaken by the government-in-exile, and Radio Free Bangladesh started regular programs to keep morale high in the occupied and the liberated areas. The noncooperation movement against the regime was continued, and was especially successful in the factories and educational institutions. West Pakistani goods were boycotted. During this second phase, struggles of the liberation movement became multidimensional.

As there was a cessation of frontal battle in the second phase, the Yahya regime tried to settle down and "normalize" life in the occupied areas. To counter the publicity of the Bangladesh movement, the regime also started external publicity. Foreign journalists who were thrown out of Dacca on March 25 were invited to return; amnesty was granted to returning refugees from India, and much-publicized (but not effective) reception centers were opened to welcome them back. The regime also attempted to restore a sham civilian government. On June 28, 1971, Yahya announced his long-awaited plan for a "political settlement" with the Awami League.[27] He promised a constitutional government and restoration of civilian rule in the next three or four months. The Awami League remained banned as a political organization, though individual Awami Leaguers who were not guilty of "subversive" and "criminal" actions were allowed to retain their seats in the assemblies.[28] Such settlement terms were obviously not acceptable to the government-in-exile, who in rejecting them said that "The people of Bangladesh will never accept a constitution from a foreign source."[29] In the next three months the regime continued its plan of "civilianization" of its administration. A long list of names of Awami League members of the National Assembly was published, against whom the regime brought specific "criminal" charges; and by-election dates for these "vacant" seats were announced. In September, the military governor in East Pakistan, General Tikka Khan, was replaced by a civilian governor, and a civilian cabinet (composed of members of several parties) was installed as an interim arrangement to facilitate by-elections.

To counter the guerrilla activity of the liberation movement, the regime started its own counterinsurgency programs. After the military crackdown, some prominent Bengali politicians, who were opponents of the Awami League, mostly from the Muslim League and the Jama'at, emerged as defenders of the unity of Pakistan and collaborated with the

---

[27] After the military crackdown in East Pakistan, Yahya came under pressure from foreign countries to come to a political settlement with the Awami League. It was expected both at home and abroad that in his June 28 broadcast Yahya would offer some compromise formula to the Awami League government-in-exile. Yahya's plan of establishing a quisling government by dividing the Awami League could hardly be regarded as a compromise solution. Its rejection by the Awami League was a foregone conclusion.

[28] *The Pakistan Observer* (Dacca), June 29, 1971.

[29] Quoted in Rashiduzzaman, "Bangladesh Movement," p. 198.

Pakistan army. Peace committees were formed in different cities and localities under their auspices, with the backing of the army. Later, *razakars* (armed volunteers corps) were raised and given arms by the regime to oppose the freedom fighters. Both threats and monetary incentives were used to recruit the razakars. The liberation movement at first adopted a policy of extermination of the "collaborators," which included both peace-committee members and razakars. But as the number of collaborators swelled, the policy became more tolerant. The razakars were tolerated mainly because their arms were a potential source of strength to the Mukti Bahini. Also their deployment in rural areas in place of the better-trained Pakistani army allowed the Mukti Bahini relative freedom of operation in those areas. The attitude toward non-Bengali collaborators also changed during this phase. In the first phase many non-Bengalis living in East Pakistan were killed, mostly by mob action. In the second phase an attempt was made to neutralize or even win them over. Thus Radio Free Bangladesh started an Urdu program, beamed at the Urdu speakers in Bangladesh and urging them to join the liberation movement.

The second phase thus was a period of high tacit resistance, though active resistance was less visible. By September the people of Bangladesh, in both the liberated and the occupied areas, were psychologically prepared for a long war.

The third phase of the liberation movement saw stepped-up guerrilla activity and the resumption of conventional war, especially in the border districts. From October on, some of the urban guerrilla units had completed their training and became active in the occupied cities, nearly paralyzing normal life there. Communications and power lines were broken, and by November Dacca and other major cities were without electricity nearly half the time. Guerrilla actions in the rural areas were also intensified. In retaliation, the Pakistan army started its "search and destroy" operation, which in effect meant destruction of a certain number of villages every day. During October and early November the liberation movement appeared to be trying to liberate a few border districts in order to install the government-in-exile there; but in the last week of November that strategy was abandoned. Then, in a brief, three-week war a combined force of the Indian army and the Mukti Bahini liberated the whole of Bangladesh. On December 15, the Pakistan army with 93,000 soldiers surrendered in Dacca. The involvement of the Indian army in the last phase had been decisive. After nine months of bloody conflict, Bangladesh as a state had finally been born.

The birth of Bangladesh is in many ways a unique phenomenon and poses a number of interesting questions to students of political development. Pakistan is the first among the new states of Asia and Africa, with illogical boundaries and plural societies, to break down. Bangladesh is the first country to emerge out of a successful struggle against "internal colonialism" in the Third World countries. The emergence of Bangladesh, and especially the decisive Indian involvement in the last phase of the liberation movement, sent shock waves through the developing countries, many of whom are engaged in their own struggle to build nations out of disparate subnational groups. The question naturally arises: Was Bangladesh a special case or would it have a "domino" impact on other, similar movements? As this analysis has tried to show, the emergence of Bangladesh was indeed the result of a configuration of a number of forces which may not necessarily be repeated in other cases. Several factors may be cited to explain why the Bangladesh movement succeeded while similar movements in other countries have failed or are likely to fail.

First, the Bangladesh movement was truly a nationalist as well as a democratic struggle. The Bengalis formed the majority of Pakistan's population, but their efforts to participate in the decision-making process of the country through democratic electoral processes were thwarted repeatedly, in 1954, 1958, and 1971. The actual liberation movement started in Bangladesh in March 1971, when the Pakistani army tried to reverse with bullets the gains the Bengalis had achieved through the ballot box in the election of 1970. Unlike Biafra, where the liberation struggle was led by a military general, the Bangladesh movement was led by a political party, the Awami League, which had won an overwhelming election victory. The movement involved extensive mass participation and mass support, which was spontaneous. What the movement lost in organization from these spontaneous actions, it gained in numbers and popular support.

Second, the savage brutalities of the Pakistan army and the genocidal nature of their killings aroused a keen sense of unity among the Bengalis, broke down primordial sentiments, and stiffened their resistance. It was looked upon not only as a struggle for liberation but in fact as a struggle for the survival of a people. It is true that the Pakistan army had a number of select target groups, i.e., students, intellectuals, Hindus, Awami League supporters, slum dwellers, Bengali members of the army and police, etc.; but the burning of villages en masse and mass graves justified the Bengalis' apprehension over their survival as a group. Between one and three million people were reportedly killed during the nine-month struggle. The brutalities of the Pakistan army created worldwide sympathy for the Bengali cause, and the regime found it difficult to replenish its depleted defense budget from foreign sources. The brutalities of the army thus proved to be counterproductive.

Third, the separation of East and West Pakistan by a thousand miles of Indian territory created insurmountable logistic problems for Pakistan, which played a decisive role in the struggle. The cost of shipping men and arms across the Indian Ocean for nine months nearly bankrupted Pakistan. And when the actual war broke out at the end of November, Pakistan could not continue supplying its army in Bangladesh because of an effective Indian naval blockade.

Finally, the Indian sanctuary and Indian help played a key role. It would have taken Bangladesh several more years to emerge had India not joined with the Mukti Bahini in the third phase of the struggle. An India unfriendly to the cause of the liberation movement would, of course, have spelled disaster for the movement. Thus, the birth of Bangladesh was not only the culmination of a long struggle; it was the result of a combination of factors which might not be present elsewhere.

With the birth of Bangladesh, the major problem of Pakistan's integration is removed from the scene. The two successor states, Pakistan and Bangladesh, however, still face their own problems of national integration. For Pakistan it is the task of building a national community out of the four remaining subnational groups; for Bangladesh it is the task of building a national political system. One hopes that the policy-makers in both states have learned from the mistakes of the sixties; and that in the seventies, they will give priority to the task of nation-building through participation.

Statistical appendix

Table 1 / Interwing air travel, 1955–65

	NUMBER OF PASSENGERS			NUMBER OF PASSENGERS	
	EAST TO WEST	WEST TO EAST		EAST TO WEST	WEST TO EAST
1955–56	15,226	14,676	1960–61	40,075	40,708
1956–57	20,825	20,182	1961–62	51,893	48,421
1957–58	26,264	24,880	1962–63	55,494	55,668
1958–59	20,299	28,338	1963–64	73,330	67,147
1959–60	34,565	33,897	1964–65	39,471*	37,933*

Source: East Pakistan, Bureau of Statistics, *Statistical Digest of East Pakistan, 1966*, p. 153.
* Note: The figures are for six-month periods, not full years.

Table 2 / East Pakistan population density

DISTRICT	POPULATION (MILLIONS) 1961 CENSUS	DENSITY (PERSONS/ACRE) (THOUSANDS)		
		ON TOTAL LAND AREA	ON NET SOWN AREA	ON GROSS CROPPED AREA
Chittagong	2.98	1.80	5.65	2.90
Comilla	4.39	2.80	4.60	2.30
Dacca	5.10	3.00	4.30	3.10
Noakhali	2.38	2.30	4.15	2.30
Faridpur	3.18	2.05	2.95	1.80
Sylhet	3.49	1.15	2.60	1.70
Pabna	1.96	1.80	2.55	1.75
Barisal (Bakarganj)	4.26	1.85	2.55	1.70
Mymensingh	7.02	1.80	2.50	1.70
Khulna	2.45	.95	2.40	1.95
Chittagong Hill Tracts	.38	.10	2.35	2.05
Bogra	1.57	1.70	2.30	1.70
Rangpur	3.80	1.75	2.20	1.70
Kushtia	1.17	1.40	2.20	1.50
Jessore	2.19	1.35	1.80	1.65
Rajshahi	2.81	1.25	1.75	1.45
Dinajpur	1.71	1.05	1.65	1.40
Total	50.84	1.55	2.70	1.85

Source: Adapted from Roger Revelle and H. A. Thomas, Jr., "Population and Food in East Pakistan," Cambridge: Harvard Center for Population Studies, Harvard University, 1970.

Table 3 / Industrial disputes in East and West Pakistan, 1949–64

	NUMBER OF DISPUTES		NUMBER OF WORKERS INVOLVED		NUMBER OF MAN-DAYS LOST	
	EAST	WEST	EAST	WEST	EAST	WEST
1949	53	19	32,565	12,017	78,804	22,919
1950	21	11	8,231	8,605	35,334	47,830
1951	23	41	11,628	11,182	35,792	41,679
1952	53	42	12,251	15,784	50,026	76,147
1953	52	34	24,308	9,468	64,452	24,606
1954	35	70	19,558	49,795	82,018	213,909
1955	25	50	16,221	25,882	38,940	82,372
1956	56	94	69,923	41,908	179,843	195,064
1957	72	78	145,825	42,176	583,318	227,283
1958	51	42	45,913	14,566	147,451	169,420
1959	7	22	22,488	10,005	35,492	15,500
1960	12	30	6,086	19,663	17,947	60,818
1961	9	45	4,342	21,961	5,711	73,480
1962	34	87	19,627	49,855	119,461	268,386
1963	60	153	109,459	109,142	920,908	902,288
1964*	76	109	170,257	79,910	3,857,775	406,736

Source: Pakistan, Ministry of Economic Affairs, Central Statistical Office, Pakistan, *Statistical Year Book 1965; and '66*, p. 52.
*Figures for 1964 are provisional.

Table 4 / Riots in East and West Pakistan, 1948–66

YEAR	EAST	WEST	YEAR	EAST	WEST
1948	3,125	1,833	1958	4,550	1,346
1949	3,200	1,655	1959	3,232	913
1950	4,039	1,825	1960	4,499	1,114
1951	2,887	1,542	1961	4,777	1,681
1952	2,861	1,818	1962	4,792	609
1953	3,182	1,826	1963	5,182	758
1954	3,620	1,818	1964	5,723	1,086
1955	2,925	1,917	1965	5,626	995
1956	3,723	1,804	1966	6,135	967
1957	4,881	1,575			

Source: Pakistan, Ministry of Economic Affairs, Central Statistical Office, Pakistan, *Statistical Year Book 1967*, p. 516.

Table 5 / Revenue receipts of East Pakistan (million rupees)

YEAR	CUSTOMS	CENTRAL EXCISE DUTIES	CORPORATION TAX	TAXES ON INCOME OTHER THAN CORPORATION TAX	SALES TAX	LAND REVENUE	STAMPS	REHABILITATION TAXES	OTHER SOURCES	TOTAL
REVISED ESTIMATES										
1948–49	35.0	—	—	7.9	—	20.7	20.2	—	71.6	155.4
1949–50	29.2	—	—	6.7	18.0	19.0	17.2	—	38.1	128.2
1950–51	42.5	—	—	7.8	16.5	22.4	20.3	—	46.0	154.5
1951–52	57.9	—	—	6.6	29.1	26.3	25.8	—	25.8	171.5
1952–53	45.3	—	—	18.3	33.3	37.8	24.3	—	37.4	196.4
1953–54	40.0	—	—	21.6	19.3	43.5	23.6	—	40.1	188.1
1954–55	39.7	—	—	25.0	20.3	50.2	21.5	—	41.8	198.5
1955–56	58.1	14.6	—	29.7	20.3	50.8	25.1	—	33.7	232.3
1956–57	45.1	17.5	—	29.8	25.2	51.5	27.5	0.2	37.1	233.9
1957–58	43.3	18.7	—	35.3	25.9	67.5	27.7	0.4	43.4	262.2
1958–59	51.7	26.2	—	57.6	36.2	130.5	40.2	2.0	65.4	409.8
1959–60	47.5	21.6	—	36.9	33.7	93.5	43.5	1.9	55.3	333.9
1960–61	33.0	27.7	—	39.1	52.1	106.7	46.0	3.2	58.1	365.9
1961–62	61.9	26.5	—	44.0	62.2	145.5	45.8	2.5	69.6	458.0
1962–63	45.8	50.9	26.8	106.2	139.7	76.5	45.1	2.7	72.2	565.9
1963–64	44.3	60.5	40.0	125.1	187.1	127.6	43.8	5.3	74.5	708.2
1964–65	26.7	60.3	43.6	135.2	202.6	121.5	45.4	5.9	79.0	720.2
1965–66	14.3	89.0	75.3	190.4	200.1	133.6	57.6	6.6	94.6	861.5
1966–67	18.4	132.3	49.5	203.9	259.8	143.7	57.5	3.9	108.2	977.2
BUDGET ESTIMATES										
1967–68	15.0	120.7	77.2	205.6	257.3	180.0	60.0	4.0	113.8	1,033.6

Source: Pakistan, Ministry of Economic Affairs, Central Statistical Office, *Twenty Years of Pakistan in Statistics, 1947–67*, p. 286.

Table 6 / Revenue receipts of the central government of Pakistan (million rupees)

YEAR	CUSTOMS	CENTRAL EXCISE DUTIES	INCOME TAX AND CORPORATION TAX	SALES TAX	SALT	OTHER SOURCES	TOTAL
REVISED ESTIMATES							
1948–49	329.2	53.4	65.9	41.7	37.6	11.1	538.9
1949–50	422.5	51.5	115.5	89.4	24.4	15.1	718.4
1950–51	776.2	67.2	132.4	71.1	22.2	23.7	1,092.8
1951–52	821.5	70.9	172.3	145.1	25.0	34.0	1,268.8
1952–53	658.9	69.9	175.9	180.1	23.4	39.7	1,097.9
1953–54	361.0	131.6	180.7	86.5	24.4	42.0	826.2
1954–55	416.1	115.5	194.1	106.0	22.1	45.6	899.4
1955–56	557.9	135.0	214.2	137.2	24.0	44.9	1,113.2
1956–57	469.6	144.8	211.4	132.3	19.5	44.2	1,021.8
1957–58	420.5	193.7	240.4	142.7	0.5	50.5	1,048.3
1958–59	493.6	264.1	398.1	170.2	−0.6	64.8	1,390.2
1959–60	561.7	285.5	319.7	170.4	1.0	60.6	1,398.9
1960–61	587.7	343.5	320.6	247.4	6.2	66.2	1,571.6
1961–62	669.0	367.6	358.2	255.2	2.6	37.4	1,717.0
1962–63	735.8	412.8	279.6	244.3	—	8.4	1,680.9
1963–64	703.7	605.6	309.5	256.6	—	2.0	1,877.4
1964–65	1,030.2	697.0	342.3	268.6	—	66.3	2,404.4
1965–66	1,051.0	822.8	280.2	345.5	—	45.1	2,546.6
1966–67	1,229.4	1,227.6	260.8	430.2	—	54.5	3,192.5
BUDGET ESTIMATES							
1967–68	1,441.3	1667.9	346.9	239.4	—	62.1	3,757.6

Source: Adapted from Pakistan, Ministry of Economic Affairs, Central Statistical Office, *Twenty Years of Pakistan in Statistics, 1947–67*, p. 278.

Table 7 / Development loans made available to the provincial governments by the Center

YEAR	MILLION RUPEES		PERCENTAGE DISTRIBUTION	
	EAST	WEST	EAST	WEST
1960–61	298	335	47	53
1961–62	246	317	44	56
1962–63	431	429	50	50
1963–64	677	682	50	50
1964–65	564	540	51	49
Second Five Year Plan annual average	447	461	49	51
1965–66	370	154	71	29
1966–67	958	263	78	22
(Revised budget) 1967–68 (budget)	912	452	67	33
Third Five Year Plan annual average	747	290	72	28

Source: Pakistan, Planning Commission, *The Mid-Plan Review of the Third Five Year Plan 1965–70*, p. 36.

Table 8 / Central Government's grants-in-aid to the two provinces, 1960–68 (budget estimates in million rupees)

	EAST	WEST		EAST	WEST
1959–60	3.4	31.2	1964–65	51.6	222.8
1960–61	4.1	23.7	1965–66	36.1	192.9
1961–62	1.0	241.2	1966–67	44.5	161.3
1962–63	21.5	222.3	1967–68	3.7	148.4
1963–64	42.6	219.2			

Source: Pakistan, Ministry of Economic Affairs, Central Statistical Office, *Twenty Years of Pakistan in Statistics, 1947–67*, pp. 287, 295.

Table 9 / Industrial sanctions given by the Central Investment Promotion and Co-ordination Committee

	NO. CASES	INVESTMENT (RS. IN LAKHS)		APPROVED TOTAL
		INTERNAL	EXTERNAL	
SECOND FIVE YEAR PLAN (1960–65)				
East Pakistan	96	1,123.90	1,680.43	2,304.33
West Pakistan	385	4,627.89	7,981.34	12,609,43
Total	481	5,751.79	9,661.97	15,413.76
1965–67				
East Pakistan	164	1,106.71	1,365.87	2,472.58
West Pakistan	297	3,370.05	4,170.78	7,540.83
Total	461	4,476.76	5,536.65	10,013.41

Source: Pakistan, "Draft Report on Dearth of Private Enterprise in East Pakistan."

Table 10 / Distribution of IDBP loans by regions, 1961–67

	MILLION RUPEES		PERCENTAGE DISTRIBUTION	
	EAST	WEST	EAST	WEST
1961–62	87	81	52	48
1962–63	110	69	62	38
1963–64	195	149	57	43
1964–65	86	150	36	64
1965–66	47	149	24	76
1966–67	151	173	47	53
Total	676	771	47	53

Source: Pakistan, Planning Commission, *The Mid-Plan Review of the Third Five Year Plan 1965-70*, p. 41.

212 / Statistical appendix

Table 11 / Distribution of PICIC loans by regions, 1961–66

	MILLION RUPEES		PERCENTAGE DISTRIBUTION	
	EAST	WEST	EAST	WEST
1961–62	29.01	95.39	23.32	76.68
1962–63	47.02	102.99	31.35	68.65
1963–64	9.06	131.87	6.43	93.57
1964–65	38.21	227.06	14.44	85.56
1965–66	75.63	139.90	35.09	64.91
Total	198.93	697.21	22.20	77.80

Source: Pakistan, Planning Commission, *The Mid-Plan Review of the Third Five Year Plan 1965–70*, p. 41.

Table 12 / Distribution of NIT loans by region, 1962–67 (rupees in lakhs)

	NIT NET SALES	NIT INVESTMENT
East Pakistan	1,13,88,822	279.33
West Pakistan	9,41,21,976	464.50
Jointly in East and West Pakistan		166.22

Source: "Draft Report on Dearth of Private Enterprise in East Pakistan."

Table 13 / Allocation of resources in works program (million rupees)

YEAR	EAST	WEST
1962–63	100.00	
1963–64	200.00	100.00
1964–65	150.00	100.00
1965–66	100.55	87.70
1966–67	121.08	19.60

Sources: Adapted from Pakistan, Planning Commission, *The Mid-Plan Review of the Third Five Year Plan 1965–70*, pp. 267–68. and *Final Evaluation of the Second Five Year Plan*, pp. 130.

Table 14 / Physical achievements of works program in East Pakistan

ITEMS OF WORK	1962–63	1963–64	1964–65	1965–66	1966–67
Kutcha roads (miles)	20,920	27,553	28,410	17,841	16,678
Pucca roads (miles)	48	4,928	1,080	742	446
Bridges and culverts (nos)	7,428	103,798	300,415	8,585	20,565
Drainage and canals (miles)	920	1,248	5,357	953	1,562
Embankments (miles)	258	1,842	3,654	1,560	1,560
Union community centers		2,307	1,742	586	
Coastal community centers		79		22	
Thana training and development centers		244	230	225	

Sources: Adapted from Pakistan, Planning Commission, *The Mid-Plan Review of the Third Five Year Plan 1965-70* p. 262. and *Final Evaluation of the Second Five Year Plan,* p. 132.

Table 15 / Export earnings of East and West Pakistan
(million rupees)

YEAR	EAST	WEST	EAST PAKISTAN'S SHARE IN TOTAL EARNINGS (PERCENT)
1900–01	1,259	540	70
1961–62	1,301	543	70
1962–63	1,249	998	55
1963–64	1,224	1,070	54
1964–65	1,268	1,140	53
1965–66	1,514	1,204	55
1966–67	1,660	1,325	56
Annual rate of Growth (compounded)	4.6	16.1	

Source: Pakistan, Planning Commission, *The Mid-Plan Review of the Third Five Year Plan 1965-70,* p. 38.

Table 16 / Development of medical facilities in East and West Pakistan, 1959–66

YEAR	HOSPITALS		MATERNITY AND CHILD WELFARE CENTERS		BEDS IN HOPITALS AND DISPENSARIES		REGISTERED DOCTORS		NURSES	
	EAST	WEST	EAST	WEST	EAST	WEST	EAST	WEST	EAST	WEST
1959	71	338	38	349	4,472	22,658	5,060	5,615	321	2,167
1960	71	343	48	384	4,973	22,100	5,492	6,132	349	2,311
1961	71	345	55	422	5,295	22,394	5,841	6,902	384	2,417
1962	71	365	55	449	5,295	22,775	6,149	7,543	439	2,580
1963	72	369	55	488	5,507	23,429	6,373	8,269	442	2,829
1964	72	368	55	524	5,829	23,664	6,608	9,061	493	2,989
1965	76	383	55	554	6,984	25,603	6,864	9,725	534	3,292
1966	76	393	55	711	6,984	26,200	6,989	10,488	564	3,438

Source: Pakistan, Ministry of Economic Affairs, Central Statistical Office, *Twenty Years of Pakistan in Statistics, 1947–67*, pp. 162–63.

Table 17 / Student enrollment, 1959–66

YEAR	PRIMARY SCHOOLS		SECONDARY SCHOOLS		COLLEGES		UNIVERSITIES	
	EAST	WEST	EAST	WEST	EAST	WEST	EAST	WEST
1959–60	3,180,367	1,547,910	530,485	912,485	52,145	88,128	3,766	4,092
1960–61	3,330,582	1,705,962	532,902	960,606	51,883	82,794	3,970	5,084
1961–62	3,423,232	1,907,058	574,867	982,290	62,257	84,198	5,817	7,214
1962–63	3,636,497	2,086,228	659,345	1,109,149	80,452	108,387	7,140	9,464
1963–64	3,852,322	2,299,738	755,617	1,239,961	100,171	131,661	7,664	10,078
1964–65	4,044,179	2,532,324	848,512	1,369,416	115,264	141,779	9,714	14,381
1965–66	4,236,036	2,763,670	949,486	1,481,094	133,228	155,848	8,831	18,708

Source: Adapted from Pakistan, Ministry of Economic Affairs, Central Statistical Office, *Twenty Years of Pakistan in Statistics, 1947–67*, pp. 170–73, 184–86.

Statistical appendix

Table 18 / Regional growth of transport and communications, 1959–67

YEAR	ROUTE MILEAGE OF RAILWAYS		ROAD MILEAGE		NO. OF MOTOR VEHICLES	
	EAST	WEST	EAST	WEST	EAST	WEST
1959–60	1,715	5,237	1,040	19,684	14,410	109,228
1960–61	1,713	5,327	1,190	20,381	16,850	126,848
1961–62	1,713	5,327	1,342	20,990	23,742	145,181
1962–63	1,713	5,327	1,542	21,007	30,114	165,303
1963–64	1,713	5,327	1,794	21,397	35,805	189,070
1964–65	1,713	5,334	2,113	21,758	42,560	218,466
1965–66	1,713	5,335	2,262	22,036	47,471	234,626
1966–67	1,713	5,335	2,588	22,508	56,285	259,395

Source: Pakistan, Ministry of Economic Affairs, Central Statistical Office, *Twenty Years of Pakistan in Statistics, 1947–67*, pp. 149–51, 153–54.

Table 19 / Regional differences in cost of living, 1959–67*

YEAR	EAST	WEST	YEAR	EAST	WEST
1959–60	100.0	100.0	1963–64	102.6	106.4
1960–61	102.8	104.8	1964–65	111.3	113.6
1961–62	106.8	104.7	1965–66	122.8	112.0
1962–63	106.2	102.9	1966–67	141.4	124.5

Source: Pakistan, Ministry of Economic Affairs, Central Statistical Office, *Twenty Years of Pakistan in Statistics, 1947–67*, p. 198.
*Note: The year of 1959–60 is taken as the base (=100).

Table 20 / Development of communications, 1958-66 (by region)

YEAR	RADIO LICENSES ISSUED		ENGLISH NEWSPAPERS AND PERIODICALS		BENGALI NEWSPAPERS AND PERIODICALS		URDU NEWSPAPERS AND PERIODICALS	
	EAST	WEST	EAST	WEST	EAST	WEST	EAST	WEST
1959	28,861	284.977	57	166	152		4	780
1960	37,713	293,607	65	82	182		6	626
1961	41,213	369,923	64	65	197		8	596
1962	3,125	438,990	73	62	210		6	587
1963	115,714	455,767	81	205	229	1	3	772
1964	190,008	491,938	87	185	250	1	3	710
1965	242,361	592,602	95	175	265	1	3	706
1966	283,755	725,188	92	184	271	1	4	716

Sources: Pakistan, Ministry of Economic Affairs, Central Statistical Office, *Pakistan Statistical Year Book, 1965-66*, p. 289; and *Twenty Years of Pakistan in Statistics, 1947-67*, p. 190.

Table 21 / Membership in Registered Trade Unions in Pakistan (at year end)

	NUMBER OF UNIONS	TOTAL MEMBERSHIP		NUMBER OF UNIONS	TOTAL MEMBERSHIP
1950	251	....	1959	618	3.47,522
1951	209	3.93,137	1960	708	3.50,604
1952	352	3.94,923	1961	723	3.98,723
1953	394	4.24,563	1962	789	4.17,248
1954	382	4.10,755	1963	831	4.87,355
1955	474	3.25,610	1964	898	4.02,322
1956	524	3.16,642	1965	965	5.12,225
1957	611	3.66,317	1966	1,010	5.22,161
1958	621	3.37,064			

Source: Pakistan, Ministry of Health, Labour and Social Welfare, *Pakistan Labour Gazette* XVI (1968), 440.

Bibliography

PUBLIC DOCUMENTS

Government of East Bengal (unless otherwise indicated, published in Dacca by the East Bengal Government Press)

East Bengal. *Memorandum on Allocation of Revenue Between the Central and the Provincial Governments of Pakistan for Presentation to the Export Committee,* 1951.
— *The Report of Enquiry into Firing on 21 February, 1952.*
— Legislative Assembly, *Debates.* Vols. 1-8 (1948-1952).
— S. & G. A. Department. *The East Bengal Civil List, 1950; 1955.*

Government of East Pakistan (unless otherwise indicated, published in Dacca by the East Pakistan Government Press)

East Pakistan. *Assembly Proceedings.* Official Report. Vol. 9 (1955-57).
— Basic Democracies and Local Government Department. *Rural Works Programme Report,* 1963-64.
— Basic Democracies and Local Government Department. *Works Programme for 1964-65 for East Pakistan,* 1965.
— Basic Democracies and Local Government Department. *Performance Report on Rural Works Programme, 1964-65; 1965-66.*

—— National Planning Board. *The First Five Year Plan, 1955–60.* 1957.
—— Pakistan Academy for Rural Development, Comilla. *An Evaluation of the Rural Public Works Programme, East Pakistan, 1962–63.*
—— Pakistan Academy for Rural Development, Comilla. *A Manual for Rural Public Works.* August 1962.
—— Pakistan Academy for Rural Development, Comilla. *The Public Works Program and a Development Proposal for East Pakistan.* May 1963.
—— Pakistan Academy for Rural Development, Comilla. *Report on a Rural Public Works Programme in Comilla Kotwali Thana.* June 1962.
—— Pakistan Academy for Rural Development, Comilla; and Bureau of National Reconstruction. *An Analysis of the Working of Basic Democracy Institutions in East Pakistan.* 1961.
—— Pakistan Academy for Rural Development, Comilla; and Bureau of National Reconstruction. *Four Studies in Basic Democracy.* n.d.
—— Planning Commission. *Report of the Panel of Economists on the Second Five Year Plan.* 1959.
—— Planning Commission. *The Second Five Year Plan, 1960–65.* 1961.
—— Planning Commission. *Preliminary Evaluation of Progress During the Second Five Year Plan.* 1965.
—— Planning Commission, *Final Evaluation of the Second Five Year Plan.* 1966.
—— Planning Commission. *The Guidelines for the Third Five Year Plan.* 1963.
—— Planning Commission. *Outline of the Third Five Year Plan, 1965–70.* 1964.
—— Planning Commission. *The Third Five Year Plan, 1965–70.* 1965.
—— Planning Commission. *The Mid-Plan Review of the Third Five Year Plan 1965–70.* April 1968.
—— Planning Commission. *Socio-economic Objectives of the Fourth Five Year Plan, 1970–75.* 1968.
—— Planning Commission. *An Outline of the Fourth Five Year Plan (1970–75).* 1970.
—— Planning Division. *Growth Rates of Labor Productivity and Related Coefficients Needed for Projecting Sectoral Employment Composition of the Fourth Plan.* 1967.
—— Planning Division, Manpower Section. *Selected Tables on Projections of Education and Labor Force for Pakistan and Provinces, 1960–1990.* 1969.
United Nations. Department of Economic and Social Affairs. *Statistical Year Book, 1967.*
—— Economic Commission for Asia and the Far East. *Economic Bulletin for Asia and the Far East.* Vols. X–XIX (1959–68).
West Pakistan. *Land Reforms Commission Report, 1959.* Lahore: West Pakistan Government Press, 1959.

OTHER MATERIALS

Abbot, Freeland K. "Pakistan's New Marriage Law: A Reflection of Quranic Interpretation." *Asian Survey*, I (1962), 26–32.

— "The Jama'at-i-Islami of Pakistan," *Middle East Journal,* XI (1957), 37-51.
Afzal, K. Ali. "Bengali Muslim's Art of Warfare," *The Pakistan Observer,* September 6, 1966.
Ahmad, Abul Mansur. *Āmār Dekha Rajnitir Panchāsa Bachara* [Fifty years of politics as I saw it]. Dacca: Nauroj, 1968.
— "Are We in for One Party System," *The Pakistan Observer,* August 14, 1965.
— "Assassination of a Grand Concept," *The Pakistan Observer,* October 27, 1966.
— "Is Parity a Practical Proposition," *The Pakistan Observer,* December 25, 1963.
— *Pak Banglar Culture* [Culture of East Bengal]. Dacca: Ahmad Publishing House, 1966.
— "Political Development vis-a-vis National Integration," *The Pakistan Observer,* August 14, 1966.
— "Secularism versus Religion in Pakistan," *The Concept of Pakistan,* No. 4, November, 1964.
Ahmad, Aziz. "Cultural and Intellectual Trends in Pakistan," *Middle East Journal,* XIX (1965), 35-44.
Ahmad, Jamilud Din, ed. *Speeches and Writings of Mr. Jinnah,* Vol. I. Lahore: Ashraf, 1960; Vol. II. Lahore: Ashraf, 1964.
Ahmad, Kamruddin. *A Social History of East Pakistan.* Dacca: Crescent Bookstore, 1967.
— "Whither East Pakistan," *The Dacca Times,* February 21, 1965.
Ahmad, Khurshid. *An Analysis of the Munir Report.* Karachi: Jama'at-i-Islami, 1956.
— ed. *Studies in the Family Law of Islam.* Karachi: Chiragh e Rah Publications, 1959.
Ahmad, Muneer. *The Civil Servant in Pakistan.* Karachi: Oxford University Press, 1964.
Ahmad, Mushtaq. *Government and Politics in Pakistan.* Second Edition. Karachi: Pakistan Publishing House, 1963.
Ahmad, Nafis. *The Economic Geography of East Pakistan.* London: Oxford University Press, 1958.
Ahmed, Manzooruddin. *Pakistan: The Emerging Islamic State.* Karachi: Allies Book Corporation, 1966.
Ahmed, Mohammad, *My Chief.* Lahore: Longmans, Green & Co. 1960.
Ali, Chaudhri Muhammad. *An Appraisal of Pakistan's Economic Development.* Karachi: Nizam-i-Islam, 1966.
— *Corruption as an Impediment to Economic Development.* Karachi: Nizam-i-Islam, n.d.
— *The Emergence of Pakistan.* New York: Columbia University Press, 1967.
— *A Programme for Pakistan.* Karachi: Nizam-i-Islam, 1963.
Ali, Choudhury Rahmat. *Pakistan.* London: Pakistan National Liberation Movement, 1946.

Ali, Tayyeb. *Pakistan: A Political Geography.* London: Oxford University Press, 1966.
Allana, G. *Pakistan Movement Historic Documents.* Karachi: Paradise Subscription Agency, n.d.
Almond, Gabriel A. and J. S. Coleman, eds. *The Politics of the Developing Areas.* Princeton: Princeton University Press, 1960.
—— and B. Powell. *Comparative Politics.* Toronto: Little, Brown & Company, 1966.
—— and Sidney Verba. *The Civic Culture.* Princeton: Princeton University Press, 1963.
Ambedkar, R. R. *Pakistan or the Partition of India.* Bombay: Thacker, 1946.
Andrus, J. R. *The Economy of Pakistan.* Stanford: Stanford University Press, 1958.
—— and Azizali F. Mohammad. *Trade, Finance and Development in Pakistan.* Stanford: Stanford University Press, 1966.
Apter, David. *The Politics of Modernization.* Chicago: University of Chicago Press, 1965.
Ayub Khan, Mohammad. *Friends Not Masters: A Political Autobiography.* London: Oxford University Press, 1967.
—— *Pakistan Perspective.* Washington, D.C.: Embassy of Pakistan, n.d.
—— "Pakistan Perspectives," *Foreign Affairs,* XXXVIII (1960), 547–56.
—— *Speeches and Statements, 1958–1964.* 8 Vols. Karachi: Ferozsons, n.d.
Azam, Ghulam. *A Guide to the Islamic Movement.* Dacca: Azami Publications, 1968.
Barth, Frederick. *Political Leadership among the Pathans.* New York: Humanities Press, 1959.
Bartlett, Harvey. "Organizing Rural Development in Bengal." Paper presented at the Center for International Affairs Seminar, Harvard University, 1967.
Becker, Mary L. "The All India Muslim League, 1906–1947: A Study of Leadership in the Evolution of a Nation." Ph.D. dissertation, Radcliffe College, Cambridge, Mass., 1957.
Bertocci, Peter J. "Patterns of Social Organizations in Rural East Bengal." Paper presented at the Fifth Annual Conference on Bengal, Urbana, Ill. 1968.
Bessaignet, Pierre. *Social Research in East Pakistan.* Dacca: University of Dacca, 1960.
—— *Tribesmen of the Chittagong Hill Tracts.* Dacca: Asiatic Society of Pakistan, 1958.
Bhasani, Maulana Abdul Hamid Khan. *Mao Tse-tung er Deshe* [In the land of Mao Tse-tung]. Dacca: Punthi Patra, 1968.
Bhutto, Z. A. *The Myth of Independence.* Lahore: Oxford University Press, 1969.
—— *The Political Situation in Pakistan.* Karachi: n.d.
Binder, Leonard. "National Integration and Political Development," *American Political Science Review,* LVIII (1964), 622–31.

—— *Religion and Politics in Pakistan.* Berkely: University of California Press, 1961.
Birkhead, Guthrie S., ed. *Administrative Problems in Pakistan.* Syracuse: Syracuse University Press, 1966.
Black, Cyril E. *The Dynamics of Modernization: A Study in Comparative History.* New York: Harper and Row, 1966.
Bolitho, H. *Jinnah: Creator of Pakistan.* London: J. Murray, 1954.
Bondurant, John V. *Regionalism and Provincialism: A Study in Problems of Indian Nationality.* Berkeley: University of California Press, 1958.
Bose, Swadesh R. "Labour Force and Employment in Pakistan, 1961–1986: A Preliminary Analysis," *The Pakistan Development Review,* III (1963), 371–98.
—— "Trend of Real Income of the Rural Poor in East Pakistan, 1949–66," *The Pakistan Development Review,* VIII (1968), 452–88.
Braibanti, Ralph. "The Civil Service of Pakistan: A Theoretical Analysis," *South Atlantic Quarterly,* LVIII (1959), 258–304.
—— "Pakistan: Constitutional Issues in 1964," *Asian Survey,* V (1965), 79–87.
—— "Reflections on Bureaucratic Corruption," *Public Administration,* XL (1962), 357–72.
—— *Research on the Bureaucracy of Pakistan.* Durham, N.C.: Duke University Press, 1966.
—— and J. Spengler, eds. *Administration and Economic Development in India.* Durham, N.C.: Duke University Press, 1963.
—— et al. *Asian Bureaucratic Systems Emergent from the British Imperial Tradition.* Durham, N.C.: Duke University Press, 1966.
Brines, Russell. *The Indo-Pakistani Conflict.* London: Pall Mall Press, 1968.
Broomfield, J. H. *Elite Conflict in a Plural Society: Twentieth Century Bengal.* Berkeley: University of California Press, 1968.
Burki, S. J. "Interest Group Involvement in West Pakistan's Rural Works Program." Seminar paper, Harvard University, 1968.
—— "Twenty Years of the Civil Service in Pakistan: A Reevaluation," *Asian Survey,* IX (1969), 239–54.
—— "West Pakistan's Rural Works Program: A Study in Political and Administrative Response," *Middle East Journal,* XXIII (1969), 321–42.
Callard, Keith. *Pakistan: A Political Study.* New York: The Macmillan Company, 1957.
—— *Political Forces in Pakistan, 1947–59.* New York: Institute of Pacific Relations, 1959.
—— "The Political Stability of Pakistan," *Pacific Affairs,* XXIX (1956), 5–20.
Campbell, Robert D. *Pakistan: Emerging Democracy.* Princeton: Von Nostrand, 1963.
Caroe, Olaf. *The Pathans.* London: The Macmillan Company. 1958.
The Challenge of Disparity. Dacca: National Association for Social and Economic Progress, n.d.

Chaudhuri, M. A. *The Civil Service in Pakistan.* Dacca: National Institute of Public Administration, 1963.
Choudhury, G. W. *Constitutional Development in Pakistan.* New York: Institute of Pacific Relations, 1959.
—— *Democracy in Pakistan.* Dacca: Green Book House, 1963.
—— "Democracy on Trial in Pakistan," *Middle East Journal,* XVII (1963), 1–13.
—— *Documents and Speeches on the Constitution of Pakistan.* Dacca: Green Book House, 1967.
—— "The East Pakistan Political Scene," *Pacific Affairs,* XXX (1957), 312–20.
—— "Failure of Parliamentary Democracy in Pakistan," *Parliamentary Affairs,* XII (1959), 60–70.
—— and Parvez Hasan. *Pakistan's External Relations.* Karachi: Pakistan Institute for International Affairs, 1958.
Coleman, James S. and Carl G. Roseberg, eds. *Political Parties and National Integration in Tropical Africa.* Berkeley, Calif.: University of California Press, 1962.
Committee for Restoration of Democracy in Pakistan. *Betrayal in Pakistan: Story of a Country Oppressed by Its Defenders.* London: F. J. Lamb (printers), n.d.
Curle, Adam. *Planning For Education in Pakistan.* Cambridge, Mass: Harvard University Press, 1965.
Dahl, R. A. *Modern Political Analysis.* Englewood Cliffs: Prentice-Hall, 1964.
—— *Who Governs?* New Haven: Yale University Press, 1964.
Davis, Kingsley. *The Population of India and Pakistan.* Princeton: Princeton University Press, 1951.
Deane, Philip. "The Men Who Really Run Pakistan," *The Reporter,* January 7, 1955, pp. 30–34.
Deutsch, Karl W. *Nationalism and Social Communication.* Cambridge, Mass. M.I.T. Press, 1966.
—— *The Nerves of Government: Models of Political Communication and Control.* New York: Free Press of Glencoe, 1963.
—— "Social Mobilization and Political Development," *American Political Science Review,* LV (1961), 493–514.
—— and William J. Foltz, eds. *Nation-Building.* New York: Atherton Press, 1963.
Dil, Anwar S., ed. *Perspectives on Pakistan.* Abbottabad, Pakistan: Book Service, 1965.
Dorfman, R. "Economic Strategy for West Pakistan," *Asian Survey,* III (1963), 217–23.
D'yakov, A. M., ed. *Pakistan: History and Economy.* Moscow: U.S.S.R. Academy of Science, Institute of Oriental Studies, 1959.
East Pakistan Awami League. *Gathantantra o Niomabali* [Constitution and rules]. Dacca: General Secretary, East Pakistan Awami League, 1954; 1964.

—— *Niti o Karmasuchi* [Manifesto]. Dacca: August 1, 1969.
—— "Proceedings of the Meetings of the Working Committee." Typescript. Dacca, July 4–5, 1964.
—— "Proceedings of Meetings of the Working Committee." Typescript. Dacca, June 5–6, 1965.
—— *Report of the General Secretary* [in Bengali]. Dacca: June 4, 1970.
—— *Why Autonomy?* Dacca: n.d.
Easton, David. *A Systems Analysis of Political Life.* New York: John Wiley and Sons, 1965.
Eglar, Zekiye. *A Punjabi Village in Pakistan.* New York: Columbia University Press, 1960.
Emerson, Rupert. *From Empire to Nation.* Cambridge, Mass: Harvard University Press, 1960.
Faruqi, M. I. *Jama'at-e-Islami Pakistan.* Lahore: Secretary, Information Bureau, Jama'at-i-Islami, 1957.
Feldman, Herbert. *Revolution in Pakistan: A Study of the Martial Law Administration.* London: Oxford University Press, 1967.
—— *A Constitution for Pakistan.* Karachi: Oxford University Press, 1956.
Franda, M. F. "Communism and Regional Politics in East Pakistan," *Asian Survey,* X (1970), 588–606.
—— *West Bengal and the Federalizing Process in India.* Princeton: Princeton University Press, 1968.
Frankel, Francine. "India's New Strategy of Agricultural Development: Political Costs of Agrarian Modernization," *Journal of Asian Studies,* XXVIII (1969), 693–710.
Frey, Frederick. *The Turkish Political Elite.* Cambridge, Mass: M.I.T. Press, 1965.
Friedman, Harry J. "Pakistan's Experiment in Basic Democracies," *Pacific Affairs,* XXXIII (1960), 107–25.
Gafur, Abdul. "A Comparison of the Interregional Wages in Pakistan," *The Pakistan Development Review,* VII (1967), 533–43.
Gankovsky, Y. V. and L. R. Gordon-Polonskaya. *A History of Pakistan.* Moscow: "NAUKA" Publishing House, 1964.
Geertz, Clifford, ed. *Old Societies and New States.* New York: Free Press of Glencoe, 1963.
Ghouse, Agha M., ed. *Economic Planning and Development in Pakistan.* Karachi: Trade and Industry Publications, 1965.
Ghulam Muhammed, Chaudhry. *Jama'at-e-Islami and Foreign Policy.* Karachi: Dar-ut-Tansif, n.d.
Gilbert, Richard V. "Works Programme in East Pakistan," *International Labour Review,* LXXXIX (1964), 213–26.
Goodnow, Henry F. *The Civil Service of Pakistan: Bureaucracy in a New Nation.* New Haven: Yale University Press, 1964.

Gordon, Leonard. "Bengal and the Indian National Movement." Ph.D. dissertation, Harvard University, Cambridge, Mass., 1969.
Gorvine, Albert. "The Civil Service Under the Revolutionary Government in Pakistan," *Middle East Journal*, XIX (1965), 321–36.
Gould, Peter. "Tanzania, 1920–63: The Spatial Impress of the Modernization Process," *World Politics*, XXII (1970), 149–70.
Griffiths, Percival J. *The British Impact on India*. London: Macdonald, 1952.
Gupta, Sisir K. "Some Aspects of Pakistani Planning," *India Quarterly*, XVIII (1962), 111–33.
Habibullah, M. *Some Aspects of Rural Capital Formation in East Pakistan*. Dacca: Dacca University, Bureau of Economic Research, 1963.
Hai, Mohammad Abdul. *Sahitya o Sanskriti* [Literature and culture]. Dacca: Student Ways, 1965.
Haq, Khadiza. "A Measurement of Inequality of Urban Personal Income Distribution in Pakistan," *The Pakistan Development Review*, IV (1964), 623–64.
Haq, Mahbub ul. "Plan: Agriculture Takes Second Place," *The Times* (London), Supplement on Pakistan, August 14, 1963.
—— "Planning Machinery in Pakistan," *Finance and Industry*, IV (1965), 39–46.
—— "Planning Strategy in East Pakistan," *Trade and Industry*, IX (1965), 437–55.
—— "Problems of Formulating a Development Strategy for Pakistan's Third Plan," *Pakistan Management Review*, V (1964), 16–27.
—— *The Strategy of Economic Planning: A Case of Study of Pakistan*. Lahore: Oxford University Press, 1963.
Harrison, Selig S. *India: The Most Dangerous Decades*. Princeton: Princeton University Press, 1960.
Hashim, Abul. *Integration of Pakistan*. Dacca: Syed Mujuballah, 1962.
Hayes, Carlton J. *Essays on Nationalism*. New York: The Macmillan Company, 1926.
—— *Nationalism: A Religion*. New York: The Macmillan Company, 1960.
Hossain, Tafazzal. "From Sovereign Bengal to Civil War," *The Dacca Times*, March 25, 1966.
Hunter, William W. *The Indian Mussalmans*. London: Trubner and Co., 1872.
Huntington, Samuel P. *Political Order in Changing Societies*. New Haven: Yale University Press, 1968.
—— ed. *Changing Patterns of Military Politics*. New York: Free Press of Glencoe, 1962.
Huq, A. M. "Pakistan's Economic Development (1949–58)," *Pacific Affairs*, XXXII (1959), 144–61.
Huq, Mahfuzul. *Electoral Problems in Pakistan*. Dacca: Asiatic Society, 1966.
—— "The Electorate System in Pakistan: An Analysis of the Problem of Minority Representation." Ph.D. dissertation, Columbia University, 1964.
—— "Federalism and Provincialism," *The Pakistan Observer*, March 23, 1965.
Hurewitz, J. C. *Middle East Politics: The Military Dimension*. New York: Praeger, 1969.

Husain, A. F. A. *Human and Social Impact of Technological Change in Pakistan.* Dacca: Oxford University Press, 1956.

—— and M. N. Huda. *Problems of Economic Reform and Development in Pakistan.* Karachi: Pakistan Institute of International Affairs, 1950.

Husain, Muhammad. *East Pakistan: A Cultural Survey.* Karachi: Pakistan P.E.N. Centre, 1955.

Husain, Syed Sajjad. "The Problem of National Integration in Pakistan," *The Pakistan Observer,* June 17, 1967.

—— ed. *East Pakistan: A Profile.* Dacca: Orient Longmans, 1962.

—— ed. *Pakistan: An Anthology.* Dacca: The Society for Pakistan Studies, 1964.

Ikram, S. M. *Modern Muslim India and the Birth of Pakistan.* Lahore: S. M. Ashraf, 1965.

—— and P. Spear, eds. *The Cultural Heritage of Pakistan.* London: Oxford University Press, 1955.

Inayatullah. *Basic Democracies, District Administration and Development.* Peshawar: Pakistan Academy for Rural Development, 1964.

—— *Bureaucracy and Development in Pakistan.* Peshawar: Academy for Rural Development, 1963.

Irshad Khan, Mohammad. "A Note on Consumption Patterns in the Rural Areas of East Pakistan," *The Pakistan Development Review,* III (1963), 399–413.

Islam, Nurul. "Concepts and Measurement of Unemployment and Underemployment in Developing Economies," *International Labour Review,* LXXXXIX (1964), 240–56.

—— "Private and Public Enterprises in the Economic Development of Pakistan," *Asian Survey,* III (1963), 338–46.

—— *A Short Term Model for Pakistan.* Karachi: Oxford University Press, 1965.

—— "Some Aspects of Interwing Trade and Terms of Trade in Pakistan," *The Pakistan Development Review,* III (1963), 1–36.

Ispahani, M. A. H. *Quaid-e-Azam Jinnah: As I Knew Him.* Karachi: Forward Publication, 1966.

Jafri, Rais Ahmad, ed. *Ayub Soldier and Statesman.* Lahore: Mohammad Ali Academy, 1966.

Jama'at-i-Islami. *Arthanayitik Samassayar Islami Samadhan* [Islamic solution of economic problems]. Dacca: n.d.

—— *Bhabiswater Karya Shuchi* [Program for the future]. Dacca: n.d.

—— *Islami Adarshe Nirbachan* [Election according to Islamic principles]. Dacca: n.d.

—— *Islami Beplaber Path* [Path to Islamic revolution]. Dacca: n.d.

—— *Islami Samaje Mozoorer Adhikar* [Labor's right in an Islamic society]. Dacca: n.d.

—— *Islami Shashantantra Moolnity* [Principles of Islamic constitution]. Dacca: n.d.

—— *Jama'at-e-Islami Gathantantra* [Constitution of the Jama'at-i-Islam]. Dacca: n.d.

—— *Programme for Social Uplift.* Karachi: n.d.
Janowitz, Morris. *The Military in the Political Development of New Nations.* Chicago: University of Chicago Press, 1964.
Jennings, Sir Ivor. *Constitutional Problems in Pakistan.* London: Oxford University Press, 1957.
Jillani, M. S. "Changes in Levels of Educational Attainment in Pakistan," *The Pakistan Development Review,* IV (1964), 69–92.
Jinnah, Quaid-i-Azam M. A. *Quaid-i-Azam Mohamed Ali Jinnah Speaks: Post-Independence Speeches* Comp. by Syed Muhammad Latif. Lahore: Ferozsons, n.d.
—— *Selected Speeches and Statements of the Quaid-i-Azam Mohamed Ali Jinnah: 1911–34 and 1947–48.* Ed. by M. R. Afzal. Lahore: Research Society of Pakistan, 1966.
—— *Speeches: As Governor-General of Pakistan, 1947–48.* Karachi: Pakistan Publications, n.d.
Johnson, J., ed. *The Role of the Military in Underdeveloped Countries.* Princton: Princeton University Press, 1962.
Kahin, George M., ed. *Government and Politics of Southeast Asia.* Ithaca: Cornell University Press, 1963.
Karim, Nazmul. *Changing Society in India and Pakistan: A Study in Social Change and Social Stratification.* Dacca: Oxford University Press, 1956.
Kaufman, R. H. "Problems in Pakistan's Prosperity," *Pacific Affairs,* XXXV (1962), 59–65.
Kautsky, John H., ed. *Political Change in Underdeveloped Countries: Nationalism and Communism.* New York: John Wiley and Sons, 1962.
Khaliquzzaman, Choudhury. *Pathway to Pakistan.* Lahore: Longmans, 1961.
Khan, Aftab Ahmad. "On Planning in Pakistan," *The Pakistan Development Review,* IV (1964), 107–21.
Khan, Ali Ahmad. *Jama'at-e-Islami, Pakistan.* Dacca: Al Helal Press, n.d.
Khan, Ataur Rahman. *Ojaratir Dui Pachar* [Two years of chief ministership]. Dacca: Avijan Printing House, 1964.
Khan, Azizur Rahman. "A Multi Sector Programming Model for Regional Planning in Pakistan," *The Pakistan Development Review,* VII (1967), 29–65.
—— "What Has Been Happening to Real Wages in Pakistan?" *The Pakistan Development Review,* VII (1967), 317–47.
—— and A. MacEwan. "A Multi Sectoral Analysis of Capital Requirements for Development Planning in Pakistan," *The Pakistan Development Review,* VII (1967), 445–84.
Khan, Ayub, *see* Ayub Khan, Mohammad.
Khan, Azam, *see* Khan, Mohammad Azam.
Khan, Fazal Muqeem. *The Story of the Pakistan Army.* Karachi: Oxford University Press, 1963.
Khan, Liaquat Ali. *Pakistan: The Heart of Asia.* Cambridge: Harvard University Press, 1950.

Khan, Mohammad Azam, "National Integration: Unfettered Democracy Is a Must," *The Pakistan Observer,* August 14, 1965.
Khan, Muin-ud-Din Ahmad. *Muslim Struggle for Freedom in Bengal (1757-1947).* Dacca: Orient Longmans, 1955.
Khan, S. U. "A Measure of Economic Growth in East and in West Pakistan," *The Pakistan Development Review,* I. (1961), 49-54.
Khan, Tahawar Ali, ed. *Bibliographical Encyclopedia of Pakistan.* Lahore: Bibliographical Research Institute, 1961.
Khilafat-e-Rabbani Party. *Election Manifesto.* Dacca: 1954.
Khokhar, B. "Changing Rural Panorama: Land Reforms in West Pakistan," *Dawn,* February 6, 1966.
Kohn, Hans. *Nationalism: Its Meaning and History.* Princeton: Von Nostrand, 1955.
— *Prophets and Peoples: Studies in Ninetheenth Century Nationalism.* New York: The Macmillan Company, 1946.
Lambert, Richard D. "Factors in Bengali Regionalism in Pakistan," *Far Eastern Survey,* XIII (1959), 49-58.
— "Religion, Economics and Violence in Bengal," *Middle East Journal,* IV (1950), 307-28.
La Palombara, Joseph, ed. *Bureaucracy and Political Development.* Princeton: Princeton University Press, 1963.
— and Myron Weiner, eds. *Political Parties and Political Development.* Princeton: Princeton University Press, 1966.
Lerner, Daniel. *The Passing of Traditional Society.* Glencoe, Ill.: Free Press, 1958.
Lewis, Stephen. "Some Problems in the Analysis of Dual Economy," *The Pakistan Development Review,* III (1963), 527-46.
Linck, Orville F. *A Passage through Pakistan.* Detroit: Wayne State University Press, 1959.
Livingston, W. S. *Federalism and Constitutional Change.* London: Clarendon Press, 1966.
Macaulay, Thomas B. *Critical, Historical and Miscellenous Essays.* Boston: Houghton Mifflin, 1860.
Mahmood, Abu. "Language Movement: Social and Economic Background," *The Dacca Times,* February 21, 1965.
Majumdar, R. C. *Glimpses of Bengal in the Nineteenth Century.* Calcutta: Firma K. L. Muknopadhay, 1960.
— ed. *History of the Freedom Movement in India.* 3 vols. Calcutta: Firma K. L. Mukhopadhay, 1963.
Malik, Hafeez. *Moslem Nationalism in India and Pakistan.* Washington, D.C.: Public Affairs Press, 1963.
Mallick, A. R. *British Policy and the Muslims in Bengal, 1757-1856.* Dacca: Asiatic Society of Pakistan, 1961.
Maniruzzaman, Talukdar. "'Crises in Political Development' and the Collapse

of the Ayub Regime in Pakistan," *The Journal of Developing Areas*, V (1971), 221–38.

—— "Group Interest in Pakistan Politics 1947–58," *Pacific Affairs*, XXXIX (1966), 83–98.

—— "The Leftist Movement in East Pakistan—Leadership, Factionalism, Doctrinal and Tactical Dilemmas." Unpublished paper, Rajshahi University, 1970.

—— "National Integration and Political Development in Pakistan," *Asian Survey*, VII (1967). 876–85.

—— "Political Activism of the University Students in Pakistan. Unpublished paper, Rajshahi University, 1970.

—— "Political Development in Pakistan, 1955–58." Ph.D. dissertation, Queen's University, Kingston, 1966.

Maron, Stanley. "A New Phase in Pakistan Politics," *Far Eastern Survey*, XXIV (1955), 161–65.

—— "The Problems of East Pakistan," *Pacific Affairs*, XXVIII (1955), 132–44.

—— ed. *Pakistan: Society and Culture*. New Haven: Human Relations Area Files, 1957.

Marshall, Charles B. "Reflections on a Revolution in Pakistan," *Foreign Affairs*, XXXVII (1959), 247–56.

—— "Testimony Before the Committee on Foreign Affairs," U.S. Congress, House, Committee on Foreign Affairs. *Review of the Mutual Security Programs, Hearings: Before a Sub-Committee of the Committee on Foreign Affairs*. Washington, D.C.: U.S. Government Printing Office, 1959.

Matheson, Sylvia A. *The Tigers of Baluchistan*. London: Arthur Barker, 1967.

Maudoodi, Maulana. *Islamic Law and Constitution*. Third Edition. Lahore: Islamic Publications, 1967.

Meenai, S. A. *Banking System in Pakistan*. Karachi: State Bank of Pakistan, 1964.

Mills, C. W. *The Power Elite*. New York: Oxford University Press, 1957.

Misra, K. P., M. V. Lakhi, and V. Narain. *Pakistan's Search for Constitutional Consensus*. New Delhi: Impex, 1968.

Mohammad, Qazi Din. *Bangla Sahityer Itihas* [History of Bengali literature]. 2 Vols. Dacca: Student Ways, 1968.

Montgomery, J. D. and William J. Siffin, eds. *Approaches to Development: Politics, Administration and Change*. New York: McGraw-Hill, 1966.

Mosca, G. *The Ruling Class*. New York: McGraw Hill, 1939.

Mosley, Leaonard. *The Last Days of the British Raj*. New York: Harcourt, Brace, 1962.

Motheral, Joe R. "The Effect of Government Policy and Programs on Agricultural Production in Pakistan." Cambridge: Center for International Affairs, Harvard University, 1960.

Muhith, A. M. A. "Political and Administrative Roles in East Pakistan's Districts," *Pacific Affairs*, XL (1967–68), 279–93.

Mujahid, Sharif al-. "The Assembly Elections in Pakistan," *Asian Survey*, V (1965) 538–51.
—— "Pakistan's First Presidential Elections," *Asian Survey*, V (1965), 280–94.
Munir, Muhammad. *Constitution of the Islamic Republic of Pakistan*. Lahore: All Pakistan Legal Decisions, 1965.
Muslim League. *Resolutions of All India Muslim League* [May 1924–December 1936]. General Secretary, All India Muslim League.
Myrdal, Gunnar. *Asian Drama: An Inquiry into the Poverty of Nations*. 3 vols. New York: Pantheon, 1968.
—— *Rich Lands and Poor: The Road to World Prosperity*. New York: Harper and Row, 1957.
Naqvi, M. B. "The Ruling Regime: A Hot House Growth," *The Pakistan Observer*, October 27, 1966.
National Awami Party. *Constitution and Rules*. Dacca: 1957.
—— *Objectives and Aims*. Dacca: 1957.
—— (Pro-Moscow faction). *Resolutions*. Dacca: 1968.
National Democratic Front. *Declaration of Objectives*. Dacca: 1964.
—— "Resolutions of the Meeting of N.D.F." Mimeographed. Dacca, April 30 and May 1, 1966.
The New Constitution of Pakistan: Martial Law in a New Garb. London: F. J. Lamb (printers), n.d.
Newman, K. J. "Basic Democracy as an Experiment," *Political Studies*, X (1962), 46–64.
—— "The Constitutional Evolution of Pakistan," *International Affairs*, XXXVIII (1954), 70–74.
—— "The Dyarchic Pattern of Government and Pakistan's Problems," *Political Science Quarterly*, LXXV (1960), 94–108.
—— *Essays from Pakistan*. Lahore: Publishers United, 1954.
—— *Essays on the Constitution of Pakistan*. Dacca: Cooperative Book Society, 1956.
—— "Pakistan's Preventive Autocracy and Its Causes," *Pacific Affairs*, XXXII (1959), 19–33.
Nizam-i-Islam Party. *Aims and Objectives of the Pakistan Nizam-e-Islam*. Lahore: n.d.
—— *Purbo Pakistan Jamiat-e-Ulema-e-Islam o Nizam-e-Islam Party ebong Pakistan Nizam-e-Islam Party'r Gathantantra* [East Pakistan Jamiat-e-Ulema-e-Islam and Nizam-i-Islam and Pakistan Nizam-i-Islam Party's constitution]. Dacca: 1967.
Noon, Firoz Khan. *From Memory*. Lahore: Ferozsons, 1966.
Nuruzzaman, Md. *Who's Who*. Dacca: Eastern Publications, 1968.
Owen, John, ed. *Sociology in East Pakistan*. Dacca: Asiatic Society of Pakistan, 1962.
Pakistan Democratic Movement. *Constitution and Rules Including Eight-Point Programme*. Dacca: 1968.

—— *Resolutions of the National Executive* [May 1967–February 1968]. Dacca: 1968.

Pakistan Muslim League. *Constitution of the Pakistan Muslim League.* Rawalpindi: Pakistan Muslim League, 1968.

Pakistan People's Party. *Foundation and Policy.* Lahore: n.d.

Palmer, Norman D. "Pakistan's Mood: The New Realism," *Current History*, XLIII (1962), 263–71.

Papanek, Gustav F. *Pakistan's Development: Social Goals and Private Incentives.* Cambridge: Harvard University Press, 1967.

Papanek, Hanna. "Entrepreneurs in East Pakistan." Paper presented at the Fifth Annual Conference on Bengal Studies, Urbana, Ill., May 16, 1969.

Park, Richard L. "East Bengal: Pakistan's Troubled Province," *Far Eastern Survey*, XXIII (1954), 70–74.

—— "The Rise of Militant Nationalism in Bengal: A Regional Study of Indian Nationalism." Ph.D. dissertation, Harvard University, 1950.

—— and R. S. Wheeler. "East Bengal Under Governor's Rule," *Far Eastern Survey*, XXIII (1954), 129–34.

Peach, W. N., M. Uzair, et al. *Basic Data of the Economy of Pakistan.* London: Oxford University Press, 1959.

Pehrson, Robert N. *The Social Organization of the Marri Baluch.* Chicago: Aldine Publishing Company, 1966.

Pirzada, S. Sharifuddin. *Constitutional Remedies in Pakistan.* Lahore: All Pakistan Legal Decisions, 1965.

—— *Fundamental Rights and Constitutional Remedies in Pakistan.* Lahore: All Pakistan Legal Decisions, 1966.

—— *The Pakistan Resolution and the Historic Lahore Session.* Karachi: Pakistan Publications, 1968.

—— ed. *Qaid-e-Azam Jinnah's Correspondence.* Karachi: Guild Publishing House, 1966.

Pre-Requisites of Democracy in Pakistan. Dacca: National Association for Social and Economic Progress, n.d.

Pye, Lucian W. *Aspects of Political Development.* Boston: Little, Brown and Company, 1966.

—— *Politics, Personality and Nation Building: Burma's Search for Identity.* New Haven: Yale University Press, 1962.

—— ed. *Communications and Political Development.* Princeton: Princeton University Press, 1963.

—— and S. Verba, eds. *Political Culture and Political Development.* Princeton: Princeton University Press, 1965.

Qureshi, Anwar I. *Pakistan Marches on Road to Prosperity, 1959–64.* Rawalpindi: Ferozsons, 1965.

—— ed. *The Third Five Year Plan and Other Papers.* Karachi: Ferozsons, 1965.

Qureshi, Ishtiaq H. *The Muslim Community of the Indo-Pakistan Subcontinent.* The Hague: Mouton, 1962.

—— *The Pakistani Way of Life*. New York: Praeger, 1956.
—— *The Struggle for Pakistan*. Karachi: University of Karachi, 1965.
Qureshi, Saleem M. M. "Party Politics in the Second Republic of Pakistan," *Middle East Journal*, XX (1966), 456–72.
Rab, Abdur. *A. K. Fazlul Huq: Life and Achievement*. Lahore: Ferozsons, 1967.
Rahim, Muhammad A. *Social and Cultural History of Bengal*. Karachi: Pakistan Historical Society, 1963.
Rahman, A. T. R. *Basic Democracies at the Grass Roots*. Comilla: Pakistan Academy for Rural Development, 1962.
—— *An Evaluation of the Rural Works Programme East Pakistan 1963–1964*. Comilla: Pakistan Academy for Rural Development, 1964.
—— "Rural Institutions in India and Pakistan," *Asian Survey*, VIII (1968), 792–805.
Rahman, Hasan H., ed. *Ekushe February* [21 February]. Dacca: Granthana, 1967.
Rahman, Fazlur. *Pakistan One and Indivisible*. Karachi: Pakistan Educational Publishers, 1960.
Rahman, M. Akhlaqur. *Partition, Integration, Economic Growth, and Interregional Trade: A Study of Interwing Trade in Pakistan, 1948–1959*. Karachi: Institute of Development Economics, 1963.
Rahman, Muhammad Anisur. *East and West Pakistan: A Problem in the Political Economy of Regional Planning*. Cambridge: Center for International Affairs, Harvard University, 1968.
—— "The Logic of Regional Investment Allocation: An Aggregate Study in the Theory of Development Programming." Ph.D. dissertation, Harvard University, 1962.
Rahman, Sheikh Mujibur. *Amader Banchar Dabi: Chaya Dafa Karmasuchi* [Six Points: Our Demand for Survival]. Dacca: General Secretary, East Pakistan Awami League, 1966.
Rajput, A. B. *Muslim League: Yesterday and Today*. Lahore: S. M. Ashraf, 1948.
Rashid, Haroun er-. *East Pakistan: A Systematic Regional Geography and Its Development Planning Aspects*. Lahore: Sh. Ghulam Ali, 1965.
Rashiduzzaman, M. "The Awami League in the Political Development of Pakistan," *Asian Survey*, X (1970), 574–87.
—— "The National Assembly of Pakistan under the 1962 Constitution," *Pacific Affairs*, XLII (1969–70), 481–93.
—— "Pakistan's Local Bodies and Social Change: The Emerging Pattern of Local Leadership," *Orient*, IX (1968), 125–28.
—— *Politics and Administration in the Local Councils*. Dacca: Oxford University Press, 1968.
Ray, Jayanta K. *Democracy and Nationalism on Trial: A Study of East Pakistan*. Simla: Indian Institute of Advanced Study, 1968.
Razee, Aleem al-. "Basic Democracies and the New Regime," *The Pakistan Observer*, January 12, 1967.

— "Constitutional Obligation of Parity and Its Implementation," *The Pakistan Observer*, August 14, 1966.
— *Process of Economic Disparity*. Dacca: n.d.
Revelle, Roger, and Harold Thomas. "Population and Food in East Pakistan." Cambridge: Harvard Center for Population Studies, Harvard University.
Richard, Sandra. "A View of Pakistan's Industrial Development," *Asian Survey*, V (1965), 590-95.
Riggs, Fred. *Administration in Developing Countries: The Theory of Prismatic Society*. Boston: Houghton Mifflin, 1964.
Riker, William H. *Federalism: Origin, Operation, Significance*. Toronto: Little, Brown and Company, 1964.
Rose, Richard. "Dynamic Tendencies in the Authority of Regimes," *World Politics*, XXI (1969), 602-28.
Rose, Saul, ed. *Politics in Southern Asia*. London: Macmillan, 1963.
Rudolph, Lloyd I. "From Politics of Status to Politics of Opinion." Ph.D. dissertation, Harvard University, 1956.
Russett, Bruce, *et al*. *World Handbook of Political and Social Indicators*. New Haven: Yale University Press, 1964.
Sadeque, A. *The Economic Emergence of Pakistan*. Part I. Dacca: East Bengal Government Press, 1954; Part II. Dacca: The Provincial Statistical Board (Planning Department), 1956.
— *Pakistan's First Five Year Plan in Theory and Operation*. Dacca: East Pakistan Government Press, n.d.
Saiyid, M. H. *Mohammad Ali Jinnah*. Lahore: M. Ashraf, 1953.
Sardar, Fazlul Karim, ed. *Pakistan Andolan O Muslim Sahitya* [Pakistan movement and Muslim literature]. Dacca: Bengali Academy, 1968.
Sayeed, Khalid B. "The Capabilities of Pakistan's Political System," *Asian Survey*, VII (1967), 102-10.
— "Collapse of Parliamentary Democracy in Pakistan," *Middle East Journal*, XIII (1959), 389-406.
— "Federalism and Pakistan," *Far Eastern Survey*, XXIII (1954), 139-43.
— "Jama'at-i-Islami Movement in Pakistan," *Pacific Affairs*, XXX (1957), 59-68.
— "1965: An Epoch-Making Year in Pakistan—General Elections and War with India," *Asian Survey*, VI (1966), 76-85.
— "Pakistan's Basic Democracy," *Middle East Journal*, XV (1961), 249-63.
— "Pakistan's Constitutional Autocracy," *Pacific Affairs*, XXXVI (1963-64), 365-77.
— *Pakistan: The Formative Phase*. Second edition. London: Oxford University Press, 1968.
— "Pakistan: New Challenges to the Political System," *Asian Survey*, VIII (1968), 97-104.
— "Pathan Regionalism," *South Atlantic Quarterly*, LVII (1964), 478-506.

—— "The Political Role of Pakistan's Civil Service," *Pacific Affairs*, XXXI (1958), 131-46.
—— *The Political System of Pakistan*. Boston: Houghton Mifflin, 1967.
—— "Religion and Nation-Building in Pakistan," *Middle East Journal*, XVII (1963), 279-91.
Schuler, Edgar A. and Kathryn R. *Public Opinion and Constitution Making in Pakistan, 1958-62*. East Lansing: Michigan State University Press, 1967.
Schuman, Howard. "Economic Development and Individual Change: A Social-Psychological Study of the Comilla Experiment in Pakistan." Occasional Papers in International Affairs, Center for International Affairs, Harvard University, No. 15, 1967.
—— "Social Change and Validity of Regional Stereotypes in East Pakistan," *Sociometry*, XXIX (1966), 428-40.
Seth, K. L. "Some Aspects of the Second and Third Five Year Plans of Pakistan," *Indian Quarterly*, XXII (1966), 369-85.
Shahidullah, Dr. Mohammad. *Bangla Sahityer Katha* [History of Bengali literature]. Vol. II. Dacca: Renaissance Printers, 1965.
Sheikh, Shaukat Mahmood. *The Second Republic of Pakistan*. Karachi: Islamic Kutub Khana, 1963.
—— *A Study of the Constitution of Pakistan*. Lahore: Pakistan Law Times Publications, 1962.
Sherwani, Latif A. "The 1962 Pakistan Constitution: Two Views—The Constitutional Experiment," *Asian Survey*, II (1962), 9-14.
Silvert, Kalman H., ed. *Expectant Peoples: Nationalism and Development*. New York: Random House, 1963.
Singh, S. Nihal. "Integration of Two Wings of Pakistan," *The Statesman Weekly*, September 9, 16, 1967.
Singhal, D. P. "The New Constitution of Pakistan," *Asian Survey*, II (1962), 15-23.
Smith, Cantwell W. *Islam in Modern History*. Princeton: Princeton University Press, 1957.
Sobhan, Rehman. *Basic Democracies, Works Programme and Rural Development in East Pakistan*. Dacca: Oxford University Press, 1968.
—— "Beyond Parity," *The Dacca Times*, October 18, 1963.
—— "The Challenge of Inequality," *The Pakistan Observer*, July 12-15, 1965.
—— "East Pakistan Demands Her Due," *The Times*, August 14, 1963.
—— "Imbalance in Economic Development in Pakistan," *Asian Survey*, II (1962), 31-37.
—— "Two-Way Stretch in Basic Democracies," *The Times*, (London) April 6, 1968.
Spain, James W. *The Pathan Borderland*. The Hague: Mouton, 1963.
—— *The People of the Khyber: The Pathan of Pakistan*. New York: Praeger, 1963.

Spate, O. H. K., and A. T. A. Learminth. *India and Pakistan: A General and Regional Geography.* London: Methuen, 1967.
Spear, Percival. "Equal But Different," *The Times,* (London) February 26, 1966.
Stephen, Ian. *Pakistan.* London: Ernest Benn, 1963.
Stern, Joseph J. "Growth, Development and Regional Equity in Pakistan." Ph.D. dissertation, Harvard University, 1967.
— and Walter P. Falcon. *Growth and Development in Pakistan, 1955-1969.* Cambridge: Center for International Affairs, Harvard University, 1970.
Suhrawardy, H. S. "Political Stability and Democracy," *Foreign Affairs,* XXV (1956-57), 422-31.
Suleri, Z. A. *My Leader.* Lahore: Lion Press, 1946.
— *Pakistan's Lost Years.* Lahore: Progressive Papers, 1962.
— *Politicians and Ayub.* Lahore: Lion Press, 1965.
Symonds, Richard. *The Making of Pakistan.* London: Faber and Faber, 1950.
Tepper, Elliot. *Changing Patterns of Administration in Rural East Pakistan.* East Lansing, Mich.: Asian Studies Center, Michigan State University, 1966.
Thomas, John W. "Rural Public Works Program and East Pakistan's Development." Ph.D. dissertation, Harvard University, 1968.
— "Rural Public Works Program in East Pakistan." Paper presented at Development Advisory Service Conference, Sorrento, Italy, September 5-12, 1968.
Tilman, Robert O. "Integration and Disintegration in Malaysia: The Case of Singapore." Paper presented at the American Political Science Association Meeting, New York, September 1966.
Tinker, Hugh. *India and Pakistan: A Political Analysis.* New York: Praeger, 1962.
— *South Asia: A Short History.* New York: Praeger, 1966.
Umar, Badruddin. *Sampradayikata* [Communalism]. Dacca: Janamaitri Publications, 1966.
— *Sanskritik Sankat* [Crisis in culture]. Dacca: Granthana, 1967.
— *Sanskritik Sampradayikata* [Communalism in culture]. Dacca: Granthana, 1969.
United Front. "Twenty-One Point Manifesto." Mimeographed. 1954.
Von Vorys, Karl. *Political Development in Pakistan.* Princeton: Princeton University Press, 1965.
Ward, Barbara. "Pakistan's Ambitious Planners," *Economist,* June 5, 1965, pp. 1142-43.
Waterston, Albert. *Planning in Pakistan.* Baltimore: Johns Hopkins Press, 1963.
Weekes, Richard. *Pakistan: Birth and Growth of a Muslim Nation.* Princeton: Van Nostrand Company, 1964.
Weiner, Myron. "Political Integration and Political Development," *The Annals of the American Academy of Political and Social Sciences,* CCCLVIII (1965), 52-64.
Wheeler, Richard S. "Changing Patterns of Local Government and Administration in Pakistan," *South Atlantic Quarterly,* XXXII (1963), 67-77.

—— "Government and Constitution-Making in Pakistan." Ph.D. dissertation, University of California, Berkeley, 1957.
—— "Governor General's Rule in Pakistan," *Far Eastern Survey*, XXIV (1955), 1-8.
—— "Pakistan: New Constitution, Old Issues," *Asian Survey*, III (1963) 107-15.
Wilber, Donald N. *Pakistan: Its People, Its Society, Its Culture*. New Haven: Human Relations Area Files Press, 1964.
—— *Pakistan: Yesterday and Today*. New York: Holt, Rinehart, and Winston, 1964.
Wilcox, Wayne A. "Alternative Strategies of Political Elite Survival in Southern Asia." Paper presented at the American Political Science Association Meeting, September 1966.
—— "A Decade of Ayub," *Asian Survey*, IX (1969), 87-93.
—— *Pakistan: The Consolidation of a Nation*. New York: Columbia University Press, 1963.
—— "The Pakistan Coup d'Etat of 1958," *Pacific Affairs*, XXXVIII (1965), 142-63.
—— "Pakistan in 1969: Once Again at the Starting Point," *Asian Survey*, X (1970), 73-81.
—— "Political Change in Pakistan: Structure, Function, Constraints, and Goals," *Pacific Affairs*, XLI (1968), 341-54.
—— "The Politics of Distributive Policy in Pakistan." Paper presented at the Eastern Universities Summer Consortium on South Asia Conference on Pakistan, Rochester, New York, July 29-31, 1970.
—— "Problems and Processes of National Integration in Pakistan," *The Pakistan Student*, March-April 1967.
Williams, L. F. Rushbrook. *The State of Pakistan*. London: Faber and Faber, 1962.
Woodruff, Philip. *The Men Who Ruled India*. 2 vols. New York: Schocken Books, 1964.
Wriggins, Howard. *Ceylon: Dilemmas of a New Nation*. Princeton: Princeton University Press, 1960.
Zaidi, S. Wiqar Husain. *An Analysis of the District Census Reports of East Pakistan*. Research Report no. 49. Karachi: Pakistan Institute of Development Economics, 1966.
Zaman, Hasan. *Samaj Sanskriti Sahitya* [Society, culture, literature]. Dacca: Bengali Academy, 1967.
Ziring, Lawrence. "The Failure of Democracy in Pakistan: East Pakistan and the Central Government, 1947-58." Ph.D. dissertation, Columbia University, 1962.

Index

Adamjee riots, 29*n*, 173*n*
Administrative Reorganization Committee, 93–94
Afghanistan: Pakistani tribes in, 14–15
Agartala conspiracy case, 100*n*, 106, 171, 173, 174
Agriculture: East Pakistan, 11, 18, 19, 30, 31, 77, 86, 89, 181, 182; West Pakistan, 11, 30, 31, 57*n*; *see also* Landownership; Land reform
Ahmad, Abul Mansur, 30*n*, 42
Ahmad, Farid, 125*n*, 127*n*, 170*n*
Ahmad, Kamruddin, 42
Ahsan, Qamrul, 127*n*
Air transportation, 205; *see also* Transportation
Ali, Chaudhri Muhammad, 141, 150
Ali, Choudhury Rahmat, 21*n*
All Parties Students Action Committee (SAC), 172; Eleven-Point Program, 172, 174, 189
Army, *see* Military
Assam, 40, 42, 140

Assembly, Constituent: pre-1954, 36; pre-1948, 37; 1947–58, 61; 1947, 146*n*; 1955, 146*n*
Assembly, National, 60–61; 1955–56, 36; 1962, 57, 61, 127–28, 146, 147, 148, 149; 1947–58, 61; 1965, 61, 146, 147, 155–56; under 1962 constitution, 144, 145; 1970, 187, 188, 190, 192, 193; 1971, 193, 194, 195, 196, 201
Assembly, Provincial, 60–61; 1962, 57, 61, 161; 1965, 61; under 1962 constitution, 145; 1970, 187, 190–91
Aurangzeb, Mian Gul, 146
Autonomy, demand for, 29–30, 35, 37, 39, 42–43, 46, 47, 48, 49, 67–68, 87, 89, 96, 100–107, 131, 135, 145, 157, 159–60, 166–76 *passim*, 180, 181, 182, 186, 187, 194, 195–96, 197; Ayub on, 66, 157–58, 175; National Awami Party, 135–36, 150, 151, 172–73, 174, 189; Awami League/Six-Point Movement, 138, 139, 150, 151, 167–75 *passim*, 186, 191, 194, 195–96;

239

240 / Index

Autonomy, demand for, *(Cont.)*
  Pakistan Democratic Movement,
  170-71, 173, 174; Democratic Action
  Committee, 172-73, 175; Legal
  Framework Order, 187
Awami League, 36, 37, 41-42, 45, 48,
  49, 114, 170; Communists, 41; East
  Bengal Awami League, 41-42, 48;
  Murree Pact, 47; Awami Mahaz, 48;
  Pir of Manki Sharif's Awami League,
  48; West Pakistan, 48, 49, 138-39,
  150, 189, 191, 194; and National
  Awami Party, 49, 137, 138, 140, 155n,
  170n, 171; Six-Point Program, 68, 88,
  137, 139-40, 160, 161-62, 167-71,
  172, 174, 176, 187, 189, 192, 194,
  195-96; and Ayub regime, 127-28,
  135, 138-40, 170; and East Pakistan
  Students League, 134n, 139, 141, 196n;
  demand for autonomy, 138, 150, 151,
  167-75 *passim*, 186, 191, 194, 195-96;
  and Council Muslim League, 140, 170;
  and Nizam-i-Islam, 140, 170; and
  Pakistan People's Party, 140, 190-94
  passim, 196; *Ittefaq,* 162, 170;
  newspapers attack, 162, 170, 197;
  elections (1970), 188-92 *passim*, 197,
  203; and Bangladesh independence,
  193-204 *passim*; and Yahya regime,
  193, 194-95, 196; *see also* Combined
  Opposition Parties; Democratic Action
  Committee, United Front
Ayub, Capt. Gauhar, 60
Ayub Khan, Mohammad, 6-8, 21, 51-172
  passim, 179-80; modernization, 4, 5,
  23, 65, 67, 93, 96, 180-81; economy, 7,
  60, 62, 65, 67-89, 93, 97, 103, 104,
  179, 180; draft for 1956 constitution,
  53; on politicians, 55, 109; on East
  Bengalis, 63-64; on nation-building,
  64-65; on autonomy, 66, 157-58, 175;
  on bureaucracy, 93; election (1965),
  122-24, 128, 151, 152; uprisings
  against, 126, 170, 172-77 *passim*; and
  Pakistan Muslim League, 128-31, 132,
  141; election (1964), 130; resignation,
  174, 176; farewell address, 175, 186;
  see also Basic Democracies;
  Constitution (1962)
Azam, Ghulam, 133
Azam Khan, Gen., 150, 160, 161

Baluchi (language), 12
Baluchis/Baluchistan, 14, 15, 149n, 175,
  190-91
Bangladesh, 6, 197-204; events leading
  up to, 185-98; Indian involvement,
  199, 200, 202-203, 204
Banking and currency: Industrial
  Development Bank of Pakistan, 75,
  98n, 100; Six-Point Program, 167-68;
  Pakistan Democratic Movement, 171;
  All Parties Students Action Committee,
  172
Bari, Mian Abdul, 127n
Barisal (Bakarganj): election (1965), 123,
  153; population, 206
Basic Democracies, 57, 59, 61, 64, 94,
  110-27, 129, 130, 143, 151, 155n;
  rural works program, 59, 64, 113-14,
  115, 117, 119, 122, 124, 125-26; Ayub
  on, 111; as electoral college, 113, 119,
  124, 126, 159; District Council, 115,
  116; Divisional Council, 115, 116;
  Thana Council, 115, 116, 118-19;
  Union Council, 115-21 *passim*
Basic Principles Committee Report (BPC),
  37, 42; anti-BPC movement, 42-43
Bengali (language), 12, 13, 14, 162, 168;
  controversy over state language, 37-38,
  40, 43-45, 46, 48, 96, 163; as state
  language, 38; newspapers and
  periodicals, 216; *see also* Vernacular elite
Bengalis, 5-6, 15, 18, 24-26; *see also*
  Bangladesh; East Pakistan; West Bengal
Bhasani, Maulana Abdul Hamid Khan, 40,
  48, 114; Awami League, 41-42;
  Muslim League, 42; National Awami
  Party, 136, 137, 171, 172, 173, 176,
  194n; election (1965), 150, 154;
  election (1970), 189
Bhutto, Zulfikar Ali: and Ayub Khan,
  56n, 131, 173; and Pakistan People's
  Party, 140, 141, 172, 190, 193; election
  (1970), 190, 192n; and Sheikh Mujibur
  Rahman, 193-94, 196; and Yahya
  Khan, 193, 196
Biafra, 203
Bihar, 134
Bogra: election (1965), 123, 153;
  population, 206
BPC, *see* Basic Principles Committee
  Report

Braibanti, Ralph, 92
Bureaucracy, 20, 24, 25–26, 52–53, 63, 92–93, 180; Civil Service of Pakistan, 25, 26, 29, 59–60, 92, 94–95, 105, 106, 107; British influence on, 52, 92; Ayub regime, 57–61 *passim*, 63, 65, 67, 91–107, 110, 129; East Pakistan, 60, 61–62, 63, 95, 96, 98–102 *passim*, 105, 106, 107, 165, 180, 181, 195, 199; West Pakistan, 63, 95–96, 101, 107; Ayub on, 93; Yahya regime, 186; *see also* Basic Democracies
Business and industry, 34, 59, 60–61, 172, 180; East Pakistan, 26, 27, 30, 31, 35, 61, 62, 63, 74, 87–88, 180, 181, 211, 212; West Pakistan, 27, 30, 31–32, 49, 61, 63, 86, 87, 88, 211, 212; Central Investment Promotion and Co-ordination Committee, 75, 211; *see also* Economy; Labor force

Castes, Muslim, 15, 17
Central Development Working Party (CDWP), 103, 104
Central Investment Promotion and Co-ordination Committee, 75, 211
Central Treaty Organization, 49*n*
China: and Pakistan, relations, 136, 137, 171; Pakistan People's Party, 140; *see also* National Awami Party
Chinioti, 27
Chittagong, 16, 18, 19; population, 11, 206; election (1965), 123, 153
Chittagong Hill Tracts, 16, 18, 19; election (1965), 153; population, 206
Choudhury, Hamidul Huq, 158*n*
Choudhury, Yousuf Ali, 158*n*
Chowdhury, Fazlul Qader, 160*n*, 161*n*
Christianity, 23
Civil Service of Pakistan (CSP), 25, 26, 29, 59–60, 92, 94–95, 105, 106, 107; *see also* Bureaucracy
CML, *see* Council Muslim League
Combined Opposition Parties (COP), 137, 150–51, 154, 155, 161
Comilla, 16, 17; population, 11, 18, 206; Rural Academy, 94; rural public works program, 113; election (1965), 123, 153, 154
Committee for Co-ordination of Economic Policies, 103

Communications, 66, 171; East Pakistan, 31, 33, 66, 182, 199, 200, 202, 206, 215, 216; West Pakistan, 31, 33, 215, 216; censorship and control during Ayub regime, 55, 141, 156, 162; *see also* Press; Radio
Communism: East Pakistan, 18*n*, 40–41, 157; Awami League, 40; Jama'at-i-Islami, 133; *see also* National Awami Party
Congress party, 40, 43
Constituent Assembly, *see* Assembly, Constituent
Constitution of 1956, 53, 102; Basic Principles Committee Report draft, 37, 42–43; "Grand National Convention" draft, 42–43; abrogation of, 51, 55; Ayub Khan draft, 53
Constitution of 1962, 56, 68–69, 70, 102, 110, 127, 143–45, 156, 159; Bengali opposition to, 68, 69, 145, 146, 156–57, 158–59, 161; Union Council membership changed, 116; assembly, 144; presidency, 144, 159; distribution of power, 144–45, 159; changes proposed, 173, 175; changes proposed in Legal Framework Order, 187–88; changes proposed by Awami League, 189
Cost of living, 81, 215; East Pakistan, 88, 215
Council Muslim League (CML), 135, 139, 140, 141, 170; and Awami League, 140, 170; election (1970), 188, 190, 191; *see also* Combined Opposition Parties
CSP, *see* Civil Service of Pakistan
Culture, *see* Society and culture
Currency, *see* Banking and currency

DAC, *see* Democratic Action Committee
Dacca, 16, 17, 18, population, 11, 206; election (1965), 123, 153, 154; massacres (1971), 198
Dacca faction (Muslim League), 39–40
Dacca University, 46; strikes and riots over language controversy, 37–38, 43, 44, 96; strikes and riots (1962), 158, 161; strikes and riots (1966), 163; National Students Federation, 164; strikes and riots (1968–69), 169*n*, 173, 174; army attacks on (1971), 196–97

242 / Index

Daulatana, 132
Dawood (family), 60
Dawood, Siddiq, 60n
Dawoodi Bohra, 27
Defense, 43, 46, 76, 84, 166, 204; Six-Point Program, 167, 168
Democratic Action Committee (DAC), 172, 173, 176
Deutsch, Karl W., 2
Dinajpur: election (1965), 123, 153; population, 206

East Bengal, 25
East Bengal Regiment (EBR): Bangladesh conflict, 196n, 198, 199, 200
Easton, David, 3
East Pakistan: national liberation movement and Bangladesh independence, 6, 185–204; politics, 7, 8, 16n, 20, 21–22, 24–30 passim, 35–49 passim, 53, 54, 56, 61–66 passim, 68, 69, 85, 88–89, 96, 98, 100, 106, 107, 113, 114, 124–42 passim, 149–77 passim, 180, 185–204 passim; geography, 10, 11, 189n, 191; agriculture, 11, 16, 19, 30, 31, 77, 86, 89, 181, 182; population, 11–12, 15, 16, 17, 18, 114, 181, 206; economy and trade, 12, 16, 18, 19, 30–37, 67, 68–89, 114, 166–67, 180, 181, 200, 210, 211, 212, 213; migration, 12, 18–19, 134, 149, 154, 181, 196, 199; languages, 12–24 (see also Bengali); Muslims, 12n, 13, 14, 19, 22, 23, 25–29 passim, 38, 41–42, 45, 183; culture and history, 12n, 14, 15, 18–19, 20–21, 25, 37–38, 162–63; Hindus, 12n, 18–19, 22, 23, 26, 27, 157, 163, 204; landownership, 12n, 18–19, 117, 122; labor force, 16, 18, 35, 63, 88, 89, 124, 168–69, 173, 174, 175, 180, 181–82, 183, 207, 216; education, 17, 30–31, 33, 81–82, 163–65, 182, 214; religion, 22–23; business and industry, 26, 27, 30, 31, 35, 61, 62, 63, 74, 87–88, 180, 181, 211, 212; per capita income, 31, 32, 71–72, 79–81; communications 31, 33, 66, 182, 199, 200, 202, 206, 215, 216; transporation, 31, 33, 81, 182, 199, 200, 205, 213, 215; medical facilities, 33, 81, 182, 214; foreign aid allocation, 34, 35; riots, disturbances, and uprisings, 37–38, 40, 43–45, 46, 48, 96, 126, 163, 168–69, 170, 172–77 passim, 183, 207; students and politics, 37–45 passim, 63, 96, 114, 124, 134, 139, 141, 158, 161, 163, 164, 168, 169, 172, 173, 174, 182–83, 194n, 196–97, 200, 204; land reform, 39, 48; election (1959), 53, 122; bureaucracy, 60, 61–62, 63, 95, 96, 98–102 passim, 105, 106, 107, 165, 180, 181, 195, 199; military, 62, 95, 174, 194–204 passim; 1962 constitution opposed, 68, 69, 145, 146, 156–57, 158–59, 161; taxation, 69, 70, 71, 73, 208; cost of living, 88, 215; works program, 89, 113–14, 122, 124, 125–26, 212, 213; Basic Democracies, 112–26 passim; election (1953), 114; election (1960), 119; election (1964), 119, 122, 124–25, 158, 161; election (1965), 122–24, 152, 153, 154, 155, 158, 161; election (1954), 129, 131–32, 203; election (1962), 145, 146, 147, 158; election (1970), 188–89, 190, 203; election (1971), 201; election (1958), 203; see also Autonomy, demand for; Bengalis; Monem Khan, Abdul
East Pakistan Planning Board, 104
East Pakistan Rifles (EPR): Bangladesh conflict, 196n, 197, 198, 199, 200
East Pakistan Students League, 134n, 138, 141, 194n, 196n
East Pakistan Students Union (EPSU), 41, 134n, 141
EBDO, see Elective Bodies Disqualification Ordinance
EBR, see East Bengal Regiment
Economy, 4, 5, 6, 7, 10–11, 209; Ayub regime, 7, 60, 62, 65, 67–89, 93, 97, 103, 104, 179, 180; East Pakistan, 12, 16, 18, 19, 30–37, 67, 68–89, 114, 166–67, 180, 181, 200, 210, 211, 212, 213; West Pakistan, 12, 30–37, 67–89, 134, 210, 211, 212, 213; GNP, 80, 88, 180; two-economy thesis, 85–89, 180; National Economic Council, 97, 103, 104; Pakistan Muslim League, 130; Jama'at-i-Islami, 133; Council Muslim League, 135; National Awami Party, 136; Pakistan People's Party, 140;

Six-Point Program, 168; Pakistan Democratic Movement, 171; *see also* Business and industry
Education, 186; East Pakistan, 17, 30–31, 33, 81–82, 163–65, 182, 214; West Pakistan, 30–31, 33, 81–82, 214
Elections: 1959, 53, 57, 122; 1964, 65n, 119, 121, 122, 124–25, 130, 149, 158, 161; 1965, 65n, 122–24, 129, 132, 139, 149–56, 158, 161; Basic Democracies as electoral college, 113, 119, 124, 126, 159; 1953, 114; 1960, 119–20; 1962, 127, 145–47, 158; 1954, 128n, 129, 131–32, 203; 1970, 187–92 *passim*, 197, 203; 1971, 201; 1958, 203; *see also* Suffrage
Elective Bodies Disqualification Ordinance (EBDO), 55, 128, 145, 156
Eleven-Point Program, 172, 174, 189
Emerson, Rupert, 1, 9
English (language), 12, 13, 14; newspapers and periodicals, 216
EPR, *see* East Pakistan Rifles
EPSU, *see* East Pakistan Students Union

Faridpur, 16, 17; population, 11, 206; election (1965), 123, 153
Faruque, Gulam, 160
Five Year Plans: Second (1960–65), 68, 73, 74, 75, 78, 83, 85; Third (1965–70), 69, 71–76 *passim*, 78, 83, 85, 87; First (1955–60), 73, 85
Foreign aid, allocation of, 34, 35
Foreign policy: Bengali demands, 43, 46, 48; Jama'at-i-Islami, 133; Council Muslim League, 135; National Awami Party, 136, 151; Pakistan People's Party, 140; Awami League, 151, 167
Fundamentalist parties, *see* Ulema

Gaffar Khan, Abdul, 136
Ganatantri Dal, 41, 45; *see also* United Front
Gauhar, Altaf, 56
Geertz, Clifford, 2n, 5
Geography, 10–11; floods, 10, 11, 187n; cyclones, 189n, 191
Gilbert, Richard, 114n
Governor's Conference, 97–98, 104
Great Britain: colonial administration, 20, 25, 52, 63, 64, 92, 112; business interests in Pakistan, 27
Gross National Product (GNP), 80, 88, 180

Habibullah, Gen., 60
Halali Memon, 27
Hasan, Fida, 56
Health, *see* Medical facilities
Hindus, 13, 26, 135; East Pakistan, 12n, 18–19, 22, 23, 26, 27, 157, 163, 204; landownership, 12n, 18, 26; castes, 15; West Pakistan, 22; business, 26, 27
Huntington, Samuel P., 51
Huq, Fazlul, 28n, 47n; Muslim League, 39, 40; Krishak Sramik Party, 45; United Front, 48
Huq, Shamsul, 42

IDBP, *see* Industrial Development Bank of Pakistan
Income, per capita, 30, 31, 71–72, 79–81
India: and Pakistan, migration, 6, 199; bureaucracy, 52; and Pakistan, Kashmir conflict (1958), 52; and Pakistan, conflict (1965), 83–84, 139, 140, 159, 160, 166–67; panchayats, 112; and autonomy, 157; cultural domination, 163; and East Pakistan independence (Bangladesh conflict), 199, 200, 202–203, 204; *see also* West Bengal
Indus Basin Project, 76
Industrial Development Bank of Pakistan (IDBP), 75, 98n, 100, 211
Institute of Public Administration, 95
Iqbal, 13n, 21n
Iran: Pakistani tribes in, 14–15
Islam, 13, 14, 20–23, 65, 66; East Pakistan, 12n, 13, 14, 19, 22, 23, 25–29 *passim*, 38, 41–42, 45, 183; West Pakistan, 14, 23; caste, 15, 19; business, 26, 27; Muslim Family Laws Ordinance, 180–81; *Islam Pasand*, 191, 192; *see also* Jama'at-i-Islami; Jamiat-ul-Ulema-i-Islam; Markazi Jamiat-ul-Ulema-i-Pakistan; Muslim League; Nizam-i-Islam
Islamabad, 76
Ittefaq, 162, 170

Jagannath College, 165
Jama'at-e-Talaba, 134
Jama'at-i-Islami, 132–35, 141, 150, 170; and Awami League, 140; election (1970), 188, 189, 190, 191; Bangladesh conflict, 201–202; *see also* Combined Opposition Parties

Jamiat-ul-Ulema-i-Islam: election (1970), 188, 190
Jatoi, Ghulam Mustafa, 146n
Jessore: election (1965), 123, 153; population, 206
Jilani, Makhdum Zada Syed Mahid Raza, 146n
Jinnah, Fatima: election (1965), 123, 151–55 *passim*
Jinnah, Quaid-i-Azam Mohammad Ali, 21n, 37, 39n, 55
Judiciary, 46

Kaji Kader, 131, 160n
Karachi, 32
Kashmir: Indo-Pakistani conflict (1948), 52; Indo-Pakistani conflict (1965), 83–84, 139, 140, 159, 160, 166–67
Khaliquzzaman, Choudhury, 28n
Khan, Abdul Jabbar, 159
Khan, Abdus Sabur, 131, 160n, 161n
Khan, Abdus Salam, 42, 171n
Khan, Akram, 39
Khan, Akhter, 113–14
Khan, Ataur Rahman, 30n, 42
Khan, Ayub, *see* Ayub Khan, Mohammad
Khan, Liaquat Ali, 21n, 52, 55
Khan, Nasrullah, 139
Khan, Sardar Bahadur, 127n
Khan, Gen. Tikka, 201
Khoja Ismaili, 27
Khoja Isnashari, 27
Khulna: election (1965), 123, 153; labor riots, 181; population, 206
Krishak Sramik Party (KSP), 45; *see also* United Front
Kushtia: election (1965), 123, 153; population, 206

Labor force: East Pakistan, 16, 18, 35, 63, 88, 89, 124, 168–69, 173, 174, 175, 180, 181–82, 183, 207, 216; United Front, 46; West Pakistan, 63, 174, 207, 216; Jama'at-i-Islami, 133; All Parties Students Action Committee, 172; Yahya regime, 186
Lahore Resolution, 21–22, 46
Landownership, 15–22, 26, 56–58, 63; East Pakistan, 12n, 18–19, 117, 122; West Pakistan, 15, 56, 117, 146; zamindars, 18, 122; kulaks, 57–58; talukdars, 122; *see also* Agriculture

Land reform: East Pakistan, 39, 48; Ayub regime, 56–57; West Pakistan, 56, 57; Jama'at-i-Islami, 133
Languages, 12–14; controversy over state language(s), 37–38, 40, 43–45, 46, 48, 96, 163; newspapers and periodicals, 216; *see also* Baluchi; Bengali; English; Punjabi; Pushtu; Sindhi; Urdu
La Palombara, Joseph, 91–92
Leftist movements, 20, 40–41, 49, 106, 134, 141, 171–72, 175, 176, 177, 188, 189; *see also* Communism; National Awami Party; Pakistan Democratic Party; Riots, disturbances, and strikes; Socialism; Students (and politics)
Legal Framework Order (LFO), 187–88

Macaulay, Thomas B.: on Bengalis, 63, 64n
Mahmud Ali, 158n
Malik, Muzaffar Khan, 146n
Mamdot: Jinnah Muslim League, 48
Markazi Jamiat-ul-Ulema-i-Pakistan: election (1970), 188, 190
Marriage customs, 15
Martial law: 1958–62, 49, 51, 54, 55–56, 96–97; 1968–69, 175, 186; 1971, 195
Marwari, 26, 27
Maudoodi, Maulana Abul Ala, 133
Medical facilities: East Pakistan, 33, 81, 182, 214; West Pakistan, 33, 81, 214; family planning, 180
Mian Iftikharrudin, 136
Migration: India, 6, 199; East Pakistan, 12, 18–19, 134, 149, 154, 181, 196, 199; West Pakistan, 12, 31–32, 134, 149
Military, 20, 24, 25–26, 52; British colonial administration, 20, 25; Rawalpindi Conspiracy, 52; Ayub regime, 52, 53–54, 54–55, 58, 59, 60, 61; East Pakistan, 62, 95, 174, 194–204 *passim*; Yahya regime, 185, 192; civil war (Bangladesh), 196–204 *passim*; East Pakistan Rifles, 196n, 197, 198, 199, 200; East Bengal Regiment, 196n, 198, 199, 200; Mukti Bahini, 200, 202, 204; razakars, 202; *see also* Bureaucracy; War with India
Mirza, Iskander, 28n, 52n, 53, 54, 58
Mohammad Ali, 27, 47, 127n, 193
Monem Khan, Abdul, 130n, 131, 152n, 160–66

Mughal (Muslim caste), 19
Mughal period, 21
Mukti Bahini, 200, 202, 204
Murree Pact, 47
Mushashid, Maulana, 127
Muslim Family Laws Ordinance, 180–81
Muslim League, 21–22, 28, 29, 39, 40, 47, 60, 127–29, 135, 162–63; East Pakistan, 21, 22, 28, 29, 39–40, 44–45, 46, 47, 114, 128, 131–32, 134, 135, 139, 201; Lahore Conference and Resolution (1940), 21–22, 46; Huq faction, 39; Suhrawardy faction, 39, 40; Dacca (Nazimuddin) faction, 39–40; Murree Pact, 47; Pakistan Muslim League, 128–32, 139, 141, 155, 188, 190; convention (1962), 129; Council Muslim League, 135, 139, 140, 141, 170, 188, 190, 191: election (1970), 188, 189, 190; Qayyum Muslim League, 188, 190, 194
Muslims, see Islam
Mymensingh, 16, 17, 18; election (1965), 123, 153; population, 206

NAP, see National Awami Party
Narayanganj, 18; election (1965), 123; demonstrations and riots, 169n
National Assembly, see Assembly, National
National Awami Party (NAP), 49, 127–28, 134, 135–38; and Awami League, 49, 137, 138, 140, 155n, 170n, 171; East Pakistan Students Union, 134n, 141; autonomy demands, 135–36, 150, 151, 172–73, 174, 189; Moscow/Peking split, 136–37, 137–38, 171–72, 188–89n, 194n; election (1965), 154, 155n election (1970), 188–89, 190, 191; see also Combined Opposition Parties; Democratic Action Committee
National Democratic Front (NDF), 170; East Pakistan, 139, 150, 155, 158; West Pakistan, 155
National Economic Council (NEC), 97, 103, 104
National Finance Commission, 68, 69–70, 70–71, 78
National Investment Trust (NIT), 75, 212
National Students Federation (NSF), 164
Nazimuddin, Khwaja, 27, 39–40, 132, 135, 150, 193

NDF, see National Democratic Front
NEC, see National Economic Council
New Nation Press, 162
Newspapers and periodicals, see Press
NIT, see National Investment Trust
Nizam-i-Islam, 45, 134, 141, 150, 170; and Awami League, 140, 170; see also Combined Opposition Parties; United Front
Noakhali: population, 11, 206; election (1965), 123, 153, 154
Noon, Firoz Khan, 28n
Noon, Noor Hayat Khan, 146n
North-West Frontier Province, 14, 48, 175; election (1970), 190–91
NSF, see National Students Federation
Nurul Amin, 158n, 160, 170n, 173n, 193
Nurul Islam, A.B.M., 125n

Pabna: election (1965), 123, 153; population, 206
Pakistan: creation of, 21, 22; origin of name, 21
Pakistan Democratic Movement (PDM), 137, 139, 170–71; see also Democratic Action Committee
Pakistan Democratic Party: election (1970), 188, 189, 191, 192
Pakistan Industrial Credit and Investment Corporation (PICIC), 75, 212
Pakistan Industrial Development Corporation (PIDC), 27, 60n, 68
Pakistan Muslim League (PML), 128–32, 139, 141, 155; Central Working Committee, 130, 131; Central Parliamentary Board, 131; Finance Committee, 131; election (1970), 188, 190
Pakistan People's Party, 140–41, 172, 192; and Awami League, 140, 190–94 passim, 196; election (1970), 188, 190, 191
Parsi, 27
Pathan (Muslim caste), 15, 19, 27, 64
PDM, see Pakistan Democratic Movement
Per capita income, see Income, per capita
Perspective Plan, see Twenty Year Perspective Plan
PICIC, see Pakistan Industrial Credit and Investment Corporation
PIDC, see Pakistan Industrial Development Corporation

246 / Index

Pir Mohsenuddin, 158n
Pir of Manki Sharif: Awami League, 48; National Awami Party, 136
Planning Commission, 95, 97, 100, 103, 104, 113–14
PML, see Pakistan Muslim League
Political parties act, 128, 132
Politics, 5, 8, 17, 20, 23–24, 28–30; power elite, 4–5, 5–6, 7, 10, 13, 24–30 passim, 37, 38, 40, 45–48, 54–63 passim, 186, 192–93, 197 (see also Bureaucracy); Ayub regime, 6–8, 53, 54–66, 91–107, 109–42, 145, 148–56, 158, 161, 169–75, 179–80; vernacular elite, 26, 29, 38–49, 53, 54, 56, 96, 107; factionalism, 141–42, 183; after Ayub's resignation, 175–76, 183; Yahya regime, 186–97 passim, 201, 203; see also East Pakistan, politics; Leftist movements; Students (and politics); Ulema; West Pakistan, politics; individual parties
Population, 6, 11–12; East Pakistan, 11–12, 15–16, 18, 19, 114, 181, 206; West Pakistan, 11–12, 14–15
Press, 68, 216; control and censorship under Ayub, 55, 141, 156, 162; see also Communications
Press Trust, 162
Provincial Assembly, see Assembly, Provincial
Public and Representative Offices (Disqualification) Act (PRODA), 29
Punjabi (language), 6, 12, 13, 14
Punjabis/Punjab, 6, 15, 20, 21, 48, 175, 186; riots, 23; election (1970), 190, 191
Pushtu (language), 12, 13, 14

Qadir, Manzur, 56
Qayyum, 132
Qayyum Muslim League, 194; election (1970), 188, 190

Radio, 216; see also Communications
Radio Free Bangladesh, 200, 202
Radio Pakistan, 163
Rahman, Mashihur, 149n
Rahman, Sheikh Mujibur, 42, 138, 174–75, 176; Six-Point Movement, 139, 140, 167, 169, 170, 174; election (1965), 150, 155n, 171; and Ayub regime, 158n, 162, 169, 173, 186; election (1970), 189, 192n; and Yahya regime, 193, 194–95, 196; and Bhutto, 193–94, 196; Bangladesh independence declared by, 197
Railways, 68, 102; East Pakistan, 31, 33, 199, 200, 215; West Pakistan, 31, 33, 215; see also Transportation
Raisman Award, 69, 70
Rajshahi: election (1965), 123, 153; population, 206
Rajshahi University, 46
Rangamati: election (1965), 123
Rangpur: election (1965), 123, 153; population, 206
Rawalpindi Conspiracy, 52
Religion, 21–23, 65; see also Hindus; Islam
Riots, disturbances, and strikes: East Pakistan, 37–38, 40, 43–45, 46, 48, 96, 126, 163, 168–69, 170, 172–77 passim, 183; West Pakistan, 172, 173, 174, 176–77, 190, 207
Roads, 77, 81, 213; see also Transportation
Round-table conference (1969), 173, 175, 176, 186, 187
Rural areas, 19, 20, 25, 39, 40, 46, 59, 64, 66, 89, 175–76; Basic Democracies, 59, 64, 111–19 passim, 122, 124, 125–26; works program, 59, 64, 69, 76–78, 89, 113–14, 115, 117, 119, 122, 124, 125–26, 181, 212, 213

SAC, see All Parties Students Action Committee
Sakar, A. H., 158n
Shahab, Q. A., 56
Shaikh (Muslim caste), 19, 27
Shoaib, 56
Sibli Nomani, 13n
Sikh, 27
Sindhi (language), 12, 13, 14
Sindhis/Sind, 15, 48, 175; election (1970), 190, 191
Six-Point Movement, 68, 88, 137, 139–40, 160, 161–62, 167–71, 172, 174, 176, 187, 189; details, 167–68
Sobhan, Rehman, 78
Socialism, 88–89, 131, 133, 136
Society and culture, 14–22, 37–38; East Pakistan, 12n, 14, 15–17, 20–21, 37–38, 162–63; West Pakistan, 14–15, 17, 20–21, 37–38
South-East Asia Treaty Organization, 49n

Standing Organization Committee, 102–103
Strayer, Joseph R., 9
Students (and politics): East Pakistan, 37–45 passim, 63, 96, 114, 124, 134, 141, 158, 161, 163, 164, 168, 169, 172, 173, 174, 182–83, 194n, 196–97, 200, 204; Youth League, 41; East Pakistan Students Union, 41, 134n, 141; Awami League, 42, 134, 139, 141, 192, 194n, 196n; West Pakistan, 63, 134, 141, 192; Jama'at-e-Talaba, 134; Jama'at-i-Islami, 134; National Awami Party, 134, 141; East Pakistan Students League, 134n, 139, 141, 194n, 196n; Pakistan People's Party, 141, 192; National Students Federation, 164; All Parties Students Action Committee, 172, 174, 189; see also Dacca University
Suffrage: United Front, 46; Council Muslim League, 135; National Awami Party, 136; Combined Opposition Parties, 151; Ayub regime, 175; Yahya regime, 187, 188; see also Elections
Suhrawardy, H. S., 39, 40, 48–49, 138, 158, 161
Syed (Muslim caste), 19, 27
Syed, G. M., 136
Sylhet, 16, 17, 18; election (1965), 123, 153, 154; population, 206

Tagore, Rabindranath, 163
Talpur, Mir Ghulam Ali, 146n
Talukdars, 122
Taxation: anti-BPC movement, 43; East Pakistan, 69, 70, 71, 73, 208; West Pakistan, 69, 70, 209; Six-Point Movement, 168; All Parties Students Action Committee, 172
Thomas, John, 78, 119
Trade, see Economy
Transportation: railways, 31, 33, 68, 102, 199, 200, 215; East Pakistan, 31, 33 81, 182, 199, 200, 205, 213, 215; West Pakistan, 31, 33, 81, 205, 215; roads, 77, 81, 213; air, 205
Tribal population, 14–15, 16
21 Points, 36, 44, 45–47
Twenty Year Perspective Plan (1965–85), 69, 71, 87

Ulema, 23, 63, 180–81; see also Jamiat-ul-Ulema-i-Islam; Markazi Jamiat-ul-Ulema-i-Pakistan

Union of Soviet Socialist Republics: Pakistan People's Party, 140; see also National Awami Party, Moscow/Peking split
Unions, see Labor force
United Front, 29, 47; 21 Points, 36, 44, 45–47
United States: business interests in Pakistan, 27; aid to Pakistan, 35; aid cut in war with India (1965), 167
Uprisings, see Riots, disturbances, and strikes
Urdu (language), 12, 13, 14; controversy over state language, 37, 38, 43, 48; as state language, 38; newspapers and periodicals, 216
Usmani, Mahmoodul Huq, 136

Vernacular elite, 26, 29, 38–40, 41, 43–45, 48–49; and national elite, 47, 48, 162–63, 175; and Ayub coup, 55, 56; and CSP, 96, 100, 106, 107; and Constitution of 1962, 145, 146, 148–49
Voting, see Elections; Suffrage

Wahiduzzaman, 131
War, civil (1971), 6, 197–204
War with India: Kashmir conflict (1948), 52; Kashmir conflict (1965), 83–84, 139, 140, 159, 160, 166–67
Weiner, Myron, 3
West Bengal, 20, 25, 40n, 163
West Pakistan: politics and government, 6, 7, 20, 21–22, 25, 26, 27, 28–30, 48–49, 63, 131–36 passim, 138–39, 140–41, 146, 150, 155, 156, 189–94 passim, 197 (see also Politics, power elite); geography, 10; agriculture, 11, 30, 31, 57n; population, 11–12, 14–15; economy and trade, 12, 30–37, 67–89, 134, 210, 211, 212, 213; migration, 12, 31–32, 134, 149; languages, 12–14; Muslims, 14, 23; culture and history, 14–15, 17, 20–21, 37–38; ownership of land, 15, 56, 96, 117, 146; military, 20, 25; religion, 22–23; business and industry, 27, 30, 31–32, 49, 61, 63, 86, 87, 88, 211, 212; per capita income, 30, 31, 71–72, 79–81; education, 30–31, 33, 81–82, 214; transportation, 31, 33, 81, 205, 215; communications, 31, 33, 215, 216; medical facilities,

West Pakistan: politics and government *(Cont.)*
33, 81, 214; foreign aid allocation, 34, 35; land reform, 56, 57; bureaucracy and civil service, 63, 95-96, 101, 107; students and politics, 63, 134, 141, 192; labor force, 63, 174, 207, 216; taxation, 69, 70, 209; Basic Democracies, 116, 117, 119; election (1960), 19-20; election (1964), 121; election (1962), 146, 147; election (1965), 152, 155; riots, disturbances, and strikes, 172, 173, 174, 176-77, 190, 207; election (1970), 189-90, 190-91; works program 212; cost of living, 215

Williams, Rushbrook, 54

Works program, *see* Rural areas, works program

Yahya Khan, Aga Mohammad, 186-98; proposed changes for constitution, 187-88; election (1970), 187-92 *passim;* and Bhutto, 193, 196; Bangladesh conflict, 196, 201, 204

Youth League, 41

Zamindars, 16, 122